More praise for

The Thinking Parent's Guide to College Admissions

"College admissions is about finding a school that's a good match for the child, not about the parent's deferred dreams or a 'name brand' decal on the Volvo. Following Eva Ostrum's step-by-step program will make parents and students happier with the process."

—Patrick F. Bassett, President, National Association of Independent Schools (NAIS)

"Ostrum offers a sensitive, thoughtful, and detailed approach to help guide parents successfully through the maze that is selective college admissions."

—Jim Bock, Dean of Admissions and Financial Aid, Swarthmore College

"Eva Ostrum brings all of her considerable experience and intelligence to create a highly useful guide for parents as they navigate the college search process with their child. This is a fantastic tool for educating and assisting families.... I plan to recommend this book to every college counselor I know!"

—Julie M. Browning, Dean for Undergraduate Enrollment, Rice University

"Sensitive—comprehensive—thoughtful—empowering. *The Thinking Parent's Guide to College Admissions* is a powerful guide for any parent going through the college admissions process, whether it is with their first-generation or third-generation college-bound child. Bring this book with you on college tours, have it open when completing applications, and consult it when making the final college choice. You can rely on Eva Ostrum as your personal escort through the labyrinth of terms, deadlines, and paperwork of college admissions...helping you to help your student feel comfortable and confident in approaching this important process."

—Arlene Wesley Cash, Vice President for Enrollment Management, Spelman College

"*The Thinking Parent's Guide to College Admissions* is a thought-provoking, engaging, and comprehensive analysis of the college admissions process. Eva Ostrum does a remarkable job capturing the nuances of the process while giving readers an easy, step-by-step guide to college admissions."

> —Robert P. Jackson, Associate Director of Undergraduate Admissions, Yale University

"*The Thinking Parent's Guide to College Admissions* offers terrific advice for parents who are eager to guide their sons and daughters through a complicated process. Eva Ostrum's knowledgeable approach and experiential wisdom will inspire confidence among parents with college-bound students."

> —Eric Kaplan, Dean of Admissions and Financial Aid, Lehigh University

"An important new book. Eva Ostrum combines the experience of a talented admissions professional with the skill of a clear and thoughtful writer to present a thorough and comprehensive approach to navigating the college admissions process successfully. I found her book both enjoyable and enlightening."

> —James M. Sumner, Dean of Admissions, Grinnell College

"Finally, a detailed and sensible guide to help parents through the college admissions process! Practical and thorough . . . encapsulates the essence of finding the right college fit. Read it, fill in the charts, and feel your anxiety fade away; it is that good!"

> —Paul Thiboutot, Dean of Admissions, Carleton College

THE
THINKING PARENT'S GUIDE
TO
COLLEGE ADMISSIONS

*The Step-by-Step Program
to Get Kids into
the Schools of Their Dreams*

EVA OSTRUM

PENGUIN BOOKS

PENGUIN BOOKS

Published by the Penguin Group

Penguin Group (USA) Inc., 375 Hudson Street, New York, New York 10014, U.S.A.
Penguin Group (Canada), 90 Eglinton Avenue East, Suite 700, Toronto, Ontario,
Canada M4P 2Y3 (a division of Pearson Penguin Canada Inc.)
Penguin Books Ltd, 80 Strand, London WC2R 0RL, England
Penguin Ireland, 25 St Stephen's Green, Dublin 2, Ireland
(a division of Penguin Books Ltd)
Penguin Group (Australia), 250 Camberwell Road, Camberwell, Victoria 3124,
Australia (a division of Pearson Australia Group Pty Ltd)
Penguin Books India Pvt Ltd, 11 Community Centre, Panchsheel Park,
New Delhi—110 017, India
Penguin Group (NZ), cnr Airborne and Rosedale Roads, Albany,
Auckland 1310, New Zealand (a division of Pearson New Zealand Ltd)
Penguin Books (South Africa) (Pty) Ltd, 24 Sturdee Avenue, Rosebank,
Johannesburg 2196, South Africa

Penguin Books Ltd, Registered Offices:
80 Strand, London WC2R 0RL, England

First published in Penguin Books 2006

1   3   5   7   9   10   8   6   4   2

ISBN 0-14-303741-2

Printed in the United States of America
Set in Stempel Schneidler Light
Designed by Level C

To my mother, Andrea Ellen Ostrum—my beginning—
and to her grandson, Ezekiel—the joyful future.

Contents

Contents

Acknowledgments

The final version of this book looks very different from (and better than!) what I had initially envisioned, a result that I never could have achieved without substantial assistance from other people. Bob Mecoy, my eternally supportive and patient agent, made me rewrite my book proposal three times before he accepted it as done. His holding the bar at such a high level from the very beginning set the standard that prepared me to work with Brett Kelly, my equally supportive and patient editor. Brett taught me through her insights and feedback how to communicate knowledge and experience to a wider audience, something that I could not have done without her.

In the college admissions world, I have many people to thank. Rob Jackson at Yale offered practical as well as moral support when I shared this project with him in its early stages. Jim Bock (Swarthmore College), Jane Brown (Mount Holyoke College), Julie Browning (Rice University), Arlene Cash (Spelman College), Doris Davis (Cornell University), Marilee Jones (Massachusetts Institute of Technology), Eric Kaplan (Lehigh University), Arnaldo Rodriguez (Pitzer College), Myra Smith (at Yale University when I interviewed her and now at the College Board), Ted Spencer (University of Michigan), Jim Sumner (Grinnell College), Paul Thiboutot (Carleton College), and Harold Wingood (Clark University) all gave generously of their time in lengthy interviews and then in subsequent e-mail correspondence and telephone conversations when I had follow-up questions. Above and beyond getting invaluable information from them for this book, I feel fortunate to have collaborated with individuals so clearly committed to higher education and to the young people they want to see benefit from it.

Patrick Bassett (National Association of Independent Schools) and Mark Sklarow (Independent Educational Consultants Association) shared their thoughts with me on independent schools and independent educational consulting, respectively, and I thank them for it.

I had the immense good fortune to meet Laura Clark (Fieldston School) when I approached her for an interview for this book. Laura is known in the college admissions world as one of the best counselors in the business. Her interview confirmed that recommendation and then led to an ongoing collegial relationship and friendship, for which I am grateful. Laura introduced me to Tim Levin (Tim Levin Tutoring, Inc.), whom I consider the test-prep "guru," and who has also grown into a colleague and friend. Ron Inniss (Boston Public Schools) used to share his thoughts on college guidance with me when we carpooled to work together in the 1990s. I have continued to draw on his wisdom and friendship over the years, including as I worked on this manuscript.

Dr. Robert Sternberg (at Yale University when I interviewed him and now at Tufts University), whom I still remember from my admissions office days at Yale, gave me a helpful overview of standardized testing. Ed Colby (ACT, Inc.) shared his time unstintingly when I needed background information on the ACT. Brian O'Reilly (College Board) educated me on some of the complexities of the SAT Reasoning Test and Subject Tests. Author David Owen generously responded to my questions after I read his informative book *None of the Above: The Truth Behind the SATs*.

Shelly Goch (Garfield, Seltzer & Curcio CPA PC) and Dwight Raiford (MetLife) contributed their time and intellectual capital to this book, both of which I appreciate. I want to recognize Bonnie Wong, executive director of Asian Women in Business, as well as the New York City chapter of the National Association of Women Business Owners (NAWBO). Both of these organizations gave me networking opportunities that contributed to the creation of this book.

I'd like to give a special shout out to my friends and neighbors in the Mount Morris Park section of Harlem—especially Laura Hope, Ray Acevedo, and their son, "Little Ray." A change of scenery every now and then as I was writing this manuscript also helped me move forward and for that I owe a debt of gratitude to my friend and former BPS colleague, Paul Harrison, who generously extended to me a standing invitation to use his lovely home on Cape Cod as a writing retreat.

I have saved for last the people closest of all to my heart. Nina Glickson and Worth David, my dear, dear friends, started out years ago as the two people who welcomed me into and taught me about the world of college admissions. Their influence in my life and their ongoing advice and support continue to help me grow, both professionally and personally. They also gave me extensive and invaluable feedback on this manuscript, for which I thank them. Vivian Shulman—my cousin, an incredible educator, and the ultimate thinking parent—made me feel while I was writing this book that I had my own personal cheerleading squad. Troi Lefkowitz, Laura Podalsky, and Richard Reimer, my dearest friends from college, have supported me in more ways than I can describe here, during the writing of this book and beyond. They take the definition of friendship to new levels each and every day and I only hope that I reciprocate in ways that let them know how much they mean to me. Finally, I want to recognize my two brothers, Ethan and Judah, whose presence in my life means more than I can say. I have dedicated this book to our mother, and hope that my doing so fills their hearts in the way it does mine.

Introduction

Stacks of applicant folders lined my office and nearly all the flat surfaces of my apartment when I worked as an admissions officer at Yale. Each one contained every piece of information that we received on a student, with a comment card at the top on which two readers (sometimes three) recorded feedback. A first reader provided an objective perspective on the application, with no detailed knowledge of a student's school or community. A second reader commented on the application in the context of school and community, as that same person scrutinized all other applications from that geographic area. For me, that meant reading every folder from California south of Los Angeles and from New York's Nassau County. I had to know the nature and character of each high school and the type of applicants that it sent us each year so that I could put individual students into context. After I narrowed down the ones that stood out to me, I then presented my "slate" of applicants to a committee that voted anonymously to determine the final outcome.

The "folder-based" admissions process that we used at Yale (and that many selective institutions employ) allowed us to take a remarkably close look at prospective students. I remember individual applicant essays and letters of recommendation, as do my former colleagues, at least one of whom I have heard occasionally interject into conversation, "strong folder, very strong folder," when the name of a current or former Yale student has come up. College admissions, not an exact science, may look unpredictable to an outsider, who only sees that an Ivy League institution rejected a number one student but accepted number fifteen. To those on the inside, though, this deeply involved and labor-intensive process consists of a team of admissions personnel poring over thousands of folders in a search for those candidates whom they can envision enriching classroom and campus life.

Families have used various strategies over the years to "strengthen" student folders. *The Washington Post* reported in March 2005 that SAT preparation has grown into a more than $300-million-a-year industry. Parents with the financial means spend thousands of dollars to send their college-bound children to exotic overseas destinations on summer community service projects. Independent consultants in major metropolitan areas charge tens of thousands of dollars for private college counseling. Throwing money at the process may have marginal value for your child (it may also make you feel better than you otherwise would) but, in the end, admissions officers prefer substance over packaging almost every time, and have grown pretty astute at distinguishing between the two.

My advice to parents may sound deceptively simple, but it works. First, concentrate 90 percent of your effort on substance and 10 percent on packaging. Your child should put her best foot forward when she applies to college, but she should not try to reinvent herself into what she (*or you*) thinks admissions officers want to see. Second, engage in honest reflection about your child, her strengths, areas in which she may need support, and the educational environment that will best meet her needs. Donating $10 million to the development office at an elite college or university may, in some cases, get your child into an institution that would have otherwise rejected her; but if her skill set or level of achievement falls markedly short of her peers on campus, you may have just bought her four years of academic and personal struggle. Third, do your homework. Educate yourself on your child's high school, on colleges and universities around the country, on the different standardized tests from which your child can choose, and on financial aid options. Last but not least, offer your child support based on what you have learned about the process, but resist the temptation to grab the reins.

Share helpful information with your child but let her make her own decisions whenever possible. It may seem like so much depends on which colleges and universities accept your child and where she chooses to spend her college career; parents sometimes feel helpless to influence this process. But by following the simple steps I've outlined in this book, you can successfully serve as a reliable, resourceful coach through this notoriously harrowing experience, and help your child find and gain admission to the best possible colleges and universities for her—without having to hire a team of high-priced experts.

Let me make two things clear. First, prestige, name recognition, and *U.S. News & World Report* rankings have nothing to do with what makes a college or university the best possible choice for your child. "Best," in this context, means the place that will nurture and encourage her so that she thrives and blossoms intellectually, socially, and as a human being. I urge you to think long and hard about this point before you embark on the college admissions process. Holding on to your own definition of "best," such as Ivy League or Big Ten only, and trying to make your child fit into that category could mean that you are shoving a round peg into a square hole. The harder you push, the more likely you are to cause harm.

Second, families with whom I work sometimes find it difficult to discard their own strategies in favor of mine and, instead, pick and choose morsels, rather than adopting the entire plan that I give them. You may already have some ideas of your own about ways in which to approach various aspects of the college admissions process. I urge you to set aside any preconceived notions you may have and pay close attention to the advice in this book. Without exception, those who faithfully follow my recommendations achieve dramatically better results than those who do not. Regardless of when you pick up this book—when your child is a freshman, sophomore, junior, or even first-semester senior—every chapter includes helpful suggestions. Even the section on paying for your child's education offers advice for those families who have not yet taken a single step to save for college and have only a few months before they have to start paying tuition.

Skip a section of the book only if you know that it does not apply to you. You may think, for example, that it does not make sense to read the chapters on standardized testing because your child already took the SAT. If she did not do as well as she had hoped, though, it might make sense to read about the ACT. College visits this past summer may have wrapped up your child's college interviews. You may still want to read the interview chapter, though, if your child has not yet completed alumni interviews, which usually take place after applications have gone in and carry significant weight at some colleges and universities. Glance at the checklist that ends each chapter for a quick and easy way to see the points that it covers and whether or not it has relevance for you.

Read this book and, while you do, open yourself up to the wonderful possibilities that await your child at the end of this process. Yes, aspects of applying to college qualify as downright grueling (you would have a hard time getting me to take my SATs again, even if you offered me a lot of money!); but the payoff can be great. I smile as I imagine my current cohort of high school seniors on various campuses around the country next year. I picture one young man thriving at Rice University in Houston—a fabulous school that many East Coast students unfortunately skip over because of its location—and another getting the academic support that he needs as well as nurturing his passion for writing at Lake Forest College, outside Chicago. I envision one of my young women at Oberlin College, in Ohio, and another at James Madison University in Virginia. Helping students find and get into the college or university at which they will realize their true potential and thrive gives me the same giddy sense of satisfaction that matchmaking does when I know that a couple has hit it off (and the ones that I set up always do!).

You can experience that same sense of satisfaction when your child's college results come in. This book will help you get there. Get ready to roll up your sleeves, do some work, and then enjoy watching your child get into the school of her dreams.

THE
THINKING PARENT'S GUIDE
TO
COLLEGE ADMISSIONS

ONE

Assessing Your Child (and Yourself)

When families walk into my office for a college admissions consultation, I take them through a series of preliminary steps. First, I ask both parents and child what each hopes to get out of the college admissions process and what they hope to accomplish by working with me. Next, I look at any supporting paperwork that the family has brought, such as transcripts, standardized test score reports, or letters of recommendation. Last but not least, I take down information on the student's extracurricular and personal profile. All of this information helps me to place the student and parents in context so that I can support and guide them in the most useful way possible. The steps that follow will help you compile the same kind of profile of your child that I would put together if we met in my office. They will also enable you to set realistic expectations for the college admissions process and then lay out a road map for how to achieve them.

CLARIFYING YOUR GOALS

It strikes me each time a new family comes to see me how dramatically people's goals for getting into college can differ. Many parents and students voice general preferences that focus on a specific geographic region of the country (Northeast versus West Coast) or on size (large university versus small liberal arts college). Parents and children occasionally differ on what makes a place "the right school" but, most of the time, they voice similar objectives—with parents underscoring their desire for their children to be happy, wherever they go.

The goals that parents and children articulate to me generally sound reasonable and attainable; at times, though, the expectations that people express in my office will either require some very hard work, or some rethinking altogether. I am assisting one young man, for example, who wants to attend a college of engineering but whose standardized test scores in mathematics and the sciences look weak and will make it difficult for him to gain admission. At my suggestion, he is now exploring liberal arts institutions with strong engineering departments, where he could receive a similar kind of training. Parents sometimes put together wish lists that limit their children's options, ignore what their children want, or exaggerate what their children's track records suggest they can achieve. One mother recently announced to me that she wanted her son to attend Columbia University, a school for which he did not look like a strong candidate. She refused to consider other options when I pointed out that her son may prefer to go elsewhere or that Columbia, a highly selective Ivy League institution, might not admit him based on his academic performance. At the end of another session, a father asked his daughter to leave the room and told me privately that he would write a check for any amount to the development office at his daughter's first-choice college or university to guarantee her admission there. I always remind parents like these that their intense focus on getting their children into a particular place at any cost, financial or otherwise, ultimately limits their children's options and does them a disservice—even if the institution in question accepts them!

An Ivy League or Division I school may well represent the ideal choice for your child, but you should arrive at that conclusion based on who he is and what he has accomplished rather than on your own personal preferences and preconceptions. The goals that you and your child put together should define the type of environment that will enable him to thrive academically, socially, and personally during his four years of college. Multiple institutions can provide that setting; your challenge lies in identifying them and helping your child complete, to the best of his ability, the necessary steps to gain admission.

Try to identify some of your own goals for the college admissions process. Have a discussion with your child to identify his. Take a few minutes to ask yourself some key questions. Does name recognition (or rank) matter to you or would you consider an institution that you did not know but that, upon examination, looks and sounds wonderful for your child? Do you see your child benefiting from large lectures with famous professors, from individualized attention in seminars, or both? If your child plays a sport, do you have your heart set on his joining a particular college team? Tease out any secret biases or hopes that may be influencing where you want your child to attend college, examine them closely, and ask yourself if they really represent the best possible options for your child.

Thinking about college admissions from a student-centered rather than a school-centered perspective requires that you understand your child's strengths, the areas in which he needs to improve, what motivates him to succeed, and the expectations that he has set for himself. You need to go through this thought process honestly and unflinchingly for it to have value. Your child, for example, may stand out as the star of his high school but may not have credentials that compare strongly to his peers from other schools. Conversely, a grade point average of B+ at a rigorous college-preparatory program could have greater value than a grade point average of A+ somewhere else. You may not be sure how to measure your child, especially in the context of the larger universe of high school students. That's what this book can help you do: assess your child so that you can understand his abilities and prospects come application time.

Keep four general questions in mind as you think about your child and his college future:

- What kind of student is my child?
- What are my child's extracurricular interests?
- What type of environment would best serve my child?
- How does my child compare to his peers?

Let's take some time to go through that process the same way that we would if we were sitting together in my office.

ASSESSING YOUR CHILD'S ACADEMIC PROFILE

Admissions officers will tell you without hesitation that they want to know how an applicant has performed academically before anything else. People frequently associate academics with grades and test scores and, yes, these criteria do carry significant weight in the admissions process, as we will discuss later in this book. You cannot stop with these objective indicators alone, though, in understanding this aspect of your child's profile. You must look further than that, at the underlying motivations that have pointed your child in the direction he has taken.

Is Your Child a Solid Student?

- Does he generally like school?

- Does he have a history of following directions closely and well?

- Does he generally get A's or B's and finish assignments without your nagging him?

- Does he see college as an obvious and natural next step after high school?

- Where do his passions lie—in academic learning or elsewhere?

I want to know two things right off the bat when I look at a student's high school transcript: the grades he has earned and the courses he has taken. Some students perform consistently well, such as Seth, who almost always earned grades in the B range, regardless of the level of difficulty of the class. Others have easily discernible areas of strength and weakness, like Brittany who always earned A's or B's in the humanities but could not get higher than a C in foreign language. Some students push themselves to take the most challenging classes available, such as Advanced Placement (AP) or International Baccalaureate (IB), even if doing so means receiving lower grades than they would otherwise. Others opt out of these rigorous courses but receive consistently high marks in the next level down. I look at all of these details and ask follow-up questions to determine how the student sitting in front of me compares to others his age: Is he a solid student, a passionate learner, an underachiever, or a struggling student?

A solid student typically studies diligently, completes all homework assignments, gets A's or B's, and elicits positive comments from teachers. He works hard when necessary and may occasionally have to wrestle with a challenging assignment, but does not appear to struggle overall with academics. He generally enjoys high school, at least parts of it, and looks forward to college as a natural next step. A solid student does not always earn standardized test results that parallel his grades and usually explains disappointing scores by describing himself as "not a strong standardized test taker." His motivation to do well can stem from external factors (a desire to please, a focus on getting into college, etc.) or from an internal, self-driven passion for learning or for a particular subject.

Is Your Child Passionate About Learning?

- Does he love to learn for the sake of learning?

- Does he display intellectual passion for a particular area?

- Has he created his own independent sources of intellectual stimulation?

- Does he invest significant time and energy in classes that he enjoys and form strong relationships with those teachers?

Plenty of applicants to selective colleges and universities submit a solid academic transcript. We were looking at Yale for the folders that conveyed a young person's clear and tangible love of learning, a passion for what he did—the students that the teachers in the school loved to teach, as my former boss explained to me. Most kids feel passionate about something in their lives, but it does not always have to do with academic learning. I can think of two current clients off the top of my head, for example, who qualify as solid students but get passionate only when they start talking about the stock market, which they follow religiously. If your child qualifies as a solid student, ask yourself if his enthusiasm for learning pushes him into the next category, i.e., the passionate learner, or if his real interests lie elsewhere. The most selective colleges and universities are looking for passionate learners, not just solid academic performers. Distinguishing between these two profiles will make a difference when the time comes to apply to college.

Some passionate learners knock the ball out of the park with their academic performance while others underperform in school if they have become disenchanted with it. My current client, Jake, for example, reveals his enthusiasm for learning when he talks about the books that he reads on his own (at least one a week) by authors such as Bellow, Kafka, and others. He hates the typical rote learning of high school, though, and does not invest a lot of time in assignments that he considers pointless. This approach has cost him a good grade on occasion and has left him with a somewhat speckled transcript. Jake responds with enthusiasm to good teachers when they come along but relies primarily on his own independent outlets for intellectual stimulation. If your child sounds like Jake, encourage his independent pursuits and help him reflect them in his college application. Admissions officers need to know that his transcript does not tell the whole story, especially about what makes him tick as a student.

An underachiever, the student whom parents browbeat or nag about schoolwork, gets his name because he performs below his ability level. Strong performance on standardized tests and/or a clear ability to understand concepts and solve problems let the adults in an underachiever's life know that he has the ability to do well in school if he chooses. An underachiever, though, typically opted out of school a long time ago. You may hear him complain about school and call it boring or stupid. For him, in fact, it is. A good teacher or an interesting curriculum might have motivated him in a heartbeat to invest in academics, but he has not encountered much of that throughout his high school experience and has checked out mentally as a result.

Is Your Child an Underachiever?

- Does he perform well on standardized tests and/or demonstrate an ability to understand concepts and solve problems even though he does not do well in school?

- Does he complain that school is boring and do the bare minimum to get by?

- Does he do a sloppy and/or erratic job completing homework assignments and studying?

An underachiever's boredom can stem from many factors, depending on his environment. Research has shown, for example, that schools disproportionately refer African American males to special education programs, a circumstance that leaves those who do not belong there academically unchallenged. Think of the movie *Ferris Bueller's Day Off*. You can feel the students' pain as they sit trapped in classrooms with teachers speaking in monotone and relying on rote exercises. The film may exaggerate for comic effect, but the number of high school students around the country who have to sit through similarly dull classes day after day would surprise you. The experience, if it happens often enough, can alienate some young people from school completely, to the point that they no longer respond to an exciting and stimulating teacher when one comes along.

A change in circumstances can sometimes push an underachiever to engage academically. One mother I know moved her son to a different school and saw his performance improve with the high level of expectations in his new environment. A young man with whom I am currently working scored well on the SAT Reasoning Test and realized that a selective college or university might accept him if he raised his grades. One of my former students from my high school teaching days decided to invest time and effort in my class when I started giving him individualized assignments to prepare for the AP European history examination (the school did not offer AP classes at the time). He requested a similar arrangement with two other teachers when he realized that he enjoyed the assignments that he was getting from me, took three AP tests that year, and scored off the charts on all of them. Several years later I ran into him on the street in Cambridge, where he was majoring in physics at Harvard. Avoid nagging, browbeating, or threatening your underachieving child, as those tactics rarely do the trick, and think instead about whether or not changing something in his environment could motivate him to kick into gear academically.

Is Your Child a Struggling Student?

- Does he perform poorly on academic assignments even though he studies hard?

- Does he have trouble keeping up with the pace of class discussion?

- Does he have ongoing difficulty with particular subjects no matter how hard he works?

I have tremendous respect for a student who puts effort into academic subjects that do not come easily—somebody you might describe as a struggling student. Brittany, whom I mentioned earlier, took three years of Latin when her school only required two. She worked tirelessly at it and, although she could never break a C in the subject, her work ethic inspired her Latin teacher to rave about her. Another client of mine, Daniel, writes so well that teachers have questioned the authorship of some of his research papers; however, he continues to teeter on the brink of failure in mathematics and science in spite of the twice-weekly support that he gets from a highly skilled private tutor. Make special efforts to support your child throughout high school if he is struggling academically. Work closely with the school guidance counselor to take advantage of school/community-based resources, such as tutoring or mentoring, and consider seeking a private evaluation for a learning disability if problems persist. Waiting until college lies on the horizon to provide support means that you risk having your struggling student throw his hands up in the air long before then and give up on school out of frustration.

THE ROLE OF STANDARDIZED TEST SCORES

Standardized test scores help me confirm, deny, or modify the impressions of a student's academic profile that I got from looking at his transcript. The scores also allow me to place a student academically in the context of his peers and give me a hint about how admissions officers will view the applicant. Finally, they give me clues about where a student can best direct his efforts if he wants to improve his academic profile.

Passionate learners, not surprisingly, do best of all on standardized tests. They may or may not have done all that their teachers asked of them. They have, however, pursued their own avenues of intellectual stimulation, like Jake who read a book a week on his own throughout high school. Jake earned almost perfect scores on every standardized test that he took. His test results reinforce the story that his application will tell of an extremely talented young person who has defined and pursued his own intellectual interests with seriousness and depth. That narrative will open doors for him at highly selective colleges and universities with a special appreciation for self-directed learners, even those with imperfect transcripts.

Good grades with middling test scores indicate to me that a solid student has diligently followed all the instructions that his teachers gave him but has probably not done much more. The average high school education does not prepare students to perform at an outstanding level on standardized college entrance examinations. The College Board's Subject Tests, for example, sometimes focus arbitrarily on a particular area within the subject, such as plants or insects on the biology test. A passionate learner who reads voraciously on biology has probably already gone through several books or journal articles about plants. A solid student who has simply followed his high school biology class curriculum, however, has touched broadly on many areas of the subject without having emphasized one. Test scores, therefore, can serve as a basic and preliminary indicator of a student's innate passion, initiative, and drive—factors critical to admission at the most selective institutions in the country.

Every so often I see a transcript with poor grades accompanied by impressive standardized test scores. This combination suggests to me either that an underachieving student also qualifies as a passionate learner who is absorbing knowledge on his own, outside of school, or that he can pick things up without studying them at length (perhaps through hearing about them in class or reading them quickly in a half-hearted attempt to complete an assignment). In these instances, I know that a student has more choices than his transcript alone suggests and that the colleges and universities to which I encourage him to apply will depend on his level of motivation more than anything else.

Poor test scores that accompany poor grades reinforce that a student is struggling with academics. Some families have already found their own strategies for success, so grades may in fact be improving. An evaluation of Brittany revealed a learning disability that resulted in her taking medication. Her grades noticeably improved thereafter. Sending a child to college without having found any strategies for success will only set up that child for renewed failure once he arrives on campus. For struggling students, the college admissions process must include establishing which kinds of academic support (tutoring, small classes, etc.) can improve performance. That determination will prove critical in identifying the right colleges and universities for your child.

ASSESSING YOUR CHILD'S EXTRACURRICULAR AND PERSONAL PROFILE

Admissions officers also care about what your child does outside the classroom. Remember, student-run organizations and events play a big role in campus life. With every client that comes to my office, therefore, I take a detailed inventory to figure out how a student spends his discretionary time. Specifically, I want to know if his extracurricular activities reflect commitment, leadership, passion, and/or independence of spirit. I also want to know if a student has any "hooks," admissions jargon for qualities that colleges and universities are aggressively seeking in applicants, usually in direct response to a shortage on campus of students who fit that particular description.

Admissions officers at the most selective institutions in the country look for the same enthusiasm and drive in a student's extracurricular life that the passionate learner displays in his academic life. Students can take on leadership roles at school (captaining a team, editing a school publication, holding student government office, directing a theatrical production) or pursue independent interests outside of school (one young man with whom I work has earned his certification as a scuba-diving instructor). Contributing to the household economy, such as working in the family business or baby-sitting for siblings while parents work, also demonstrates qualities that admissions officers value. Think about the quality of the time your child spends on what he does, rather than the quantity. Involvement that makes a difference or that suggests passion or independence of spirit will likely catch the attention of someone reading your child's folder.

Interestingly, extracurricular activities stand out in my experience as an area in which parents sometimes have a skewed vision of their child's accomplishments. I remember one mother saying to her daughter, "Now tell her about your extracurricular activities." Her father chimed in, "They are terrific!" The daughter told me that she baby-sits to earn spending money and that she had joined the one club that her school offers. "She does everything that she can," the mother pointed out, when I asked if the young woman participated in any other activities. These parents mistakenly assumed that their daughter would stand out because she had gotten involved in everything that the school had made available to her (a single activity). They had chosen to ignore, however, that they live in New York City, where opportunities and resources abound.

Take a few moments to assess your child's extracurricular profile, perhaps through completing the "Extracurricular Activity Profile" on the next page. Look at the responses that you indicate and ask yourself what they tell you about your child. Does he look like a leader who would thrive on a campus with other students who have had the experience of being a big fish? Does he prefer to focus on other parts of his life, such as his studies or his social life, instead of on organized extracurricular pursuits? Does he need a college or university with a broad range of activities or would a few in-depth opportunities to get involved suffice? We are not looking for right or wrong answers here, only details that can factor into finding the right college or university for your child.

Before we leave this part of the discussion, you need to consider whether or not your child has any admissions "hooks." Colleges and universities want students from all walks of life—those from diverse regions and backgrounds; those who demonstrate exceptional talent in fields such as music or athletics; and children of alumni, among others. A hook gives an applicant an advantage over a similar student who does not have one. It does not guarantee admission, but could mean that a folder gets closer consideration than it otherwise would (three readers instead of two, for example). We will discuss this aspect of a student's profile later in this book, but keep it in mind as you assess who your child is and what he brings to the table.

FINDING THE RIGHT COLLEGE FIT

We have focused so far on what we might call your child's resumé: courses, grades, test scores, activities, and compelling personal characteristics. Finding the right fit for your child, though, requires that you and he think about the intangible qualities that make him who he is. You may have to visit several campuses before you figure these out. Let me give you a few examples.

Brittany, the young woman who did poorly in foreign languages, told me that she wanted a Division III campus in an urban area, with strong psychology and art departments and support for learning disabled students. I sent her to look at a campus that sounded perfect for her based on these criteria. It turned out that her definition of urban

Student Name: _____   Current Grade in School: _____

Extracurricular Activity Profile

ACTIVITY	GRADES PARTICIPATED	TITLES EARNED/ AWARDS WON	LEVEL OF TALENT	PROVIDES A HOOK?
Concert Violinist	2–12	First violin in Cleveland Philharmonic	Play in nationally known symphony orchestra	Yes
Scuba Diving	8–12	N/A	Certified instructor (PADI)	No
Varsity Basketball	9–10, 12	MVP, Captain	All-state team	Maybe for Division III? (Not sure—must contact coaches)
Holy Name Society—community service	7–12	N/A	N/A	No
Baby-sitting	7–12	N/A	N/A	No

Assessing Your Child (and Yourself)

meant sophisticated and wealthy and had nothing to do with actual physical location. We went back to her list and modified it so that "collegiate" and "preppy" replaced urban. She came back much happier from her next round of campus visits than she did from her first.

Lena, a deeply religious young woman, told me the first time we met that she already knew she wanted to attend a religious university in her faith and had identified her first choice. I thought she was going to have the easiest college admissions experience of all my clients, as she fell well within the competitive range for the institution she had chosen and was planning to apply early. A few weeks later Lena came back to see me. She had visited her first choice and no longer wanted to apply there at all! A native New Yorker, she had found the campus too homogeneous and decided that a large, diverse urban institution would suit her better than one that catered to a particular group.

Finding the Right Fit: Discussion Questions

- Does your child enjoy a social life and, if so, does it center on parties and large group activities or on intimate activities with a small group of good friends?

- Does he prefer large communities with extensive resources or small ones that emphasize an intimate learning environment?

- Does he prefer the company of people like him or does he enjoy meeting people from diverse backgrounds?

- What kind of physical surroundings would he prefer? A pristine, collegiate campus or a bustling urban center?

- How far from home will he travel to attend college?

- Does he want a campus life that emphasizes athletics, such as at a Big Ten university?

- Does he want to attend religious services on campus?

- Does he want to live in the dormitories all four years?

Brittany's and Lena's stories illustrate the intangibles of finding the right college fit. Think about who your child is as a person, in addition to who he is as a student and member of his school community. Use the "Finding the Right Fit" discussion questions to brainstorm with him and start to outline where he sees himself. Then be prepared to throw everything out and start from scratch once you have made a few visits. Openness and flexibility at the start of your search may facilitate narrowing the options as the process unfolds: the more you and your child see at the outset, the better equipped he will be to define what appeals to him and what does not.

FREQUENTLY ASKED QUESTIONS

Your description of the underachiever sounds like you wrote it for our tenth-grade daughter. What can we do to get her to engage in school, do her work, and realize her full potential, so that she can go on to a college or university that truly challenges her?

Underachievers frequently disengage from school because they find it deadly dull and focused on unimportant trivia. Take my former student who wound up at Harvard, for example. His ninth-grade English teacher gave him a zero because he had forgotten to cover his textbook. He came in the next day with the book appropriately covered, but the teacher told him he was too late and the zero stood. In tenth grade, this same student took a French final that required him to use vocabulary words in sentences that demonstrated he knew the words' meanings. He did so and, in each sentence, he underlined the word in question. The teacher, however, gave him a zero on the entire section of the final because her instructions said that he was supposed to write the vocabulary word first, punctuate it with a colon, and then write a sentence that incorporated the word and showed its meaning. Experiences such as these led this talented young man to grow cynical about the inane details that he thought high school emphasized at the expense of real learning.

Sit down and talk with your daughter about the classes she is taking. Ask her which subjects interest her and which teachers she likes. See if she can show you assignments that she has enjoyed and take a look, also, at her class notes. You may find that her work focuses on rote memorization and questions at the end of a chapter, much of which would bore anyone. Find out what interests her: reading? writing? the arts? science? community service? athletics? Talk to her guidance counselor and, if possible, to the teachers she says she likes. Isolate what they are doing that catches her attention and work with your daughter to figure out how she can replicate those experiences elsewhere at school.

You may find that you grow as disenchanted with your daughter's high school as she has. In that case, explore your options. Motivated teachers may agree to give her independent projects. The district may offer alternative high school programs, such as theme-based or charter high schools. If no other options exist, try supplementing her experiences with enrichment programs or local college classes over the summer.

As your primary objective, focus on finding something academic that interests her, whether in school or outside of school, and move forward from there. Do not spend too much time worrying about what type of college will accept her. Many storied institutions around the country accept transfer students from community colleges. She will have plenty of opportunity, if she chooses, to make the transition to a selective institution, whether it happens directly from high school or via an alternative path.

Our son, who is finishing grade nine, came to his current high school when we moved here from a different town last year. His middle school did not prepare him adequately in mathematics and the department chair just informed us that, effective in grade ten, she would be moving Clark from honors mathematics down to the next level. I am concerned that the school is not giving him a chance to improve through hard work and that this decision will have an impact on his college chances. We have scheduled a meeting with the department chair. What can we say to convince her not to make the switch and what options do we have if she ignores our wishes and insists on moving Clark out of honors?

This situation has two sides to it. On the one hand, high school tracking decisions definitely influence the options available to students by the time they reach junior and senior year. In your son's case, for example, moving down from honors mathematics will likely preclude him from taking an AP mathematics class later. On the other hand, your son may welcome the opportunity to take mathematics outside of the honors track if his main interests lie elsewhere. You do not want him to overload on AP subjects further down the line in a way that might compromise his overall academic performance.

If your son wants to remain in honors mathematics, ask the department chair to give him the chance to study with a tutor over the summer. Request copies of the mathematics textbooks for this year and next year, as well as any review materials the department chair might have. Make sure your son has all of his corrected tests, so that he can review his errors with a tutor and understand what he did wrong. Impress upon the department chair that your persistence on this point reflects your son's interest in catching up to his peers and remaining in honors mathematics and that you want to give him that chance.

Do not worry about fallout from this situation in the college admissions arena if your entreaties to the department chair do not work. Look at summer enrichment opportunities in mathematics—such as on college campuses that offer summer programs for high school students—that would allow your son to cover honors-level work outside of school, if he cannot get access to it as part of his regular curriculum. Pay special attention to your son's preparation for the mathematics portion of the SAT Reasoning Test or ACT to insure that leaving the honors track does not handicap him on his standardized tests. Taking steps such as these can compensate for a high school's tracking decision, both from a practical as well as from an educational standpoint.

You used the example of Jake in your discussion of the "passionate learner" and mentioned that he had a "speckled" transcript. Our son sounds to us very much like Jake, except that he also has characteristics of the solid student (he completes all assignments and receives the highest possible grades on them, even if he does not like the class). Can a student fall into both the passionate learner and solid student categories?

A student who falls into the passionate learner category can overlap with just about any of the other areas as well. Jessica had skipped a year in every subject except science by the time she graduated from high school; she clearly had a passion, though, for French. French grammar books came with her on summer vacation, she worked multiple summer jobs so that she could afford to take a trip to France the summer before her senior year of high school, and she competed in citywide French language contests outside of school. Mark felt the same way about physics as Jessica did about French: he did well all around in high school (enough to gain admission to an Ivy League institution), but he devoured anything he could find on physics. Your passionate learner may do well in all subjects, he may have Jake's speckled transcript, or he may even struggle in certain academic areas while he pursues his passion in others.

Our son is finishing his junior year of high school and says he wants to apply to college. Every time we schedule a campus visit, however, he refuses to go. His grades have dropped since the beginning of high school so that he is now just barely passing his major subjects. He did not do well at all on the SAT Reasoning Test and has also refused every invitation from teachers or his peers to participate in extracurricular activities. What can we do to get him motivated about finishing high school and moving on to college?

Your son needs to motivate himself. You can provide support, but the impetus to apply to college must come from him. The description that you have given sounds more like a young person who has shut down rather than like somebody with an eye on his educational future. Take the focus off college for a moment and help your son unlock the source of his anxiety and, to some extent, paralysis. You may want to request the help of your son's guidance counselor or a teacher whom you know he respects. If no other options present themselves, consider going with your son to see a therapist who specializes in adolescents. The college admissions process will fall into place once your son has successfully addressed the larger issues that seem to be at play.

STEP-BY-STEP CHECKLIST:
ASSESSING YOUR CHILD AND YOURSELF

☐ Make a list of your goals and objectives for the college admissions process.

☐ Examine your list and ask yourself if it represents the best possible scenario for your child or your own personal hopes and biases.

☐ Have a discussion with your child to determine his goals and objectives for the college admissions process and see where yours and his overlap.

☐ Use your child's transcript, test scores, and what you know as his parent to assess which description fits him as a student: solid, passionate, underachieving, struggling.

❑ Use the activity worksheet in this chapter to put together his extracurricular profile.

❑ Use the discussion questions in this chapter as a springboard for a conversation with your child about the type of college or university that would fit him well.

TWO

Assessing Your Child's High School

In Chapter One, I walked you through the kind of informal assessment of your child's academic, extracurricular, and personal profile that I would perform if the two of you were sitting across from me in my office. I would also gather in this initial session information on your child's high school, a critical component of her college admissions profile. Understanding your child's high school informs me on two separate levels: First, it allows me to gauge her accomplishments and put them into context. Admissions officers go through this same mental exercise when they read folders, as they know that students at different high schools receive varying levels of academic and college guidance support. Second, an understanding of your child's high school enables me to point out to you where and how the high school will likely serve your child well in the college admissions process and where and how you may have to supplement what it is doing for you. Although you do not want to emphasize college too early, helping your child make the most of what her high school has to offer and providing her with supplementary resources as needed represent appropriate parental involvement at any point along the way.

HOW ADMISSIONS OFFICERS VIEW HIGH SCHOOLS

Let's expand a bit on the folder-based admissions process that we discussed earlier in the book, as this system relies on admissions officers knowing about and understanding different high schools around the country. Everything that your child submits as part of her application goes into an individual folder with her name on it, including materials that other parties send directly to the admissions office, such as letters of recommendation that come from the writers themselves, the Secondary School Report that the guidance counselor sends, and standardized test scores that ACT or the Educational Testing Service (ETS) forwards to the colleges and universities that your child designates. One or more individuals then read this folder and provide feedback on it, with variations in procedure depending on the institution. At Yale, we used what we called "first readers" to comment on a folder based strictly on the materials it contained, without any expected understanding of the student's high school or community. (First readers could include admissions officers, faculty members, or a pool of people that the office hired specifically for that purpose.) After the first read, your child's folder then would have gone to the admissions officer responsible for reading all folders from that territory. That person got the benefit of seeing first-reader comments highlighting the objective strengths and weaknesses of the folder and then had the additional task of putting all that information plus his own impressions into the context of your child's high school and community.

Admissions officers know their territories well. They visit them during what they call "fall travel season," when they meet with students and guidance counselors at local high schools. Challenging territories, such as New York City, that supply high numbers of applicants and require a nuanced understanding of a potentially complex environment often go to senior staff members. At Yale, for example, one associate director handles Manhattan and another oversees the Bronx. This system of dividing the world into geographic territories, each of which falls under the aegis of a different person, means that the admissions officer reading your child's application knows what kind of teaching and learning go on at her high school, how an AP course there compares with the same course at another high school across town, how a typical applicant from that high school scores on the ACT or SAT, how many of its students get in annually, which counselors provide helpful information, and, sometimes, even which teachers write substantive recommendations. The admissions officer in charge of your child's territory uses this information when he puts together his slate—the candidates he presents to a committee of his peers in the office for discussion and a vote. (The voting committee may also include faculty members, university administrators, and others, depending on the institution.)

Presenting candidates to the voting committee means providing supplementary information on school and/or community if necessary. A colleague at another Ivy League institution recently told me about the value that this type of information had in his support of a candidate whom I had encouraged to apply to his institution and about whom he felt strongly. The young man, from a struggling urban high school, had earned every academic honor possible and had even participated in his state's Governors Scholars program. His standardized test scores looked weak, though, and, as my colleague put it, "he wrote better than his teacher recommenders did." Committee members overcame their skepticism when they learned from my colleague about this young man's school and community. At a New York City elite independent school, the same student would have put together a dossier with the test scores and recommendations that were lacking here; however, he could only do so much in a severely resource-constrained environment. Understanding the expectations that admissions officers have of your child and the context in which they view her means looking at her high school and community through their eyes.

ASSESSING YOUR CHILD'S HIGH SCHOOL

High schools offer students varying levels of resources and support; you need to know exactly what your child's high school makes available to her and, if possible, supplement as needed. Schools in a particular category—such as suburban, urban, private—certainly share common characteristics. They can fall at different points along the quality spectrum, though, even when they possess similar attributes. Comparing the experiences of students within the same school building sometimes reveals a range there as well, depending on teachers, guidance counselors, the academic track in which a student has been placed, and other factors that can distinguish one young person's day-to-day reality from another's. Rather than generalize or jump to conclusions based on name or reputation, take a few moments to assess the actual strengths and weaknesses of your child's high school, as she has experienced it. Complete the "Assessing Your Child's High School" worksheet and tally the numerical averages by category (academics, college guidance, extracurriculars, overall assessment), as well as all

School type (circle one):   Suburban Public   Urban Public   Rural   Private   Charter   Exam/Magnet   Other

Assessing Your Child's High School

	Strongly Agree		Agree		Somewhat Agree		Disagree		Strongly Disagree	
Academics: Skilled and caring teachers help my child develop her academic strengths and effectively address her weaknesses.	10	9	8	7	6	5	4	3	2	1	0
Academics: Assignments interest and engage my child in school.	10	9	8	7	6	5	4	3	2	1	0
Academics: The curriculum builds my child's skill set/knowledge base.	10	9	8	7	6	5	4	3	2	1	0
Academics: My child takes classes that challenge her at an academically appropriate level.	10	9	8	7	6	5	4	3	2	1	0
Academics: My child gets individualized attention and extra help from teachers if she needs it.	10	9	8	7	6	5	4	3	2	1	0
Academics: Teachers/administrators respond quickly and with concern if I reach out to them to discuss an academic issue.	10	9	8	7	6	5	4	3	2	1	0
Academics: The high school offers advanced level courses, e.g., AP, IB, etc.	10	9	8	7	6	5	4	3	2	1	0
Academics: The high school provides students with all necessary materials and resources to succeed academically, e.g., textbooks, computer labs, science labs.	10	9	8	7	6	5	4	3	2	1	0
Academics: The curriculum includes enrichment activities, e.g., field trips.	10	9	8	7	6	5	4	3	2	1	0
Academics: The high school has created an environment that strongly encourages learning and academic success.	10	9	8	7	6	5	4	3	2	1	0
College Guidance: My child's counselor meets with her and provides helpful guidance as needed, e.g., course selection, questions about college, etc.	10	9	8	7	6	5	4	3	2	1	0
College Guidance: Guidance counselors meet with parents about college.	10	9	8	7	6	5	4	3	2	1	0
College Guidance: Guidance counselors suggest appropriate colleges and universities to which students should apply, including out-of-state options.	10	9	8	7	6	5	4	3	2	1	0
College Guidance: College-bound students at my child's high school generally get into one of their top two or three choices.	10	9	8	7	6	5	4	3	2	1	0
College Guidance: Guidance counselors recommend financial aid resources.	10	9	8	7	6	5	4	3	2	1	0
Extracurriculars: The high school offers a range of extracurricular activities.	10	9	8	7	6	5	4	3	2	1	0
Extracurriculars: Teams and clubs get the resources they need.	10	9	8	7	6	5	4	3	2	1	0
Overall Assessment: My child has grown academically at this high school.	10	9	8	7	6	5	4	3	2	1	0
Overall Assessment: My child has developed/pursued her interests.	10	9	8	7	6	5	4	3	2	1	0
Overall Assessment: My child has grown socially and developmentally.	10	9	8	7	6	5	4	3	2	1	0

Assessing Your Child's High School

around. Doing so may give you an invaluable perspective that helps you target where your involvement could add the greatest possible value for your child.

THE IMPORTANCE OF ACADEMICS

An effective high school at the very least should offer its students an academic platform from which to grow intellectually and, ideally, reach their potential as young learners.[1] Parents sometimes have a hard time knowing if and when appropriate growth and development are taking place, as an example that I will never forget from my first year of high school teaching illustrates. I received a telephone call from a disgruntled parent who thought her daughter, one of my eleventh-grade U.S. history students, had way too much work to do. "This is history, not chemistry," the mother complained when we spoke. "Chemistry is supposed to be hard, but for history class you read the chapters and answer the questions at the end of each one." My department head helped me settle the matter and I did not expect to hear anything further from this parent.

A few weeks later, the mother called again, this time to apologize. Her daughter had been working on a paper for my class and Mom, anticipating that her daughter might need help, offered to critique the first draft. "It was horrible!" she exclaimed. Report cards with A's and B's from a high school with a national reputation had led this mother to believe that her daughter was learning what she needed to know. She had never looked at her daughter's work, which she now found "so, so bad. And just think," she observed, realizing that other students, like her child, must also have slipped through the cracks. "I only have to read one paper, but you have to read them all!"

Many parents, like this mother, use report cards to judge whether or not their children are making appropriate progress in school. Understanding whether or not your child's high school is doing a good job, though, means knowing what the report card grades represent, the same way that admissions officers need to know and understand what an A or B means at one high school versus another in order to differentiate between them. Does an A in U.S. history at your child's school mean that she answers questions at the end of a textbook chapter or that she is writing analytical papers that rely on primary source documents? You can gain invaluable insight through just a few simple steps.

Sample Teacher Letter

To the parent/guardian of _____ :

We are delighted to introduce ourselves as your child's history teachers. In World History I, students will use maps, readings, discussions, and writing to gain an understanding of Africa, Europe, the Americas, and Asia. The attached syllabus describes in detail the topics that the class will explore.

We will be asking students to do a lot for our class. Their success will depend on regular attendance and on their putting effort into homework and studying on a regular basis. We would very much like to work with you in helping your child succeed and plan to do so in several ways.

First, we will call you regularly—if your child misses our class; if s/he comes unprepared; and also if s/he has done work in which you, as a parent or guardian, can take pride. Second, we will be distributing a "Weekly Planner" on the first day of class each week. The Weekly Planner will contain all classwork and homework for the entire week. It will also alert you to days when your child will be receiving a printout of his/her grade so far in the marking term. Please ask to see the Weekly Planner every Monday. Put it on the refrigerator and keep track of your child's assignments. Finally, we will be available for tutoring students after school and for meeting with parents/guardians before and after school almost every day of the week.

Please ask your child about what we are learning in class. We are hoping that you find the topics interesting and relevant and that they provoke some lively discussion or debate. We also intend for this class to prepare your child for promotion to the next grade, for the New York State Regents examination, and for applying to college.

We have attached several pieces of information to this letter so that you can have a full understanding of what your child will be learning in class:

1. A syllabus that discusses topics that students will explore, how they will be graded, and how they will be rewarded;

2. A table that displays the skills, or "competencies," that your child will gain through the work in this course;

3. A sample Weekly Planner from the first few days of class; and

4. A signature sheet below for you to sign, tear off, and have your child return to us so that we can be sure that you received this letter.

We thank you in advance for allowing us to work with you in educating your child. We are available to you by telephone, by e-mail, and in person. Please do not hesitate to contact us. Best wishes to you and to your family at the start of a new school year.

First, take a look at the materials readily at your disposal: a course syllabus or some kind of introductory letter that each teacher distributed at the beginning of the school year, descriptions of homework and/or project assignments that teachers have given out throughout the year, your child's class notes, and returned student work with teacher grades and comments. You want to create a story with these materials and then check for consistency or gaps. The syllabus or teacher letter (see the sample provided) in any given course tells you what your child, in theory, is learning. Class notes and assignment descriptions tell you whether the reality of what happens day-to-day in a particular classroom matches what the teacher described at the start of the year. Graded work lets you know your child's level of performance and a particular teacher's standards. Discrepancies between what a teacher stated at the outset versus what is actually occurring could reveal one type of problem. The quality of your child's work could expose others, as the mother of my eleventh-grade U.S. history student learned.

Next, compare your child's syllabus, assignments, and level of performance to what educators say she should be accomplishing. You may think that a high school mathematics class working on fractions sounds acceptable because that is what you were working on at your child's age. In fact, grade nine students routinely cover algebra these days and have long since left basic fractions behind in middle school. Find out what current educational standards call for and if your child's school is meeting them. (You can find information on state standards on either the school system or state department of education Web site.)

Last but not least, make sure you understand the level at which your child's high school has tracked her—above average, average, or below average in mathematics or English for her grade, for example—

and whether the quality of work expected in her track differs from others. Completing this step may require talking with an administrator or with your child's guidance counselor. If you have time, make these conversations a reason to visit the high school. Walk along the hallways, peer into classrooms, and get a feel for the pulse of the building. How do the corridors look during class periods—are they full of wandering students or empty because people are in class? Do students carry books? Does student work line classrooms and hallways? Do announcements over the public address system interrupt teaching and learning? Your observations on a spontaneous walk-through, when parents are not scheduled to be in the building, can tell you a lot about whether or not the school has created an environment that promotes student learning and academic success.

Assessing Academics at Your Child's High School

- Look at materials that teachers have distributed, such as the syllabus and descriptions of assignments.

- Examine your child's class notes and graded work.

- Find out how your child is tracked and how that affects the standards and expectations in place for her.

- Compare all of the above to what the district and state say your child should be learning.

- Is your child's high school teaching her to perform at an appropriate level? Above it? Below it?

Teaching and learning can take place in all different kinds of environments, from highly selective independent schools that charge steep tuition to urban public schools, like New York City's Career and Technical Education (CTE) programs at Aviation or Automotive High Schools. Do not let name and reputation lull you into a false sense of security. Conversely, do not assume the worst if your child attends the neighborhood public high school. You will likely find good and bad in every environment. The good news is that, as a parent, you can take steps to improve your child's education, both in school and outside of it.

> **Does Your Child's High School Promote Student Learning and Academic Success?**
>
> • Are corridors clear during class periods or do you see students wandering?
>
> • Do students carry books?
>
> • Has the school put student work on display in hallways and classrooms?
>
> • Do announcements over the public address system interrupt teaching and learning?

STRATEGIES FOR ACADEMIC CHANGE

Looking closely at your child's academic experience will almost certainly bring to your attention at least some small area in which you would like to see change take place. The first step in implementing effective change lies in identifying and understanding the problem. Does it lie with the school, with your child, or with both? You need to understand the ins and outs of how your child's high school works to know the recommended approach to take. You can operate in some cases from general principles and in others from characteristics specific to your situation and environment.

Let's say your child has a bad teacher in an important subject. I have seen evidence of poor teaching (usually alongside good) in every type of high school imaginable, including elite independent, suburban public, and urban "exam" schools. Every school has its bad apples on the faculty, there's no way around it. In your child's case, pay close attention to two subject areas: those about which she feels passionate and those in which she sometimes falters. A young person with an affinity for history, for example, will experience a heightened sense of frustration with a poor or mediocre teacher. She may also lose out on necessary preparation for successful performance on College Board Subject Tests, which students generally take in areas that interest them. At the other end of the spectrum, a subject that has traditionally posed problems for your child, especially a cumulative one like mathematics or foreign language, could grow into a source of ongoing discontent and/or low self-esteem with a bad teacher.

Strategies for Academic Change

- Determine the source of the problem (the school, your child, both) and whether or not it requires that you take action.

- In the case of a bad teacher, encourage your child to seek extra help from somebody else in the department and/or to take advantage of free school-based tutoring, such as peer or volunteer programs.

- Consider a class or tracking change.

- Research available enrichment or remedial programs in your area, such as those funded by the federal government or nonprofit organizations.

- Research summer enrichment programs on college campuses.

- Look into private tutoring.

- Explore high school transfer options for the beginning of grade ten.

You have a range of options here, starting with doing nothing. Talk to your child and, if possible, to other parents whose children have had the same teacher, to assess the cost of this educational shortfall. Will your child still be able to master essential pieces of the curriculum at a crucial juncture point, such as key mathematics concepts in grade eleven, the year that she is taking the ACT or SAT? If your child is having this experience early in high school, will her teacher in the same subject the following year review material that students may not have mastered? Is your child a passionate learner and will she, therefore, make up the bulk of this material through her own reading and self-directed intellectual pursuits? A positive response to any of these questions may mean that monitoring the situation will suffice, without your changing the status quo.

If the situation requires that you take action, such as if you cannot comfortably answer yes to any of the questions in the paragraph above, you have several options at your disposal. One student I know loved Spanish but had a terrible teacher. The only other Spanish class at his level met at a time that did not fit into his schedule, but the teacher of that class agreed to give him extra help after school. Encourage your child to approach other teachers in the department for extra help or to make use of peer and volunteer tutoring resources that many schools offer. You may also want to explore having your child switch classes. Keep in mind, though, that not all schools can accommodate such requests. Small magnet schools, for example, may not have more than one teacher assigned to a particular subject, while structural impediments can complicate schedule changes at large schools. Changing one class could have a domino effect on the rest of your child's schedule and leave her less satisfied than before, so explore the repercussions of this request before you make it.

Problems with a high school's academic program sometimes extend beyond one or two bad teachers in a given year. You may find that daily lessons and assignments in a number of areas do not meet state or district standards, or that they do not align with school syllabi and course descriptions. Alternatively, like the mother I mentioned earlier, you may discover that a grade of A or B does not necessarily represent high-quality work. Changing your child's academic track in the same school could make a positive difference, although you should consider this option only after close consultation with your child. I saw dedicated teachers at all levels in my almost ten years of teaching but consistently observed a higher workload in honors classes than in others. Make sure that your child is prepared for this increase in academic intensity and understand that requesting such a change will require you to make a strong case to the high school that your child will benefit from and can handle a more rigorous academic program than the one to which she has been accustomed.

Shortcomings that you identify either at your child's high school or in the work that she is producing may lead you to explore remedial or enrichment options elsewhere in the community. Choices include private tutoring, summer programs, and more. Think back to the academic assessment of your child that you completed in Chapter One and use that information in considering whether she needs support or enrichment and how best to deliver it.

Both the solid student and the passionate learner will probably fare well with options that build on their drive and initiative and/or allow them some independent direction. Those in urban areas can benefit from educational enrichment programs developed specifically for them, including national initiatives (like federally funded Upward Bound[2]), offshoots of local nonprofits (like Harlem Educational Activities Fund, New York City Mission Society, and Harlem Children's Zone, all in Central Harlem[3]), and nonprofits that serve students in multiple cities (like the Summer Search Foundation in Boston, New York City, Napa-Sonoma, Seattle, and San Francisco[4] and the Posse Foundation in Boston, Chicago, Los Angeles, and New York[5]). Solid students and passionate learners may also find helpful resources at summer programs on college campuses such as Johns Hopkins, Harvard, and Yale. Many of these institutions offer financial aid for families that cannot pay full tuition. A few hours of online searching should point you in the right direction and give you multiple alternatives to explore.

The underachiever and the struggling student may benefit from more structured and individualized attention than a classroom environment or group program typically provides. Consider private tutoring, if your family budget allows, either with a highly recommended individual or a well-regarded program. Ask for references and take the time to check them before you invest your money and your child's time in a tutor or program. Cost varies, but expect to pay the best tutors in the business what an appointment with a reputed child psychologist in your area would run, which can be as much as $350 per hour in New York City. (You can certainly find excellent tutors for less than that and should not, under any circumstances, pay more.)[6] Students who attend high schools that have been designated as failing under the No Child Left Behind (NCLB) Act may also have access to federally funded private tutoring at no charge, the availability of which your school system is supposed to advertise.

Switching schools entirely could present a viable option if the high schools in your district accept new students at the start of grade ten. Making the most of the transfer options available to your child means acting early in her ninth-grade year—September or October. Take the necessary steps sooner rather than later, even if you have not decided for sure that your child will make the change. Your child can always decline an offer of admission and choose to remain where she is.

Transferring to another high school outside of the context that I have described above could create more problems for your child than the ones that she is leaving behind at her current school. Few spots if any will remain in schools of quality after grade ten. You also do not want to jump from the frying pan into the fire. Every school has its strengths and weaknesses. The disruption to your child's education that switching schools late in the game can bring with it and the unknown pitfalls that she may encounter in her new environment could make this approach far less desirable than it initially seems.

If you and your child both agree that the benefits of switching schools after grade ten outweigh the costs, research available alternatives thoroughly and make the change as early in her high school career as you can.

Admissions officers know and understand the strength of the academics at high schools in their territories. You need to understand your child's high school to the same degree that they do so that you can help your child take advantage of the school's strengths and compensate for its weaknesses. Keep your child's profile as a student at the forefront of your mind if you need to change or supplement her academic program at all, as you always want to select options and strategies that work for her as a learner. With a thorough assessment of the academic terrain at your child's high school under your belt, you can now take a close look at the college guidance resources that the school offers students and families.

GETTING HIGH-QUALITY COLLEGE GUIDANCE, NO MATTER WHAT

A high school that does its job well provides students and families with effective college counseling, in addition to an academic platform that allows every child to thrive. Guidance departments can have strengths in some areas and fall short in others, so I ask my clients a range of questions if I do not know their counselor by name or reputation. As with academics, any type of high school can offer high-caliber as well as poor college counseling, sometimes side by side in the same building. Understanding what to expect from a college counselor enables you to gauge the quality of guidance that your child's high school delivers. A family that puts in the requisite time and effort can compensate for deficiencies in almost every case.

Communication from your child's high school on which courses and standardized tests to take should begin ideally in grade nine, either through individual meetings (with a guidance counselor or a faculty advisor) or through school bulletins, letters home to parents, and other such mass communications. One-size-fits-all prescriptions generally do not work equally well for all students, so ask a lot of questions to make sure that they meet the needs of your child. Compare, for example, the experiences that two of my client families with children in grade nine had at different high schools: One received a letter in the spring letting them know that grade nine students should discuss with their teachers whether or not to take the College Board Subject Test in biology at the end of the year. The student, in this case, decided not to take it when his teacher pointed out to him that, although he was earning an A– in the course, his test scores came in noticeably lower than his grades on lab reports and homework assignments. The other family received a blanket recommendation that the high school issued to all grade nine students to take the biology Subject Test at the end of the year. The student did not know any better and, thinking that she had to follow the school's advice, took the test and received a disappointing score. Seek guidance on issues such as these by February of your child's freshman year if the high school does not address them automatically; ask follow-up questions to determine whether or not generic suggestions meet the needs of your child.

You also want to see evidence at least by the second half of grade eleven that the counselor who will be working with your child on college applications knows her and has met you. Meeting parents can take several different forms, depending on high school size. College counselors at small, independent high schools almost always set up individual meetings with each family, while those at large public high schools generally convene a college night for parents at which those who attend hear a presentation, ask questions, and meet the counselors. If your child attends a high school that does not automatically invite families for individual meetings, do not hesitate to call the counselor to set one up yourself. Even counselors in the most resource-constrained buildings generally welcome constructive parental involvement.

The value of meeting with your child's counselor, whether individually or in a group session, depends on the quality of information that the counselor provides. Pay attention to whether your child's counselor suggests colleges and universities based on your child's profile or, conversely, appears to rely on a generic list of institutions for everybody. Keep track of whether or not he recommends options in other states and regions of the country. A counselor who only refers students to in-state institutions, for example, is probably working from a limited knowledge base. Perform some due diligence with parents of students who have graduated. Did their children wind up at colleges and universities where they have thrived? Did they get into one of their top two or three choices? Tracking details like these will tell you more about the quality of counseling at your child's high school than tallying the number of students who got into Harvard or Yale.

You should also expect to receive helpful guidance and support through the financial aid process from your child's counselor. Once again, ask members of the Parents Association or friends who have already gone through the process at your child's high school. In my experience, all counselors in a building did not necessarily demonstrate equal expertise with financial aid, but at least one person in the guidance department knew how to assist parents with the process.

Supplementary college guidance information abounds, in bookstores, online, through private companies, and through private consultants. Consulting written materials, either online or off the shelf, makes sense even if every indicator suggests that your child is working with an effective college guidance counselor. Books such as this one and online sources of information, such as www.collegebroadband.com, can, at the very least, help you formulate questions for meetings with your child's counselor and insure that you cover all the bases relevant to your individual situation. They can also help you assess whether and how to use supplementary resources for your child, as well as develop a college admissions strategy of your own if your child's high school falls short in this area. Check credentials of the authors and Web site operators, though, before you rely on their advice. Use extra caution with expensive seminars where someone promises inside connections with Ivy League institutions, as these claims generally lie *far* from the truth and amount to a colossal waste of time and money.

You can also use books and Web sites to help you target exactly how to use a private college counselor, if you decide that you need to hire somebody in this capacity. Your child's college counselor at the high school may give excellent advice on standardized testing and course selection but have limited knowledge of music conservatory programs, for example. In this case, you would look for an independent advisor who has visited campuses across the country, can recommend and help you research schools, and can guide your child on preparing performance tapes to submit with her application. Scrutinize credentials carefully and do not mistake high sticker price for quality. Some of the best private counselors I know charge a fraction of what they could and accept clients only through referrals, rather than as a result of aggressive marketing. Call a well-regarded independent school in your area and ask its college counseling office for a referral to a private counselor. Sometimes the counselors there see private clients themselves, either pro bono or for a reasonable fee; they also generally keep a Rolodex of consultants whom they trust.

The best private consultants in the business also understand the concept of "too many cooks." I take clients who genuinely lack sufficient college counseling resources at their high school. One young man with whom I am working, for example, has had a different guidance counselor for each of his four years. Families regularly approach me, though, from high schools with top-notch college guidance and academic advising resources. In these instances, I limit my involvement with a student so as not to interfere with the high school's standard operating procedures.

FREQUENTLY ASKED QUESTIONS

My daughter's high school tracks students as either "honors" or "standard." She entered high school as a standard English student but, this year, in grade ten, had a teacher who got her excited about the subject. She now wants to move to honors for junior and senior year. Unfortunately, her guidance counselor is telling us that the school will not allow the move because she has already fallen too far behind the honors curriculum in her first two years of high school. What would you recommend?

It sounds like your daughter is turning into a passionate learner in English, an evolution that I urge you to encourage strongly for a number of reasons. Newfound passion in one subject area can have a spillover effect: Your daughter may find that she becomes more excited than she has been in the past about learning overall as a result of what she is experiencing with English. Her self-esteem may also rise as she performs at new levels in a challenging subject. An interest and strong background in English could open a whole new set of academic and career possibilities for her, such as journalism. Do everything you can to encourage your daughter's newfound enthusiasm for English, regardless of what the high school says.

You have many options at your disposal, both within and outside of the high school. Start by going to the teacher who got your daughter excited about English in the first place. Let him know the effect his class had on her and ask him for his help in moving her to honors. He may be willing to tutor your daughter over the summer, for example, to prepare her for a placement examination in the fall that would demonstrate to her guidance counselor that she has caught up to the honors class. (You would, of course, have to pay the teacher for tutoring. If he cannot do it, ask him if he can recommend a colleague.) Having the teacher on your side will strengthen your case, especially if you need to continue working your way up the chain of command at the high school—to the principal, if necessary.

You may also want to look into summer enrichment programs, either in your area or on a college campus. Participating in this kind of program would expose your daughter to peers who share her passion for English, an advantage that private tutoring does not offer. Once again, consult with her current teacher and see if you can get the syllabus and textbook for the upcoming year's honors course. Your daughter can show them to her instructor over the summer and ask for extra help in covering key topics.

The high school may still tell you that your daughter may not switch to honors, for a variety of possible reasons. Large high schools frequently structure schedules so that all students taking honors English are also taking honors history, for example, a case that may not hold true for your daughter and cause a resulting scheduling conflict. Honors English may already be oversubscribed. The list could go on. The high school's inability to accommodate you only means that you need to continue pursuing enrichment opportunities in other ways, such as your daughter joining the school newspaper or literary magazine staff, enrolling in a community college course after school or on weekends, or taking an online course. Never let a high school's lack of resources or flexibility limit your child's educational options!

Our son's high school openly acknowledges that its curriculum does not prepare students for standardized tests—e.g., the SAT Subject Tests—and that many perform poorly on them as a result. The college guidance office encourages seniors to apply to colleges and universities that do not require or place much weight on standardized testing. Could this approach limit our son and, if so, what would you suggest we do, both to prepare him for standardized tests and to expose him to colleges and universities that his high school may not emphasize?

All students, no matter where they attend high school, need to study intensively for standardized college admissions tests. Your son's high school has let you know unequivocally and with sufficient advance notice that you have to find effective test-preparation resources for him. You also now have an advantage over families who mistakenly believe that their child's high school curriculum provides adequate standardized test preparation, a common and egregious misconception.

Your description of the high school and its relationships with colleges sounds like the school has created a niche for itself. That situation strikes me as far better than the high school not having relationships with any admissions officers at all (the case in many places). Reach out to your son's guidance counselor and let him know if your son, in fact, has an interest in colleges and universities with whom his high school does not usually do business. Ask the counselor to invite representatives from those institutions to visit the high school during their fall travel season. If that strategy does not work, call admissions offices yourself and ask when a representative will be traveling in your area. You may be able to attend an information session at another high school or at a local college fair.

I went to the state department of education Web site and looked at the state standards as you recommended, but found them very confusing. How else could I gauge the quality of the curriculum at my child's high school?

If your daughter has started talking about colleges that interest her, go to those Web sites and look at their educational requirements. Does it look like your child's high school curriculum is preparing her for them? You may also want to place a telephone call to an academic department at the college that interests her. Ask somebody there what an entering freshman needs to know and be able to do for introductory courses. You will know right away that a problem exists if the history department says, for example, that freshmen routinely have to write ten-page papers, while your child's high school is only asking for a five-paragraph essay by senior year (an actual example that I saw at a supposedly college-preparatory high school).

My son had the chance to enroll at an elite independent high school, but we could not afford the tuition and left him where he was. He says he wants to attend an Ivy League college but has started to languish from boredom at his current high school, both because of bad teaching and uninterested classmates. He has maintained a B+ average but could be doing so much better than that. What can we do to insure that our son reaches his potential in spite of the inadequate teaching and learning going on at his high school (he has just finished sophomore year)?

Unfortunately, many students from all kinds of backgrounds and communities find themselves in a situation similar to your son's. This scenario looks like one in which, in addition to using the strategies in this book, it may make sense to engage a private college admissions consultant. (A high school with a uniformly weak academic program may also lack effective college guidance resources.) Let the consultant know that you want your son to understand exactly what he will have to know and be able to do to have a chance at gaining admission to an Ivy League institution. Ask the consultant to suggest strategies that you and your son can use independent of his high school if he decides he wants to pursue this path. You should be able to accomplish this discussion in the course of one session (two at most). Do not sign any type of contract for a college admissions package or for repeated visits with this consultant. Instead, observe whether or not your son follows the initial pieces of advice that you got in this first session. Offer your son support where necessary, but let him drive the process.

If your son acts on the consultant's recommendations, go back to see that person at the beginning of your son's junior year. Consider at that point working with the consultant on an ongoing basis to set up a standardized testing strategy and timeline, identify colleges and universities to look at, and more. Much of the success of this approach will depend on your son acting as a self-starter, without the structure that a strong, school-based college guidance program provides. Look for evidence at the outset that your son will pull his weight to make investing time, energy, and funds in this outside resource a worthwhile endeavor.

STEP-BY-STEP CHECKLIST:
UNDERSTANDING YOUR CHILD'S HIGH SCHOOL

❏ Complete the worksheet "Assessing Your Child's High School."

❏ Look at materials—the syllabus, descriptions of assignments—that teachers have distributed.

❏ Examine your child's class notes and graded work.

❏ Find out how your child is tracked and how that affects the standards and expectations in place for her.

❏ Compare all of the above to what the district and state say your child should be learning.

❏ Come to a conclusion about whether or not your child is learning at an appropriate level.

❏ If you suspect that a problem exists, determine its source (the school, your child, both) and whether or not it requires that you take action.

❏ In the case of a bad teacher, encourage your child to seek extra help from somebody else in the department and/or to take advantage of free school-based tutoring, such as peer or volunteer programs.

❏ Look into what a class or tracking change would entail.

❏ Research available enrichment or remedial programs in your area, such as those funded by the federal government or nonprofit organizations.

❏ Research summer enrichment programs on college campuses.

❏ Explore private tutoring.

❏ Look into high school transfer options for the beginning of grade ten.

❏ Start looking in the spring of grade nine for communication from your child's high school about standardized testing and course selection as they relate to college.

❏ Examine any suggestions for an entire cohort of students (for example, all students should take the College Board Subject Test in biology at the end of grade nine) to make sure they meet the individual needs of your child.

❑ Perform some due diligence with parents whose children have gone through the college admissions process at your child's high school to determine if those students have had a positive experience in college thus far.

❑ Attend any type of meeting or college night to which the college counseling department invites you.

❑ Call to set up an individual appointment with the college counselor in January of your child's junior year if the high school does not set up this type of face-to-face meeting on its own.

❑ Seek information and/or support from external sources if you suspect that you are not getting top-quality advice from your child's counselor (for example, the counselor does not offer help with the financial aid process, he refers your child only to a generic list of colleges and universities, he seems to know and refer students only to in-state institutions, and so on).

❑ If hiring a private college admissions consultant appears necessary, get a referral from a college counselor at a well-regarded independent school in your area.

THREE

Understanding Your Child's Academic Transcript

I always ask new clients to bring with them a copy of their child's high school transcript the first time they come to see me. We have already looked at how the transcript illustrates your child's academic profile, but we are now going to examine how it factors into the admissions process, how an admissions officer would use it in evaluating your child, and what you and your child can do to strengthen his high school transcript at different points along the college admissions timeline. Academic transcripts represent one of the most sensitive and complex areas of college admissions but also an area over which your child has more control than you might think—beginning in grade nine. Understanding how it makes sense to exert that control (and how it does not) could have a profound impact on your child's quality of life in high school and his eventual college admissions results. Using the baseline assessments that you have already completed of your child's student profile and of his high school gives you a strong foundation from which to proceed.

MANAGING EXPECTATIONS (BOTH YOURS AND YOUR CHILD'S)

Before we start looking at your child's high school transcript in depth, I want to share with you a story about my own mother, who always took a hands-off approach with grades. She and I had a grand total of two conversations about them, the first when I brought home a disappointing report card in sixth grade and the second when I told her in my freshman year of college that my grades over the next four years would not match what I had earned in high school. In that first conversation, my mother let me know that the 65's and 70's on my sixth-grade report card "disappointed" her. I had previously attended an elementary school that did not believe in grading students, so I had no idea what the numbers on this green piece of cardstock represented. "Just try your hardest," she responded when I asked her what she expected of me. "But 90's or higher would be nice," she clarified after a short pause.

I decided to accept my mother's challenge, partly because I did not like the feeling that came over me when she told me that I had disappointed her, but also because I wanted to see what would result from my trying my best. By the end of sixth grade, the 65's and 70's on my report card had risen to 85's (and maybe a 90 here or there). My mother showered her pride and satisfaction on me when she saw the report card—an experience that differed dramatically from the evening several months earlier when she had stood next to the refrigerator and shaken her head in disappointment. I decided to see how much further I could go with this "doing my best" strategy and continued to make strides. Along the way, my motivation for achieving academically shifted from pleasing my mother to satisfying myself. I developed a passion for history and languages (both of which I went on to teach years later) and formed strong relationships with wonderful teachers. My mother never offered me any material reward for academic achievement and, in her own way, taught me that the most effective kind of motivation comes from within.

Now fast forward several years later to my freshman year in college when I suddenly found myself in a setting unlike anything else that I had experienced before. New people, endless activities, plus the responsibilities of a work-study job as part of my financial aid package all pulled me away from academics. Suddenly maintaining a straight-A average did not seem as compelling as it had in high school. I let my mother know that I wanted to experience more at college than just an isolated study carrel and heaved a sigh of relief when she agreed that I should live a little. I still intended to do well and kept my grades consistently at the B+ level, but I knew that I was forfeiting my chance to attend a place like Harvard Law School. Imagine my surprise then, at the end of my junior year, when my mother suggested that I look into fellowships—Rhodes, Marshall, Fulbright—all highly prestigious and awarded in large part based on academic achievement. I reminded her of our earlier discussion and explained that my transcript, while solid, would not measure up in such a competitive pool. A pause ensued at the other end of the telephone. "But you're such a good person!" she exclaimed, in maternal bewilderment. I appreciated that my mother, out of love, still wanted every door to remain open for me; I valued just as much, though, her having given me the freedom to make my own choices.

This story has a timeless quality to it. Parents have particular goals, hopes, or dreams for their children and they see getting top grades as the key to achieving them. Sometimes these adult visions of what children can or should achieve trace back to what we as adults wish we had accomplished ourselves. In other instances, they represent a desire for the next generation to experience life without any obstacles. Whatever the case, you as a parent have to walk a fine line between supporting your child's aspirations for himself without pushing him in directions that represent *your* desires more than *his*.

Your child may also need your guidance and support in clarifying his own goals and/or strategies if he has set his heart on a highly selective institution and is focusing disproportionately on his grades or, alternatively, is not giving them sufficient attention given the height at which he has set the bar. I recently met with a young man, about to enter his junior year of high school, who named Harvard, Yale, and Dartmouth when I asked him where he pictured himself for college. His transcript, on the other hand, told a different story and needed to improve—given who he was and where he was attending high school—if he expected to get into any of those top schools. In this case, the young man himself was setting the expectations; his parents simply wanted to support his goals. The day after our meeting, the boy's mother let me know via e-mail that her son understood from our discussion that he would have to "work very hard" to make it to the Ivy League, but that he had also told her that he would "not be crushed" if he ended up going elsewhere.

Understanding the role that the high school transcript plays in college admissions can help you with this balancing act. You may even find that details you thought mattered a lot do not carry much weight after all. Colleges and universities look at the transcript as a document that tells a story about who your child is and what he can comfortably accomplish. Promoting a good college match for your child means managing both your expectations and his so that he has the latitude to create his own transcript, one that tells his story as authentically as possible.

COURSE SELECTION: BALANCING YOUR CHILD'S INTERESTS WITH WHAT ADMISSIONS OFFICERS LIKE TO SEE ON A TRANSCRIPT

Deans of admission around the country can usually characterize in a phrase or two what they hope a transcript will reflect about a student. Jim Sumner at Grinnell College hopes to see "intellectual engagement." Jane Brown describes the "hallmark of the Mount Holyoke student" as "how her academic work connects to making a difference in the world." Rice University's Julie Browning searches for students "who drink deeply from the educational pond." Harold Wingood at Clark University describes the ideal entering student as "academically independent, willing to take academic risks." All of these seasoned admissions folks could expand on the intellectual qualities they seek in successful applicants, but even these brief descriptions provide windows into each institution's character and demonstrate that the value of a transcript lies in much more than the number of AP courses your child takes.[7]

Admissions officers seek four principal pieces of information about your child from his high school transcript:

1. The extent to which he challenges himself academically, relative to the resources available to him;

2. The academic areas that interest him;

3. His ability to perform, as evidenced by his grades; and

4. The degree to which these factors overlap with a college or university's character and priorities.

These four strands work together in an interconnected way, especially at the most selective colleges and universities in the country. Let's look at a couple of success stories in which students made the right decisions for themselves.

Calvin's love of history, literature, and foreign languages propelled him to the highest levels of performance at his high school. The Spanish department had to create a class for him in his senior year because he had exhausted all of its existing resources. He did not, however, feel the same way about the sciences and turned down the department chair's invitation to join an AP class his senior year. Calvin winced a little bit when he opted out of the AP science class: he hated giving up the chance to strengthen his transcript for his early action application to one of the Big Three Ivies, but science had never appealed to him, and he ultimately decided that the requirements of an AP class would take away from his ability to enjoy the courses in his senior year that he was looking forward to taking.

What Admissions Officers Look For in a Transcript

- The extent to which your child challenges himself academically, relative to the resources available to him.

- Academic areas that interest him.

- His ability to perform, as evidenced by his grades.

- The degree to which these factors overlap with a college/ university's character and priorities.

Hannah majored in art at a nationally known high school that admitted students based on competitive auditions or portfolio submissions. She enjoyed her high school experience but decided in her junior year that she wanted to attend a liberal arts college where she could explore different disciplines, rather than go to a specialized fine arts institute. AP classes gave her the chance to begin that exploration in high school. She enrolled in two as a junior and earned grades of B+ and A− but did not do well on the AP examinations at the end of the year. Undeterred, she enrolled in five AP courses as a senior, including physics because she thought it sounded interesting. She never achieved at the exceptional levels that Calvin did, but she maintained her B+/A− average and loved her classes.

Somebody with an eye on the Ivy League or near equivalent might say that Calvin and Hannah made strategically questionable decisions about which classes to take. One gave up a coveted spot in an AP class and the other decided to explore new academic areas instead of emphasizing her existing strength in art. They both, however, presented themselves to colleges in an authentic way rather than focusing on what they thought an admissions officer would want to see. Calvin, the star of his school, got in early to his first choice—an Ivy League university. Hannah, who had originally wanted to attend an Ivy League school but did not get in, accepted an offer from a small, highly respected university that admired her intellectual curiosity and spunk and pursued her energetically. Both students felt that they had found the best possible fit in a college and reported back in glowing terms in their freshman year. Calvin's and Hannah's stories illustrate general guidelines to follow when you discuss courses with your child.

Guidelines for Thinking About Course Selection

- Encourage your child to challenge himself without making himself miserable.

- Help your child balance his academic interests with the priorities of the colleges and universities that appeal to him.

- Look for colleges and universities that match your child's learning style and that value the aspects of his education that matter to him.

Encourage your child to challenge himself without making himself miserable. Yes, highly selective institutions want to see that he has stretched himself as far as the resources at his high school allow, including taking AP courses if possible (admissions officers will not penalize him if his school does not offer an AP program). I would not recommend, however, that he push himself to take upper-level courses if his heart is not in it, simply to make a good impression when he applies to college. If he has to tie himself into knots with the classes that he takes in high school just to gain admission to a college or university, imagine what he will have to do to keep up once he gets there.

Help your child balance his academic interests with the priorities of the colleges and universities that appeal to him. Your child should feel free to concentrate his efforts and energies on areas that interest him, the way Calvin did when he took AP classes in the humanities but not in the sciences. Keep in mind, though, that colleges and universities have priorities of their own. The most selective in the country, for example, want to see a heavy dose of all the bread-and-butter subjects (English, foreign language, history, mathematics, and science). Suggest to your child by the end of grade ten that he look at course requirements at a couple of colleges or universities that interest him, in case he wants to factor the information he finds there into his decisions about what to take in high school. An institution that requires several years of foreign language, for example, will appreciate the presence of foreign language courses on your child's high school transcript.

Look for colleges and universities that match your child's learning style and that value the aspects of his education that matter to him. Admissions officers use your child's transcript as a principal tool to determine whether or not a good fit exists between student and school. You should do the same. If your child has done well in classes that emphasize research, consider a small university, where he will have the chance to work closely with faculty members. If he has excelled with teachers who assign independent projects, explore institutions that encourage self-directed study. Help your child use his transcript at the end of grade eleven or beginning of grade twelve to analyze his own learning style and then look for colleges and universities that will nurture it.

GRADE POINT AVERAGE (GPA) AND CLASS RANK: DEBUNKING THE MYTHS

Believe it or not, GPA and class rank matter to admissions officers far less than you may think they do. Don't get me wrong—academic performance, measured by grades and relative to other students, weighs heavily in the evaluation process. Because the ways in which high schools calculate GPA and class rank vary so widely, however, admissions officers generally take these numbers with a grain of salt. In fact, GPA and class rank have become over time an increasingly unreliable way of judging a candidate's ability.

GPA means, by definition, that a high school assigns a point value to each grade that a student can earn (4.0 for an A, 3.0 for a B, etc.) and then averages these point values for an overall indicator of how a student is performing academically. Let's take the easiest possible example: an A is worth 4 points and your child has earned an A in each of the five classes he is taking. The point values for his five classes average out to 4, which means that your child would have a 4.0 GPA.

This method seems simple and straightforward enough, except that no uniform scale for point values exists: a high school in Tulsa could make an A worth 4 points and a high school in Santa Fe could make it worth 10. To complicate matters further, high schools frequently add bonus points to the value of grades earned in honors or AP classes. These widespread variations in policy and procedure have forced many admissions offices to discount GPA almost entirely—unless they know and understand a particular high school's calibration—or to create their own ways to use it. The University of Michigan, for example, recomputes GPA for every applicant based on core courses that appear on the transcript.

If the seemingly endless ways that high schools calculate GPA cause frustration, admissions officers simply throw their hands in the air when they hear the term "class rank." Deans of admission from some of the most selective institutions in the country used words like "elusive," "manipulated," and "politicized" in my discussions with them about class rank. Many high schools, especially those in suburban communities, have responded to political pressure from parents, who feel that a top ranking will help their children get into college. Every student with a GPA at or above a certain point, therefore, gets ranked number one. This solution has led to absurd situations, such as a single graduating class having forty valedictorians, and has dramatically diluted the value of class rank as a comparative measure. Graduating at the top of the class may still have meaning in some communities; but, as Rice's Julie Browning says, "All valedictorians are not alike!"

Colleges and universities have taken varying approaches to class rank as their ability to use it has declined. Rice University tracks the information but uses it with "caution." Pitzer College exempts applicants in the top 10 percent of their class from standardized testing (it has the same policy for applicants with a 3.5 GPA). Mount Holyoke considers class rank only when it understands an applicant's high school well. Parents and students frequently focus on GPA and class rank as the ultimate indicators of academic success. College admissions offices around the country, though, are sending a very different message.

Admissions officers also realize that mere hundredths of a point can separate number one from number fifteen in a class; as students, these two young people have almost identical profiles. This phenomenon has allowed both Massachusetts Institute of Technology (MIT) Dean of Admissions Marilee Jones and Lehigh University Dean of Admissions and Financial Aid Eric Kaplan to look more closely at applicants ranked below number one. "You could be number one, number five, or number fifteen and be equally capable," Kaplan asserts. At MIT, where at least 60 percent of the entering students are *not* number one, Jones believes that she and her staff are admitting candidates willing to "take some intellectual risks," a characteristic that MIT values.

Deans of admission with whom I spoke repeatedly pointed out that roughly half of the students that their institutions admitted came from high schools that do not calculate class rank, a clear sign that the absence of this indicator does not pose a barrier to entry for applicants. The vast majority of students that these highly selective institutions admitted from ranked high schools, however, fell within the top 10–20 percent of their graduating class. This statistic reinforces the idea that colleges and universities are looking for academically capable candidates within a certain range rather than those who have achieved a "magic number." Do not rule out your child's chances of getting into a top college or university because his class rank puts him at number fourteen rather than at number one. By the same token, do not assume that a number one ranking will guarantee admission. Selective colleges and universities look at the overall story that an academic transcript tells, a story that transcends a single numerical ranking.

INTERPRETING THE STORY THAT YOUR CHILD'S HIGH SCHOOL TRANSCRIPT TELLS

Now that you have a sense of what admissions officers value and what they do not, use the "Assessing Your Child's High School Transcript" worksheet to trace the story that your child's transcript tells. Take a moment to select the sentence in each of the four boxes that, to the best of your knowledge, accurately describes your child. Then go through each category and assess where he falls, the implications that his current transcript has for college admissions, and ways in which he can make changes if he so desires. As I mentioned earlier, who your child is and the degree of demand that exists for someone with his profile will strongly influence the academic standard to which admissions officers hold him. A student's transcript always has to demonstrate first and foremost that he can survive academically at an institution. The degree of academic excellence to which admis-

Assessing Your Child's High School Transcript

In each of the boxes below, please pick the statement that you think best describes your child.

Tracking

☐ My child's high school does not track students (skip this box).

☐ My child is taking or plans to take all of his classes in the most academically rigorous track that the high school offers.

☐ My child is taking or plans to take some but not all of his courses in the most academically rigorous track that the high school offers.

☐ My child is taking or plans to take courses in a college-preparatory track, but not in the most academically rigorous track that the high school offers.

☐ My child is not taking and does not plan to take courses in a college-preparatory track.

☐ Other: _____

Academic Performance

☐ My child's high school does not grade students (skip this box).

☐ My child consistently earns straight A's (or the equivalent if his high school uses a different grading system).

☐ My child consistently earns a combination of A's and B's (or the equivalent if his high school uses a different grading system).

☐ My child consistently earns B's and maybe an occasional A (or the equivalent if his high school uses a different grading system).

☐ My child generally earns grades below the B level (or the equivalent if his high school uses a different grading system).

☐ My child's report cards do not follow any predictable pattern, i.e., he will just as likely earn an A as an F.

☐ Other: _____

Course Selection

☐ My child's high school does not offer course selection options to students (skip this box).

☐ My child is taking or plans to take four years of each major academic subject (English, foreign language, history, mathematics, science).

☐ My child is taking or plans to take four years of some major academic subjects, but not all.

☐ My child is taking or plans to take only the major subject courses that his high school requires and will switch to elective subjects as soon as possible (psychology, art, drama, popular culture, etc.).

☐ Other: _____

Class Standing

☐ My child's high school does not rank (skip this box).

☐ My child ranks in the top 50 percent in his class.

☐ My child ranks in the top 40 percent in his class.

☐ My child ranks in the top 30 percent in his class.

☐ My child ranks in the top 20 percent in his class.

☐ My child ranks in the top 10 percent in his class.

☐ Other: _____

sions officers hold him beyond that, though, depends on the institution, its own needs, and whether or not your child meets those needs in ways that a limited number of applicants can.

Tracking, the first box on our worksheet, varies dramatically from school to school and stands out as an area at your child's high school about which you should inform yourself as comprehensively as possible. Some schools do not track at all, which means that all students take all of their classes at the exact same level of difficulty and challenge (feel free to skip ahead if your child's high school does not track). A choice, however, between honors, standard, or practical biology, for example, or between honors, Curriculum I, or Curriculum II history means his high school is tracking. Many parents do not realize that tracking can begin as early as kindergarten when teachers assign students to reading groups with seemingly innocuous names (red, yellow, blue, etc.). These early designations can follow children throughout their academic career and influence, among other things, the teachers they get, the students with whom they attend class, and whether or not they eventually gain admission to AP classes.

Tracking can also play out in different ways, depending on the policies and procedures at a particular school. Some schools track students across the board for all their classes. A student who is taking honors English is also taking honors history, foreign language, mathematics, and science, and switching out of honors for one subject means a complete change of track for all. Other schools track students subject by subject. A young woman in my class during my first year of teaching was taking honors in all subjects except history, in which she preferred to enroll at the next level down. Policies on paper sometimes conflict with the logistics of scheduling: in theory a school may allow a student to enroll in classes at all different levels, but in practice the registrar may find that most students who take honors physics also take honors mathematics and schedule courses in a way that makes only this particular combination possible. You need to understand if and how your child's high school uses tracking in order to exercise fully the options in front of you.

Highly selective colleges and universities *generally* want to see that applicants have taken many, if not all, of their classes in the most academically rigorous track available (although doing so does not in any way guarantee admission). I have emphasized the word "generally" because caveats apply here. First, admissions officers do not penalize students if their high school does not track. Second, phenomenal levels of achievement in select areas or compelling personal circumstances, such as someone who has pioneered a scientific breakthrough or the child of migrant workers who has switched schools every year, may motivate an admissions officer to look more flexibly at the transcript than he otherwise might. Third, admissions officers recognize that the demands of AP and honors classes vary across high schools; an applicant taking three such courses in a rigorous academic environment may make a greater impression than somebody taking six at a school with a less intense academic reputation. You need to understand whether or not your child has any admissions hooks and how your child's high school compares with others in order to understand how an admissions officer will interpret this part of your child's transcript.

You also need to keep your child's student profile at the forefront of your mind as you think about tracking. A passionate learner may thrive by taking rigorous classes in areas of interest. A solid student may see his self-esteem and quality of life suffer, though, if he moves from comfortably getting A's in a regular college-preparatory track to struggling for B's in an AP track. Talk with your child about how he feels and whether he's confident or not about this kind of challenge. Use this examination of your child's transcript as an opportunity to gauge his interests, comfort level, and goals. Students tend to find it easier to move from higher to lower tracked classes than the other way around (if your child wants to leave as many options open as possible). Remember, the most selective colleges and universities *generally* want to see that applicants have taken the most rigorous academic program available to them; however, doing so in no way guarantees admission.

The results of the discussion you have with your child will vary depending on when you have it. Students in grades nine and ten still have ample opportunity to switch tracks if a change feels appropriate; a conversation at this stage can focus dually on helping your child select the appropriate academic path for him and making him aware that this path will have implications for college. A discussion with an eleventh- or twelfth-grade student has more of a summary or recap focus to it, that is, the choices your child has made in high school and how they position him for college. Change can still take place at this stage, but it will require concerted and strategic effort, rather than simply making routine choices.

Always remember your overall goal, especially when you hear your neighbor talking about the perfect AP score that her brilliant child received in grade ten. You want your child to fulfill his individual academic potential in high school in order to get into the best college or university *for him*. A student who is not taking courses in a college-preparatory track has not prepared himself for a Top 20 institution; you would be doing your child a disservice by pushing him to do things with that goal in mind. Look at what your child's transcript tells you about him and then let him supplement that picture. You will find that this approach serves you far better in the long run than forcing your child down a path that does not fit him well.

Many of the same points that we visited in our discussion of tracking hold for course selection (the worksheet's second box) as well. Highly selective colleges and universities expect candidates to have taken a content-rich curriculum. Content-rich *generally* means four years of bread-and-butter subjects (English, foreign language, history, mathematics, science), rather than electives. Students sometimes have limited choices, however, for which admissions officers will not penalize them. One of my clients recently chose a feminism elective for twelfth-grade history, but explained to me that her only other options included sociology, philosophy, or historical fiction, none of which had any more content value than the option she had selected. Calvin, the student whose story we looked at earlier in this chapter, took philosophy and constitutional law in twelfth grade—after he had taken AP European history in grade ten and AP U.S. history in grade eleven. Students seeking admission to highly selective colleges and universities need to focus on bread-and-butter subjects first and electives second, when possible.

Once again, keep your child's student profile in mind. I recently met with a family wrestling with whether or not to eliminate mathematics from the son's upcoming twelfth-grade schedule. The young man disliked the teacher, had a history of weak performance in mathematics, and did not have the option of taking anything other than precalculus. He was absolutely dreading the course and I could tell immediately that it was going to overshadow his entire senior year. The father, who had attended an Ivy League university himself, expressed concern that his son's transcript would look weak with only three years of mathematics. I pointed out that, first, the transcript would look terrible if the son put all his time into precalculus and did poorly in everything else and, second, the institutions to which his son was going to apply (not very selective) would not penalize him for this decision.

I felt the same way when another one of my clients told me that she had decided to drop Latin in her senior year. This young lady had struggled with two language courses—Latin and French—throughout high school. She finally decided to give herself a break in twelfth grade and substitute a communications elective for Latin. Bound for a Top 100 rather than Top 20 institution, and with a strong athletic hook to boot, this young woman clearly did not need a fourth year of Latin and made the absolute right decision for herself, with the support of her parents.

Questions about bread-and-butter subjects versus electives usually do not come up until your child selects courses for senior year (sometimes junior year, depending on the high school). Certain tracks, however, may automatically culminate in electives rather than in more content-rich subjects in grade twelve. In history, for example, many high schools require students to take two years of world or global history in grades nine and ten and then one year of U.S. history in grade eleven. A student who is not taking an AP course in grade twelve may only have electives like feminism, psychology, or popular culture from which to choose. If you are reviewing this information while your child is still in grade nine or ten, make sure to verify whether or not your child's track will limit his course selection possibilities as he moves into junior and senior year. If you and he determine that a tracking change will work for him, then pursue that discussion with the high school.

The third box on our worksheet focuses on grades, the true litmus test for how well tracking and course selection are actually working for your child. A student attending the right high school for him and taking appropriately challenging courses should, in theory anyway, be earning primarily A's and/or B's. Let's look at some reasons why reality may differ from what makes sense in theory. First, your child may be attending a high school that is not providing the appropriate teaching and learning environment for him (see Chapter Two). Second, he may be falling short in classes that present him with too much of an academic challenge to handle. Third, he may fit the profile of either the underachiever or the struggling student that we discussed in Chapter One. Last but not least, personal circumstances—no quiet place to do homework, working too many hours at a part-time job, illness of a loved one, his own poor health—may be pulling him away from his studies. Try to tackle each possible factor one by one and see what happens before you move on to another. Changing multiple variables at once can make it difficult to determine what was creating the problem to begin with.

How you approach college admissions depends on the story that your child's grades tell by the time he reaches grade twelve and whether or not the rest of his application reinforces that narrative. Struggling students who care deeply about their education but have not yet found an appropriate learning environment will benefit from a college campus that offers them the support they need. Specific colleges and universities that offer an outstanding academic and personal support system for students include Lake Forest College outside of Chicago (www.lakeforest.edu), Marlboro College in Vermont (www.marlboro.edu), Massachusetts College of Liberal Arts (www.mcla.edu), Ohio Wesleyan (www.owu.edu), St. Bonaventure in New York (www.sbu.edu), and Susquehanna University in Pennsylvania (www.susqu.edu), to name a few. Loren Pope's book *Colleges That Change Lives* (New York: Penguin, 2000; www.ctcl.com) focuses on institutions of which you may not have heard but where students have had extraordinary educational experiences, even if they arrived on campus with a weak academic high school transcript.

I would also recommend the Pope book for underachievers, although with some specific caveats. You need to understand why your child is not achieving at his potential in order to address that issue in high school if possible (depending on the grade he is in when you read this book) and certainly in order to help him find the right environment for college. It does not pay, with today's cost of tuition, room, and board, to send a young person to college who does not plan to take advantage of it. Make sure you and your child have dealt with this issue head-on in your discussions about his postsecondary plans. An underachiever especially may benefit from spending a year or two at a community college to build up an appreciation for his education and for what a four-year program would offer him. Community college could address cumulative skill deficiencies resulting from years of failing to pay attention or complete assignments. A community college transition may also allow your underachieving child to rebuild a transcript that opens far more doors for him at four-year institutions than his high school transcript would.

The most selective colleges and universities in the country are looking for intellectual passion, curiosity, and a drive to take advantage of any and all available resources. Those qualities often (but not always) appear as A's on a transcript—the A that comes from the teacher who identifies the student as one of the top five she has encountered in twenty years of teaching rather than from the teacher who writes that Jane showed up for class on time every day. You as a parent need to do the hard work of examining what your child's A's and B's represent: the equivalent of analytical, college-level work; basic, factual response questions on homework assignments and tests; or something in between.

Class rank (the fourth box on our worksheet) may help you here. The exact numerical ranking that your child holds may not tell you much, but the decile (10 percent slice) or quintile (20 percent slice) into which he falls can prove quite informative. Top 20 colleges and universities *generally* take students in the top decile and Top 50 institutions seek the top quintile. Keep in mind, once again, that these generalizations vary depending on the high school your child attends, whether or not he has any specific qualities or interests that qualify as admissions hooks, and a variety of other factors that can vary from applicant to applicant. An unhooked candidate, from a regular high school that admits anybody who lives in the area—especially a high-volume college application area—should pay attention to these numbers.

FREQUENTLY ASKED QUESTIONS

My daughter's high school has offered her the opportunity to enroll in what the counselor described as a "dual enrollment" program for her senior year of high school. What exactly does "dual enrollment" mean and what implications does it have for her high school transcript and the college admissions process?

Dual enrollment programs offer high school students the opportunity to take college-level classes, usually at a nearby local campus that has established a relationship with a particular high school or school district. One of my clients recently told me that his high school selected him as a dual enrollment participant at a selective Manhattan-based private university where he will be taking Russian literature in eleventh grade. Another client who lives in a rural southern community and comes to see me on school vacations when she visits family members in the north is participating in a different kind of dual enrollment program: she is taking all of her classes in her senior year of high school at the local campus of the state university. All of these grades appear on students' high school transcripts, but with special designations that indicate college courses.

Roughly 5 percent of all high school students in the United States took college courses in the last school year, either through dual enrollment programs or outside of them, according to the National Center for Education Statistics.[8] The vast majority of these dual enrollment programs (85 percent) require students to meet eligibility criteria, such as a minimum GPA or test score. These statistics suggest that your daughter would be putting herself in a select academic group if she decides to take advantage of this opportunity. (A small minority of programs—5 percent—specifically target at-risk students.)

Whether or not your daughter decides to take advantage of this opportunity should depend entirely on her own motivation level. College courses will likely demand much more of her academically than she has faced in the past. Her heart needs to be in this in order for it to work to her benefit. I would guess that most passionate learners would jump at this opportunity and that some solid students might as well. If your daughter falls into the underachiever category, a different teaching and learning environment might stimulate her intellectually, although I would talk with her about the pros and cons of this scenario in great detail before encouraging her to participate. (She may enjoy classes more than she has in the past, but she may also have more work than she has had before.)

One side effect of dual enrollment presented my rural southern client with a challenge that your daughter might want to consider. The courses that she was taking met on a college schedule that did not coincide at all with her high school. She loved the academic challenge and the intellectual stimulation. She missed out, however, on the opportunity to participate in extracurricular activities at her high school because of the change in her academic schedule. (She had run on the track team every year prior to dual enrollment, for example, and could no longer continue.) If your daughter's dual enrollment program will move her entirely out of her high school environment, look into how this shift will affect her extracurricular activities and make sure that you and she have discussed how she will handle any resulting changes.

Our son, a junior in high school, is trying to decide whether to enroll in several AP classes for his senior year. He feels confident that he can earn solid B's in them, versus solid A's in honors classes (the next level down). Which looks better on the high school transcript to admissions officers from Top 20 colleges and universities?

The easy answer to this question is that admissions officers at Top 20 colleges and universities would prefer to see A's in AP courses. I described academic transcripts at the beginning of this chapter, however, as "one of the most sensitive and complex areas of college admissions," and this question illustrates why. What an admissions officer at a Top 20 institution expects a viable applicant to present on a transcript depends on the high school that the student attends, whether or not he has any admissions hooks, and a number of other variables. I suggest that you set aside what you think somebody might want to see and focus instead on your son's academic interests. Which teachers will bring out the best in him intellectually? Which of the subjects that he is considering for AP might become a major in college? In which of the subjects would he enthusiastically invest scores of hours (outside of class assignments) to study for the AP exam? Your son's answers to these questions will provide you with insight on the best possible choice for him.

I also urge you to think about teacher letters of recommendation in this context, in addition to the transcript. In which of the various classes that your son is considering will he likely have a teacher who could turn into a strong recommender? Teachers in honors classes might identify your son as one of the top students in the class, while those in AP classes might be able to cite his extraordinary work ethic and persistence. All of these characteristics have value in a recommendation, but let me suggest a compromise solution that might get your son the best of both worlds.

Counsel your son to select the classes that have the best possible teachers for his learning style. I am guessing, just based on normal probability, that using this criterion will result in a combination of both honors and AP classes in the subjects under consideration. Taking an honors class does not rule out sitting for an AP examination at the end of the year, especially if your son has the support of a good teacher. Encourage your son to get a copy of the AP syllabus for one of the subjects that he takes at the honors level with a particularly good teacher. Suggest to your son that he ask the teacher if he can complete the AP assignments for extra credit in the honors class and then sit for the examination in the spring. That type of arrangement will result in a fabulous teacher recommendation, an attractive combination of A's and B's on his transcript, evidence that he stretches himself intellectually in multiple ways (and can come up with creative strategies with which to do so), and a fabulous learning experience to boot.

Our daughter liked a particular university very much when we visited it and is thinking about applying early decision. The admissions officer who ran the information session told us that the university expects applicants to have completed precalculus. Our daughter's current mathematics teacher insists that his class covers basic precalculus principles, even though the name of the course gives no indication of that. Does our daughter need to enroll for her senior year in the formal precalculus class that her school offers to fulfill this university's requirement?

Ask your daughter's guidance counselor to speak to the mathematics teacher and write down the precalculus content that his class covers. Then request that the counselor call the admissions officers at this university and confirm with them that the mathematics class your daughter is currently taking meets their requirements. I am guessing that your daughter will not have to enroll in precalculus in her senior year.

Our daughter has a choice for her senior year of three English classes, in order of academic rigor: AP English literature, honors English, and advanced narrative and analytical writing. She refuses to consider AP and, although she debated between honors and advanced narrative, she ended up choosing the latter. We want her at least to take honors because we think it will look better for college. She argues that honors has a heavy reading load (a weak point for her) whereas advanced narrative focuses predominantly on writing, something that she loves. Is she jeopardizing her college chances by taking the least rigorous English course that her high school offers?

Your daughter has given you specific, concrete reasons why she wants to take advanced narrative: she does not want to get bogged down with the heavy reading that honors requires and she loves to write. I am guessing that she is not planning to attend a college or university that will require her to read one hundred pages each night, for these same reasons, and that she may seek out writing-intensive options in the course catalog. She sounds like a bright and self-aware young lady. I would advise you to let her make the decision that feels educationally right to her, as doing so will lead to the healthiest possible outcome, both for her high school experience and the college admissions process.

STEP-BY-STEP CHECKLIST: UNDERSTANDING YOUR CHILD'S HIGH SCHOOL TRANSCRIPT

❏ Complete the worksheet "Assessing Your Child's High School Transcript."

❏ Determine whether or not your child's high school tracks students academically and, if so, exactly how the tracking system works (students take all classes in the same track, they select the level of difficulty that they prefer subject by subject, etc.).

❏ If you are reviewing this information while your child is still in grade nine or ten, verify whether or not your child's track will limit his course selection possibilities in any subject areas to electives rather than bread-and-butter courses as he moves into junior and senior year.

❏ If your child is in grade nine or ten, discuss with him that his academic track will have implications for college and help him select the appropriate academic path for him.

❏ If your child is in grade eleven or twelve, focus this discussion instead on the tracking choices he has made in high school and how they position him for college.

❏ Discuss with your grade-eleven child that Top 50 colleges and universities prefer to see high school seniors take content-rich major subjects, rather than electives.

❏ In looking at your child's grades, examine all possible causes for those below the B range and work with your child to modify one aspect of his educational and/or home environment at a time until you have definitively identified the cause. This step has increased importance in grades nine through eleven, when you still have time to influence positively the grades on his transcript.

❑ Go through these same steps with your grade-twelve child, but with an eye toward identifying the best possible teaching and learning environment for him in college.

❑ If you conclude from the above steps that your child is struggling with academics, make special efforts to identify colleges and universities that will provide him with the academic and personal support he needs.

❑ Consult resources, such as Loren Pope's *Colleges That Change Lives* (New York: Penguin 2000; www.ctcl.com), that will help you identify those institutions.

❑ For the underachieving student in grade eleven or twelve, research and discuss with him the possibility of community college.

FOUR

Taking a Look at the Role of Extracurricular Activities and How They Influence Admissions Decisions

I mentioned in Chapter One that I ask students in a first consultation to itemize for me their extracurricular activities, including the number of years they have participated in each one, leadership positions they have held, and the amount of time they generally devote to a given pursuit. I probe a little bit to determine the pastimes about which they feel passionate, the ones to which they devote a special level of commitment. The overall picture that I get from this discussion helps me characterize a student as a leader, a committed participant, a casual joiner, an independent spirit, a special talent, or somebody not interested or involved in extracurricular pursuits at all. Admissions officers make similar characterizations as they read a folder and see in a student's essay or letters of recommendation evidence of a particular trait that extracurricular activities underscore. Alternatively, pursuits outside of class may reveal a side of a candidate that does not come out elsewhere in the application.

Extracurricular activities give your child the opportunity to show colleges and universities who she is through doing what she enjoys, whether that means gourmet cooking or ice hockey or both—admissions officers want to see it all. They understand that extracurricular activities build leadership, social skills, and self-esteem[9]—benefits that have positive implications for the college or university that your child attends. The characteristics that admissions officers at selective institutions are seeking—leadership, commitment, contributions to school and community, and, where it exists, talent—can come through in almost any pursuit, depending on how your child engages in it, including baby-sitting, bagging groceries, or shouldering household responsibilities to help out at home. The "golden rule" of extracurricular activities, if such a thing exists, boils down to this: *what* your child does matters far less than *how* she does it.

TYPES OF ACTIVITIES AND HOW TO SELECT THEM

The "Assessing Your Child's Extracurricular Activities" worksheet begins by asking you about the types of activities in which your child participates. (You may also want to refer to the extracurricular activity worksheet that you completed in Chapter One.) A student in grade nine may not yet know how she plans to spend her time, so do the best you can if your child is just starting high school. Somebody in tenth grade or beyond, though, has ideally begun to show interest in pursuits outside of class. Complete each question on the worksheet as we discuss it and, by the end of this chapter, you will have a sense of your child's extracurricular profile, how it measures up, and how your child can modify it if she so desires.

High school students can choose from a range of activities, including school-based clubs, teams, and theatrical productions; organized groups or experiences outside of school; paying jobs; and independent hobbies and interests that they pursue completely on their own, without the formal sponsorship or structure of any organization. Some young people have family responsibilities that take up significant time and prevent them from participating in standard activities that we associate with high school. Admissions officers appreciate this entire range and do not look for any specific combination of activities when they read folders.

Unfortunately, many people still believe that some perfect formula exists for a student's extracurricular profile. Students have devoted extensive time and, where budgets allow it, families have expended significant amounts of money on activities that make no difference in the admissions decision. The notion that colleges require community service, for example, has prompted young people around the country to volunteer at senior centers, deliver Meals on Wheels, and

School type (circle one):   Suburban Public   Urban Public   Rural   Private   Charter   Exam/Magnet   Other

Assessing Your Child's Extracurricular Activities

	Strongly Agree		Agree		Somewhat Agree		Disagree		Strongly Disagree	
Types of Activities: My child participates in school-based extracurricular activities, e.g., clubs, sports, theater productions, journalism, student council.	10	9	8	7	6	5	4	3	2	1	0
Types of Activities: My child participates in extracurricular activities outside of school, e.g., church youth group, United Synagogue Youth, community service volunteering, local sports team, etc.	10	9	8	7	6	5	4	3	2	1	0
Types of Activities: My child works at a paying job.	10	9	8	7	6	5	4	3	2	1	0
Types of Activities: My child has ongoing family responsibilities that take up time, e.g., working on the family farm or in the family business, baby-sitting for young siblings, translating for non-English-speaking relatives, etc.	10	9	8	7	6	5	4	3	2	1	0
Types of Activities: My child pursues independent hobbies and interests outside of any formal organizational affiliation, e.g., she goes hiking, surfs, goes sailing, paints, reads, etc.	10	9	8	7	6	5	4	3	2	1	0
Level of Commitment: My child has participated or plans to participate in two or three of any of the above types of activities for at least two to three years.	10	9	8	7	6	5	4	3	2	1	0
Level of Commitment: My child devotes at least five hours a week to the activities to which she is most committed (see statement directly above).	10	9	8	7	6	5	4	3	2	1	0
Participation Level: My child has taken on or plans to take on leadership roles in organized in-school or out-of-school activities, e.g., running for student council, editing the yearbook, directing a play, captaining a team.	10	9	8	7	6	5	4	3	2	1	0
Level of Skill: My child has received external recognition for her level of skill in at least one activity, e.g., all-state athlete, concert-level pianist, etc.	10	9	8	7	6	5	4	3	2	1	0
Story: My child's activities help tell the story of who she is as a member of her family, school, and/or community.	10	9	8	7	6	5	4	3	2	1	0
Story: My child's activities help tell the story of who she is as an individual.	10	9	8	7	6	5	4	3	2	1	0
Passion: My child has a passion for the activities to which she is most committed.	10	9	8	7	6	5	4	3	2	1	0

tutor young children—all so that they could list the activity on the college application. In fact, admissions officers want to see that your child's talents and interests contribute to the community, whether directly or indirectly. A student artist who displays her work at the local library or senior citizens' home, a poet who participates in poetry readings at a local cafe, and a budding journalist who writes for a school or community newspaper have all had a positive impact on people around them. Your child can contribute to her school and community by pursuing what she enjoys and sharing it with others.

Similar misconceptions exist about summer activities. Do not fall into the trap of thinking that your child has to do something that looks prestigious or makes her stand out. Instead, let her pursue whatever interests her, even if it lies around the corner. My own cousin had reservations about letting her son, an aspiring applicant to selective engineering programs, work at a car mechanic's shop over the summer instead of in a university laboratory. She eventually relented and, shortly thereafter, I recounted the story to an admissions colleague at a prestigious college of engineering. "Our faculty love seeing applicants who worked as mechanics!" she exclaimed. "It shows that they enjoy taking things apart and putting them back together—the crux of engineering."

My cousin's focus on a university laboratory for her son looks like small potatoes compared with what I have seen other families do. One of my clients arranged for her son to split his summer: he spent the first half at SAT camp and the second portion performing community service in Central America, all with college applications in mind. (They made these plans before they began consulting with me.) Highly selective summer academic programs, such as Telluride or a Governor's School, catch the attention of admissions officers, while those that admit any student who pays tuition generally do not. As for expensive trips overseas, Grinnell College Dean of Admission and Financial Aid Jim Sumner differentiates "between those experiences that one has exclusively because of one's family prosperity versus others. We try not to reward a student whose family has a lot of resources just because they have them."

Send your child to summer school or on an international experience if the specific program she has selected will reinforce an interest of hers (one of my clients fell in love with Jane Austen's *Pride and Prejudice* in third grade and spent two of her high school summers in England) or will visibly make an impact on her intellectual development. Lehigh University's Eric Kaplan recounted a "great" conversation with a young man from rural Ohio who, because of a Harvard Summer School experience, "was realizing, maybe for the first time in his life, that he had intellectual peers and that it was okay to be really smart. He was probably going to see himself differently from that point forward as a result of the program." Kaplan noted, however, that he also saw on his visit to Harvard Summer School "students who go to high-powered independent schools who probably work from dawn until dusk and could have used a break." If your child falls into the latter category, she should attend a summer academic program only because she wants to, not because she thinks doing so will impress admissions officers because, when all is said and done, it probably won't.

Helping Your Child Select Extracurricular Activities

- Ask your child about her interests outside of academics.

- Invite her to point out to you clubs, teams, or other organizations in the student handbook that pique her curiosity.

- Encourage her to attend organizational meetings or talk to the faculty advisor.

- If your child's high school does not offer many activities (or none that interest her), brainstorm with her about starting a new school-based club or volunteering at a community-based organization.

- Encourage a shy or reluctant child to try at least one or two activities.

- Help an overeager young person balance her academic and extracurricular commitments.

Your child can benefit from your input in several ways as she decides where and how to devote her extracurricular energies. Large high schools that offer scores of activities can overwhelm students of any age. Conversely, small ones that make only a few activities available can frustrate students who would like to get involved. Take some time to sit down with your child and ask her about her interests outside of academics. Ask her to point out clubs, teams, or other organizations in the student handbook that pique her curiosity and encourage her to attend informational meetings or talk to the faculty advisor. If her high school does not offer many activities or if none on the existing roster interests her, brainstorm with her about ways in which she could create her own extracurricular program either inside or outside of school (starting a new club, volunteering at a community-based organization, etc.). This type of discussion could prove invaluable for a student just starting high school, as well as for one approaching senior year who has not yet found her extracurricular niche (those I call "late bloomers").

A shy child or one who needs to get acclimated to high school before she commits to teams and clubs could benefit from signing up for only one or two activities, a decision that may require some encouragement from you. A young person who sees joining teams and clubs as an important vehicle for making friends, on the other hand, may need assistance limiting her activities to a reasonable number. Remember, admissions officers are looking for sincere commitment, for quality, not quantity. Help your child figure out the ideal combination of extracurricular and academic commitments for her, as well as the pursuits that she enjoys and wants to continue throughout high school.

ENCOURAGING APPROPRIATE LEVELS OF COMMITMENT AND PARTICIPATION FROM YOUR CHILD

Admissions officers at selective colleges and universities want to see commitment to activities over time rather than a series of single-year affiliations with various clubs and committees. The most selective institutions value leadership positions—for example, captaining a team, editing a school publication, holding student government office—although, once again, no single formula guarantees admission. Commitment and leadership signify, among other things, your child's interest in a particular area, her work ethic, her ability to command peer and faculty respect, and, in certain instances, her ability to stretch herself beyond normal expectations—qualities that could obviously benefit any college campus and that also bode well for future success.

Your child will do far better in the college admissions process if she focuses on activities that matter to her and sticks with them over time than if she gets involved with many but for only a short duration. Freshman and sophomore years give your child a chance to experiment with and experience the options that her high school offers. Jumping around from club to club through all four years of high school, though, can suggest that your child is trying to bolster her college application (albeit misguidedly) rather than participating in activities because they interest her. That pattern can also lead admissions officers to question her ability to make a commitment and stick to it.

If your child has made a commitment, underscore to her the importance of fulfilling it. Signing up for the school play means seeing it through until the curtain falls on the last performance and the set has been taken down. Competing on a team calls for attending every practice and meet in a season. Grades nine and ten give you the opportunity to observe how your child handles competing responsibilities and new experiences and allow your child to learn the importance of following through on what she has said she will do. Stumbling and even falling a few times in those first two years will not harm her prospects for college, as long as she learns from her mistakes. Quitting the school play in the middle of rehearsals or dropping a sport midseason as a freshman looks very different from doing the same thing as a junior or senior.

One young man from my admissions territory at Yale who had outstanding grades and standardized test scores and an impressive extracurricular profile still stands out in my memory and illustrates the importance of following through on commitments. His letters of recommendation looked puzzlingly lukewarm, given his outstanding record, so I called his high school to get additional information. His guidance counselor explained in our conversation that this young man had a history of signing up for activities, taking on leadership positions because he thought they looked good for college, and then repeatedly shirking his commitments and leaving other students to pick up the pieces. This pattern of behavior had caused both teachers and students to see him in a negative light and made it very difficult for his recommenders to write about him with the enthusiasm that one would have expected based on the rest of his profile. Sure enough, one of my colleagues on the committee stopped me to ask why we were not discussing this young man when I passed over him in the presentation of my slate. I recounted the conversation with the guidance counselor, the committee agreed that we did not need to review his candidacy further, and we moved on.

Leadership positions in the extracurricular realm, although attractive to admissions officers, do not suit all personalities, just as not all students thrive academically in AP classes. Consistent participation in high school, even without evidence of leadership, provides a platform for solid citizenship in college, a trait that could develop into leadership as a student matures. The right college or university for the "solid participant" will recognize and value that type of extracurricular profile. Admissions officers also understand that not all students have access to formally designated leadership roles. A young person working twenty hours a week to help support her family has clearly taken on a leadership role at home but will not be able to stay after school for team practice or club meetings. A child's personality, interests, and circumstances factor into whether or not a leadership role suits her; if your child has taken initiative, great, but if not, don't worry, it makes no sense from a college admissions perspective to push a round peg into a square hole.

Those students seeking spots at Top 20 colleges and universities also need to understand the broad context in which admissions officers view extracurricular leaders. Tens of thousands of team captains, editors, and student body presidents apply to these institutions each year. Your child will do little to differentiate herself from her peers in this highly competitive pool simply because she holds a title or two. Admissions officers at these institutions want to know how your child used her opportunity to lead and, ideally, that she stretched herself beyond the existing or expected parameters of her world. Assume, for example, that two high school sailing team captains demonstrate equal levels of skill: the first did not know how to swim when he came to this country from Mongolia at the age of fifteen and the second grew up spending weekends at his parents' yacht club. Sailing captain number one has a greater likelihood of catching a reader's attention than sailing captain number two. A high level of talent also represents something that admissions officers seek, as we explore in the next section.

DETERMINING YOUR CHILD'S LEVEL OF TALENT AND HOW IT CAN HELP IN THE COLLEGE ADMISSIONS PROCESS

Colleges and universities have diverse needs that people with talent in multiple areas help them meet. The symphony orchestra may need a first violin, for example, and the football team may be losing defensive linemen to graduation. Getting flagged as a recruit can give your child an edge in the admissions process, although it does not guarantee admission. Understanding where your child falls in the talent pool, however, represents a challenge in and of itself, as does bringing that talent to the attention of an admissions committee in the appropriate way.

If you think that your child demonstrates exceptional talent in a particular area but do not know for sure, get out there and seek additional opinions. Start by asking yourself who, if anybody, has recognized your child's level of skill. I still have a box of athletic trophies from my years of captaining my high school's gymnastics team—but we stood out as the "Bad News Bears" of our league and all my trophies laud effort rather than skill. Even my mother, looking through her rose-colored glasses, could not have misinterpreted my athletic awards as a sign that a college or university gymnastics team would want to recruit me. If your child's soccer team has won the state finals, however, or if her mathematics team has achieved national ranking, talk to the coach, teacher, or instructor who shares your recognition of your child's talent and get a real sense of where your child falls among her peers.

It pays to ask. Take my client, a committed volleyball player who came to me in her junior year in high school. She was playing on a junior national team, which suggests talent, but her team had a losing record. Her parents did not know how attractive she would look to college coaches, so they started talking to her junior national coach and seeking out scouts at her tournaments. They learned that the coach had been receiving letters of interest about her, primarily from Division III schools, and enlisted a scout to help their daughter put together a game tape and an athletic resumé. I learned as this book was going to press that this young woman's first-choice college had admitted her early decision, in large part because the volleyball coach there had designated her as a top recruit. (You can learn more about college athletic recruiting and the different divisions in which colleges and universities compete at www.ncaa.org.)

The earlier you and your child recognize potential talent, the more you can do to cultivate it. Another client of mine, a young woman in her freshman year of high school, showed signs at a young age of extraordinary talent in tennis. She took lessons and played in tournaments throughout middle school, but then took some time off from the game as she adjusted to her new high school. There, she joined the tennis team but found the level of play disappointing. She decided to drop the team in favor of the tournament circuit again (with private coaching) with the express goal of gaining a national ranking and preparing herself for possible college play.

Student athletes who are approaching the college application period and do not have access to private coaches or national scouts can use a little elbow grease to find out where they stand compared with their athletic peers. A javelin thrower with whom I was working had a good sense of schools that might want him because he had visited dozens of college Web sites, looked for javelin throwers of similar height and weight, and had compared his performance statistics to theirs. He concluded based on the information he gathered that he compared favorably to javelin throwers at middle to lower ranked Division III schools (rank in this case refers to athletic standing).

Many college Web sites provide detailed information on how a candidate can contact coaches to bring herself to their attention. Swarthmore College's Web site, for instance, gives an example of an online contact form that student athletes can use to get in touch with the appropriate team coach (www.swarthmore.edu/athletics/prospective_athletes.html). Look for a similar informational area on the Web sites of the colleges and universities on your child's list. Consider also sending your child to attend a summer sports clinic at the top colleges that interest her, as these summer sessions give her direct exposure to coaches and allow them to see her play. Remember that the NCAA regulates when college coaches may initiate recruiting discussions with students, so you will need to work within that time frame.

College Web sites can also provide invaluable guidelines for students with other types of talent outside of athletics, such as artists, dancers, actors, musicians, and filmmakers. Admissions offices generally want talented students to prepare samples of their work according to specific guidelines and to submit those samples to the relevant department (fine arts, music, etc.). Each institution has its own procedures and protocol for these submissions. The Duke University Web site has a helpful example of this type of information (www.duke.edu/web/ugadmissions/apply.htm). If a university Web site or application does not provide instructions, have your child call the admissions office to find out where and how to submit materials for evaluation.

In the same way that my volleyball client's parents sought guidance from a scout, your student artist or performer can seek input about the caliber of her work from her orchestra leader, choral director, fine arts instructor, or other person under whom she is studying—a step that I would recommend prior to preparing a formal submission. Once again, keep in mind the size of the universe to which this person is referring. Saying that your child compares favorably with previous students of his who went on to study at premier conservatories or fine arts institutes differs substantially from identifying your child as a standout among all the students whom he has taught in introductory art at the high school. As with athletics, recognition of your child's particular artistic or musical talent rises in value as the pool of students with whom she is being compared increases in scope and talent (state champion outranks city and region outranks state, etc.). It is worth noting that coaches transmit to admissions officers the final list of their recruits, but generally do not spend time going over students in whom they have no interest. Submissions of art, music, film, and other types of evaluated work, however, can result in a formal evaluation from the relevant department going into your child's folder. In those cases, a mediocre or poor assessment of her work gets considered as part of the admissions process.[10]

ACTIVITIES THAT TELL YOUR CHILD'S STORY

For admissions officers, a strong folder *tells a candidate's story,* which essentially means that the many pieces of the application come together and help define the student and what she brings to the table. Let me give you an example in which extracurricular activities played a key role in letting admissions officers know who an applicant was. My all-time, absolute favorite application came from a young man from a working class family who attended Catholic school. This student listed Ryu Kyu Kempo (Okinawan karate)—in which he had attained a black belt—as his primary activity and his weekend job at a local delicatessen as the next most important one on his list. Right away, this young man jumped out at me as somebody who understood and appreciated his own neighborhood and community but who also wanted to extend himself beyond it. His two essays, the longer one about karate and the shorter one about his job at the deli, underscored my initial perception and made clear that his parents encouraged his curiosity about the world. I knew that this student would drink in everything that a major university had to offer and would give back based on his own experiences and identity as well.

My Division III volleyball player has a less exotic extracurricular profile than the "karate kid," but one that I find compelling in its own right. This young woman has three interests—athletics, the arts, and promoting a sense of community within her small high school— a story that her extracurricular profile clearly tells. She has pursued two or three activities in each of these areas, most of which she began in grade nine and continued throughout high school (see sidebar). This profile makes her highly competitive at the Top 100 and Top 50 colleges and universities to which she has applied, where she sees herself thriving academically and contributing to campus life through her continued involvement in these three areas. (As I mentioned earlier, this young woman's first-choice college accepted her early decision!)

Example of a Strong Extracurricular Profile

This young woman's extracurricular activities tell a clear and consistent story of an applicant interested in athletics, the arts, and promoting a sense of community within her high school. They make her competitive at the Top 100 and Top 50 schools to which she is applying.

- JV/Varsity Volleyball (9–12)

- Junior National Volleyball (11–12)

- Varsity Basketball (9–12, Captain 11–12)

- Varsity Tennis (8–10)

- Creative Writing Club (11–12)

- Art Club (9–10)

- Students Against Drunk Driving (9–12)

- School Tour Guide (9–12)

Go back to the extracurricular profile that you completed on your child in Chapter One and ask yourself what story her activities tell.

Look for focus, consistency, and, most of all, passion, a quality that always catches the attention of Carleton College Dean of Admissions Paul Thiboutot: "Something that began as volunteer work for the homeless and expanded from there into the organizing of a soup kitchen—there's a passion that comes through. This work has clearly become a significant part of the student's life." If you do not see these characteristics, ask yourself why not. Your child may be devoting too little time to too many activities and cluttering her application. Alternatively, she may be engaging in few or no extracurricular activities and making her life outside of school look like a large, blank slate. Never push your child to get involved in activities just for the college application, but help her by letting her know the ramifications of her choices while she still has time to make changes if she so desires. If she has already entered her senior year and has begun the college application process, look for colleges and universities that suit her based on the decisions that she has made, rather than on wishful thinking or Monday morning quarterbacking.

Those students who miss the chance to get involved in organized extracurricular activities because of the family responsibilities they must shoulder also have a story to tell. I have taught young people who had to miss school because they were acting as translators for adult family members whom they accompanied to every appointment. Others had to work twenty hours a week to help pay the family bills. Carleton College, for example, sees several farm kids in its applicant pool each year. These students spend hours each day performing chores on the family farm. "We need to know that!" Thiboutot emphasizes. "Make sure you tell it as part of your story," through the application essays, letters of recommendation, or even as details that appear in the extracurricular activities section of the application.

FREQUENTLY ASKED QUESTIONS

My daughter's New York City high school offers two organized extracurricular activities and she participates in them both. Does she need to sign up for additional activities outside of school to get accepted into an Ivy League institution?

Maybe yes, maybe no. Let's assume your daughter's academic profile and standardized test scores look competitive for her peer group and would not eliminate her from contention. (Many college and university Web sites provide statistical profiles of the incoming freshman class that you can consult to see where your child would fall.) Admissions officers put folders in the context of family, school, and community when they read them, as we discussed in Chapters One and Two. A bustling metropolis offers young people extensive opportunities through which to pursue their interests, unlike, for example, an isolated rural community where students may have limited ability to get involved in activities outside of the high school. A young person whose family circumstances prevent her from participating in activities will get yet a different read, regardless of her location.

For an unhooked, New York City applicant with no extenuating family circumstances, two extracurricular activities need to stand out in a powerful way, especially if they represent the extent of her involvement, that is, she does not pursue other interests or hobbies on her own or through organizations outside of school. Captaining a state championship mathematics team and developing an award-winning Intel International Science and Engineering Fair project through the school science club would catch my attention. Chairing the school prom committee and organizing a school fund-raiser, in this context, would not. Remember that the quality of extracurricular activities matters more than the quantity, as does the collective power of those activities to tell a story about your child. In assessing what admissions officers at the most selective colleges and universities in the country want to see from your child, think about the degree to which she is taking advantage of the resources and opportunities around her—at her school and in her community—as well as what her family circumstances allow her to do.

Our eleventh-grade daughter has multiple interests outside of her schoolwork but she pursues them all independently and not through organized activities. She practices yoga in our basement for two hours every day, for example, and has two notebooks full of short stories and poetry. Will these activities help her when she applies to college or will admissions officers focus on her lack of participation in organized school clubs?

Your daughter should definitely list these activities on her application, including the amount of time that she invests in them weekly and the number of years she has been pursuing them. Ask yourself two key questions when you look at your daughter's activities to determine if you should advise her to alter her current routine. First, do these pursuits reflect your daughter's temperament and personality accurately and, second, do they reflect the level of involvement she plans to replicate in college? If your answer to either of these questions is no, you may want to brainstorm with your daughter about ways in which she could supplement what she is currently doing.

Supplementing could mean simply building on the foundation that she has already created. Practicing yoga for two hours a day over several years might make your daughter qualified to teach a class at the local senior center. Her two notebooks of short stories and poetry may contain material that the school literary magazine or a community newspaper wants to publish. Sometimes the best way for a young person to add to what she is already doing can come through sharing her knowledge and expertise with others. Selective colleges and universities value activities that young people pursue independent of any formal organization or affiliation, especially if the essays and letters of recommendation in the folder illustrate how these activities tell a story. Do not push your daughter to add commitments to her schedule simply for the sake of her college application; a good brainstorming session, though, could lead to unexpected and interesting ideas that she welcomes and decides to pursue.

My son works twenty hours a week to pay for his car, not to help support the family. This job takes up all of his time outside of school and leaves him no opportunity to get involved in other activities. Will admissions officers understand and accept the way in which he has chosen to spend his time or will his lack of organized activities hurt his chances?

Some will and some won't, depending on the institution, on the rest of your son's profile (academic transcript, standardized test scores, letters of recommendation, and family/school/community context), and on the story he tells about the importance of having a car. As with the first example above, let's assume for now that your son is applying to a college or university where the rest of his profile would not rule him out. He needs to clarify the context in which he has decided to work twenty hours per week to finance his car. Does he use the car simply to go to the mall, go on dates, and drive around with friends or does he use it to get to the closest large city and take advantage of resources there? Has he learned any automotive mechanics to maintain the car himself? Are automobiles and/or automotive mechanics his passion? Is his car a thirty-year-old Mustang that he restored himself?

Without any additional circumstances and all other factors remaining equal, I would tell you that a student working to support her family comes across as more powerful and compelling than a student working to buy luxury items or material possessions. We have discussed repeatedly in this book, however, that context influences everything in college admissions. Explore with your son how having a car and working to pay for it have exposed him to new experiences and have helped him develop unexplored sides of himself. Including the points that come up in that conversation in an application essay, for example, could paint this part of your son's profile in a much more meaningful light than simply listing the job on the application without providing any context.

Our daughter has an outstanding academic record and accompanying letters of recommendation, but has not participated in a single extracurricular activity in high school. She made this decision consciously, as she said that she wanted to spend quality time with her family and friends before she left for college. How will this decision affect her chances of admission at a Top 20 college or university?

Your daughter has set up a challenging situation for herself, assuming that she has no admissions hooks and that many of her peers applying to the same highly selective institutions have academic records that rival hers, combined with extracurricular activities. My first question centers on the level of her academic performance. You use the word "outstanding." That characterization could mean straight A's. It could signify that she stands out as one of the best students that her recommenders have taught over the course of their careers. It could also mean that she has created a new geometric proof that a mathematics journal published. Top 20 colleges and universities will de-emphasize the importance of extracurricular activities for truly brilliant academic minds, i.e., the next generation of scholars. Answering your question with accuracy means determining whether or not your daughter falls into that category.

Your daughter should also make sure to include in her application activities that may not fall into an obvious category, but that still take up her time and define who she is. One of my recent clients, for example, just completed a lovely essay on the significance to her of watching a movie with her mother every evening. She categorized this nightly ritual as the most important extracurricular activity in her life and put it in the context of her parents' divorce and her desire to bond with each of them in a special way. The essay brought tears to my eyes and made me laugh, all within a few short paragraphs. Your daughter may spend part of every evening sitting on the couch with you as you both read a good book. She may accompany her siblings to their athletic competitions or school science fairs, or she may spend quality time with her aging grandparents. Make sure she includes these details as part of her story, as they matter to admissions officers.

Whether or not your daughter has put herself at a significant disadvantage relative to her peers applying to Top 20 colleges and universities depends in part on the story she recounts about the choices she has made and how she decides to tell it. Encourage your daughter to embrace those choices and talk about them with passion in her application, instead of just leaving the extracurricular activities section of the application blank. Taking these proactive steps will make a positive difference in how admissions officers view her.

STEP-BY-STEP CHECKLIST: EXTRACURRICULAR ACTIVITIES AND HOW THEY INFLUENCE ADMISSIONS DECISIONS

❑ Complete the worksheet "Assessing Your Child's Extracurricular Activities."

❑ If at any point in high school your child has not yet signed up for extracurricular activities on her own, ask her about her interests outside of academics.

❑ Invite your child to point out to you clubs, teams, or other organizations in the student handbook that pique her curiosity.

❑ Encourage her to attend organizational meetings for different clubs and committees or talk to the faculty advisor.

❑ If your child's high school does not offer many activities (or none that interests her), brainstorm with her about starting a new school-based club or volunteering at a community-based organization.

❏ Encourage a shy or reluctant child in any grade to try at least one or two activities.

❏ Help an overeager young person in any grade balance her academic and extracurricular commitments.

❏ Look into summer academic programs and/or overseas travel if these activities relate to your child's interests or would stimulate her academic growth, rather than because you think they will help her stand out in a pool of college applicants.

❏ Research summer activities in your local community that connect to your child's interests and that she could potentially continue into the school year.

❏ Reinforce repeatedly to your child the importance of meeting commitments—such as completing an athletic season or working on the school play through the final performance—especially in grades nine and ten when you can influence her habits for the future.

❏ Suggest to your child that she pursue leadership positions in the activities that interest her, if doing so looks like a good fit for her personality.

❏ If you think your child shows exceptional talent that could make her a college recruit in a particular area (athletics, the arts, etc.), examine the evidence you have readily available. Ask yourself, has she achieved recognition for her performance in this area and, if so, from whom?

❏ Talk to experts in the field (coaches, music instructors, etc.) to get their opinion on the quality of your child's work or performance. Keep track of the pool with which they are comparing her, such as all art students in the high school's introductory drawing class or those who have gone on to prestigious fine arts academies.

❏ Work with these experts between your child's junior and senior years to prepare a game or audition tape, a portfolio of work, or other necessary materials to forward to the colleges and universities that interest your child.

❏ Research on the Web site of each college or university that interests your child how the admissions office wants you to bring her talent to its attention and to whom you should forward supporting materials, such as a game or audition tape, portfolio, etc.

FIVE

Deciding Which Standardized Tests to Take

We cannot deny, as much as we might like to, that test scores represent an important part of your child's academic profile—but many parents, students, and even guidance counselors do not realize the choices they have in fulfilling standardized testing requirements. I cringe every time I hear families hesitate to consider their options because they or their counselor is operating with incomplete or sometimes even incorrect information. Your input into your child's standardized testing takes on increased importance in the context of the poor information and advice in this area that proliferates at the high school level. This chapter prepares you to play a key role in educating your child on standardized testing and helping him make the best choices for himself.

AN OVERVIEW OF REQUIRED STANDARDIZED TESTING FOR COLLEGE ADMISSIONS

In the early 1980s, when I was applying to college, candidates for Top 20 colleges and universities had more limited testing options than they do today. Many institutions still did not accept the ACT (in existence since 1959) or had just introduced it as an alternative to the SAT (in use since 1926); the most selective colleges and universities by and large required the SAT and three Subject Tests, end of discussion. The increased choice that applicants have today, however, means that colleges and universities also have greater latitude than they did before in asking for different combinations of tests, rather than the standard formula that I encountered. One student applying to five institutions could conceivably have to submit scores from five different combinations of standardized tests. Strategizing about what to take and when to take it assumes a new level of importance in this day and age and requires that you and your college-bound child understand all available options.

In addition to the academic transcript and the extracurricular activities profile, all student folders contain another critical item, known as a "score report," that details student performance on standardized tests. Top 20 institutions generally require applicants to take at least one standardized test, sometimes more. Others recommend the submission of scores but do not require it.

Most selective colleges and universities call for applicants to take either one of two tests: the ACT or the SAT Reasoning Test (we will call this the SAT from now on). Admissions offices accept either one, so students decide which to take.[11] (Each test has advantages and disadvantages and we will talk later in this chapter about how to determine which one suits your child.) Both the ACT and the SAT run between three and four hours and assess students across several basic subject areas, including reading, writing, and mathematics. Students generally take either one of these tests in the spring of junior year and/or fall of senior year. (Many students take it more than once in an attempt to raise their score.)

Many Top 20 colleges and universities also either require or recommend SAT Subject Tests (we will call these Subject Tests from now on), in addition to the ACT or the SAT. Each Subject Test lasts one hour—as opposed to the three to four hours that the SAT and ACT each require—and probes an applicant's knowledge in a particular academic area, such as biology, U.S. history, or physics. Admissions offices that request these tests usually direct applicants to take two or three of them. Students can select those two or three from a menu of over twenty subjects when colleges have not specified which ones they want students to take. Most students sit for Subject Tests at the end of junior year or beginning of senior year, upon completion of a full-year course in the relevant area.

THE PRELIMINARY SAT (PSAT)/NATIONAL MERIT SCHOLARSHIP QUALIFYING TEST (NMSQT)

Students take the PSAT/NMSQT through their high schools in grade eleven and sometimes also in grade ten. (An increasing number of high schools are having students take the test twice.) You pay a nominal fee for your child to sit for the test, significantly less than the cost of the SAT.[12] With the exception of the essay, which the test does not include, the PSAT gives your child a preview of the SAT Reasoning Test, including a score report comparable to one for the SAT.[13] The National Merit Scholarship Corporation (NMSC) also uses the PSAT as the qualifying test for its prestigious National Merit Scholarship program (relevant only to those taking the test in grade eleven).

Clients frequently ask me if they should prepare for the PSAT and, as with almost any college admissions question, my answer depends on a student's individual circumstances. A young person who knows that he will have to compensate for extensive skill and knowledge deficiencies—either because he has struggled academically through-out high school or because he attends a school that lacks basic resources—may need to start studying for standardized tests earlier than someone who is performing well in an appropriately challenging academic program. The first student may want to begin his SAT preparation early enough so that it also encompasses the PSAT. The second student, in most cases, does not need to do so. Remember that every way in which your child uses his time incurs an opportunity cost in another area. Beginning test preparation earlier than necessary could lead your child to miss out on chances to improve his grades, his extracurricular profile, and more.

An aspiring applicant to selective colleges and universities may also want to study for the PSAT in the hope of attaining recognition through the NMSC's National Merit Scholarship program. It makes sense to gauge the likelihood of your child's achieving that goal before he invests time and energy in pursuing it. The NMSC determines a separate "selection index" cutoff for each of the fifty states and the District of Columbia and then recognizes those students who fall above that cutoff (the selection index comes from adding together the three PSAT subscores—critical reading, mathematics, and writing). You can find the selection index cutoff for your state through your child's college guidance office, which should have this information in a publication from the NMSC called *Guide to the National*

Merit Scholarship Program. I would suggest that you calculate your child's selection index from his grade ten PSAT results or, if he did not sit for the test as a sophomore, from a practice test that he took under real-life testing conditions. Compare his results to the cutoff for your state and consider formal test preparation if hitting that number looks feasible.

The PSAT/NMSQT

- Your child takes the PSAT through his high school in tenth and/or eleventh grade.

- The PSAT gives your child a preview of the SAT Reasoning Test (without the essay).

- Scores appear in a two-digit format for each section rather than the three-digit format that the SAT Reasoning Test uses. Add a zero to the end of each two-digit score to see the equivalent SAT Reasoning Test score.

- The NMSC uses the PSAT as the qualifying test for its prestigious National Merit Scholarships.

- Studying for the PSAT generally only makes sense if your child's selection index from practice tests or from his tenth-grade PSAT score falls within 10–15 points of the cutoff for NMSC recognition in your state or if he needs to begin test preparation early to compensate for skill or knowledge deficiencies.

Let me give you an example of when I would advise a student to study for the PSAT and when I would not. Let's assume that the NMSC cutoff for the District of Columbia falls at 221 (which it did in a recent year). A D.C. student with a selection index of 210 would have to raise that number by 11 points, something that he could conceivably do with test preparation. That student would then gain some of the nifty benefits that come with NMSC recognition, like the chance to select colleges or universities to which the NMSC would then refer him—a great way to let a college or university know that it lies at the top of an applicant's list! A D.C. student whose selection index falls at 191, on the other hand, would have to increase that figure by 30 points (the equivalent of raising an SAT score by 300 points—adding a zero to the end of the PSAT selection index gives you the equivalent total SAT score). Plenty of young people have raised their standardized test scores by that degree of magnitude and more, but only with extremely rigorous preparation, something that I think would incur far too great an opportunity cost at this juncture in a student's life. I would suggest in this latter case that the student focus on the PSAT as an information-gathering tool that can help in planning a subsequent test-taking strategy, rather than as a means of advancing in the NMSC's scholarship competition.

The PSAT has wonderful value in the preview that it gives you of how your child would likely perform on the SAT. I ask clients to bring their PSAT scores with them if their first appointment takes place before they have taken the ACT or the SAT. Seeing how they performed on the PSAT gives me an indication of which test (the ACT or the SAT) looks like a better option for them, how much test preparation they will need, and whether or not it makes sense for them to apply to institutions that also require Subject Tests.

Suppose, for example, that your child earned the following PSAT scores: 49 in mathematics (which would equal 490 on the SAT), 59 in critical reading (590 on the SAT), and 53 in writing (530 on the SAT). Following the test preparation plan that I outline in the next chapter could conceivably raise your child's scores by 150 points in each section. His PSAT scores already tell me, though, that extensive test preparation will prove critical for him and that he will not have a lot of time left to study for Subject Tests, which require the same intense preparation that the SAT does. Depending on your child's academic profile, I may also suggest that he try a practice ACT to see if he performs better on it than on the PSAT. Remember that you can always check a college or university's Web site for a statistical profile of the most recent entering class, including median standard-ized test scores, to see where your child's scores fall.

In most cases, I advise families to spend more time analyzing the results of the PSAT than preparing for the test itself. Students should go to bed early the night before and eat a good breakfast the morn-ing that they take the test, but that's about it. It bears repeating that, for most students, the PSAT has no impact on college admissions de-cisions. Students would do more to strengthen their chances of ac-ceptance to selective institutions by raising their grades in high school than by studying for the PSAT. The products and services that test-preparation companies and private tutors market for the PSAT often waste your money and your child's time.

DETERMINING WHICH TEST BETTER SUITS YOUR CHILD—THE ACT OR THE SAT

Students have historically chosen to take either the ACT or the SAT based largely on where they live. Those on the East and West Coasts have gravitated toward the SAT, while ACT, Inc., considers itself strongest in the Midwest, Rocky Mountain West, Southwest, and Southeast. These geographic differences stem from where the tests originated, where each parent corporation has based its headquarters, and where each organization has directed its marketing efforts. ACT, Inc., began to see a noticeable increase in test takers from traditionally SAT states when the College Board in 2005 modified the format and content of the SAT, changed the traditional 1600 scoring scale to 2400, and even updated the names of its tests. (The SAT I Reasoning Test became the SAT Reasoning Test and the SAT II became the SAT Subject Test.)

Opinion varies on how significantly the ACT and the SAT differ from each other; but, in general, educators, college admissions officers, test-preparation experts, and students have commented to me that they find the ACT a "more straightforward" test than the SAT. I agree. Both run between three and four hours and focus on reading comprehension, writing, and mathematics. The ACT also has a science section, which by and large assesses a student's ability to read scientific charts and tables and answer questions on the information they contain. The tests differ markedly, however, in style and tone.

I have spoken about this difference at length with my friend and colleague Tim Levin, the man I call the "Test-Prep Guru," and we both agree: with the ACT, you either know the material or you don't; with the SAT, knowing the trick behind the question sometimes matters just as much, if not more, than understanding the content on which it is based. Part of the difference in the character of these two tests traces back to their origins: The makers of the ACT call their test "curriculum based" and have always designed it to measure what students successfully learned in school. The SAT, on the other hand, began as an "aptitude" test, which supposedly gauged innate intelligence, such as one's ability to see through tricks built into a problem and still select the correct answer. (See the accompanying sidebars for additional details on the origins of the ACT and the SAT.)

You can argue both sides of this stylistic coin, as each has its advantages and disadvantages. If your child does not understand the content being tested, the ACT leaves him few options besides guessing, whereas he may still select the correct answer on the SAT if he can see the trick behind the question and narrow down the answer. Conversely, if he knows the material, he stands a good chance of choosing the appropriate answer on the ACT, whereas the trick behind the question may still trip him up on the SAT. This difference in approach and how it compares to your child's learning style should influence more than anything else his choice of which test to take.

The following worksheet helps you determine whether the ACT or the SAT best suits your child. Although many students, regardless of their academic profile, receive comparable scores on both tests, in my experience, the ACT tends to work better for solid students than the SAT does, while the reverse holds true for underachievers. (See "Academic Profile" section of worksheet.) "Working better" for your child could mean that he receives a higher score on one test than on the other or that he simply feels more comfortable with one than with the other. Passionate learners who are also solid students tend to do equally well on both assessments, while struggling students find both the ACT and the SAT a significant challenge.

The pattern that I have observed makes sense when you think about it. Solid students do their homework and study for tests. They have fewer gaps in their knowledge and skills base than underachievers do and, when they encounter them, they already have the disciplined study habits that enable them to learn the necessary material. They may or may not do well finding the trick behind a question, but if they have studied the relevant content they have a good chance of identifying the correct answer. Underachievers generally suffer from significant gaps in their knowledge and skills base, given that they do not rely on disciplined study habits and do not consistently complete assignments or pay attention in class. They may not know all the material being tested; but, with appropriate preparation and clever deciphering, they may be able to figure out answers to SAT questions. Struggling students generally have trouble with standardized testing overall and have to devote extensive time and energy to studying, regardless of the test they select.

Your child's current grade in school (circle one): Below grade nine Grade nine Grade ten Grade eleven Grade twelve

Determining Whether Your Child Should Take the ACT or the SAT

	Strongly Agree		Agree		Somewhat Agree		Disagree		Strongly Disagree		
Academic Profile: My child is a solid student. (See Chapter One.)	10	9	8	7	6	5	4	3	2	1	0
Academic Profile: My child is a passionate learner. (See Chapter One.)	10	9	8	7	6	5	4	3	2	1	0
Academic Profile: My child is an underachiever. (See Chapter One.)	10	9	8	7	6	5	4	3	2	1	0
Academic Profile: My child is a struggling student. (See Chapter One.)	10	9	8	7	6	5	4	3	2	1	0
Learning Style: My child picks up new concepts and ideas quickly, even when it seems like he is not paying close attention.	10	9	8	7	6	5	4	3	2	1	0
Learning Style: My child solves challenging problems and brainteasers quickly and with ease.	10	9	8	7	6	5	4	3	2	1	0
Learning Style: My child thinks over challenging problems and brainteasers carefully as he solves them.	10	9	8	7	6	5	4	3	2	1	0
Learning Style: My child struggles with challenging problems and brainteasers.	10	9	8	7	6	5	4	3	2	1	0
Writing Style: My child composes his thoughts on paper quickly.	10	9	8	7	6	5	4	3	2	1	0
Writing Style: My child prefers to respond to theoretical essay questions rather than to practical ones.	10	9	8	7	6	5	4	3	2	1	0
Test Results: My child has taken a practice or real ACT and/or a practice or real SAT (or PSAT) and his scores fell within or close to the middle 50% range for some of his top choice schools. (Skip this question if your child has not yet taken any practice or real tests.)	10	9	8	7	6	5	4	3	2	1	0
Test Results: My child has taken a practice or real ACT and/or a practice or real SAT (or PSAT) and performed significantly better on one than on the other. (Skip this question if your child has not yet taken any practice or real tests.)	10	9	8	7	6	5	4	3	2	1	0
Test Results: My child has taken a practice or real ACT and/or a practice or real SAT (or PSAT) and felt more comfortable with one than with the other. (Skip this question if your child has not yet taken any practice or real tests.)	10	9	8	7	6	5	4	3	2	1	0

Deciding Which Standardized Tests to Take

With focused and disciplined preparation, a student who picks up new concepts and ideas quickly will improve his scoring outlook for either test. (See "Learning Style" section of worksheet.) Those who master brainteasers with relative ease, though, as opposed to having to think them over, will likely have an advantage over other students on the SAT and may prefer it to the ACT. Again, look at your child's learning style and encourage him to do practice questions from both tests to see which one suits him.

The ACT

- The ACT lasts 3 hours and 25 minutes with the essay or 2 hours and 55 minutes without it.

- It contains four required sections—English, Mathematics, Reading, and Science—and an optional essay (called the Writing section).

- A student gets 30 minutes to write the essay on the ACT, versus 25 minutes on the SAT.

- A student can earn a maximum of 36 points on each section, which ACT then averages for a "composite" score. (Those who don't sit for the essay simply do not have that score averaged in.)

- Incorrect answers do not result in lost points.

- ACT offers "Score Choice." Colleges and universities see only the test results that a student wants them to see.

- A student may see his test questions, his answers, the correct answers, and a scoring conversion chart through a supplementary service called Test Information Release (TIR).

A student's writing style also factors into deciding whether to take the ACT or the SAT, as the next two items on the worksheet suggest. (See "Writing Style" section of worksheet.) Both tests include an essay question, although the ACT makes the writing optional and gives students thirty minutes to complete it, while the SAT requires it and only allows test takers twenty-five minutes.[14] As with the other sections, the essay questions on the two tests differ dramatically from each other

The Origins of the ACT

In November 1958, a University of Iowa professor of education named E. F. Lindquist gave a speech at a conference that ETS had convened to focus on problems with standardized testing. The College Board at that time still claimed that the SAT (then the Scholastic Aptitude Test) measured innate ability. Lindquist made the case in his remarks that a college entrance examination should not focus on gauging natural aptitude, but instead assess knowledge and skills that students need to learn in high school in order to prepare effectively for college. Such an emphasis, Lindquist argued, would give students an incentive to work hard in high school and would also give institutions of higher education a better indication of a student's college readiness than an aptitude test would.[1] The College Board and ETS declined to incorporate Lindquist's suggestions into their SAT program and, in 1959, Lindquist started his own organization, American College Testing—today known simply by the acronym ACT.

While the creators of the SAT intended their test to identify the cream of the crop, the designers of the "populist" ACT meant for their assessment to "reject only the hopelessly unprepared and to help teachers work with the rest more effectively [sic]."[2] Lindquist saw standardized testing as a tool to expand educational opportunity to many and considered the SAT's focus on gauging natural aptitude educationally harmful. ETS acted as a gatekeeper for the most prestigious colleges and universities in the nation. ACT built its base with public universities. Author David Owen believes that ETS acts as a lightning rod for critics of standardized testing, as opposed to ACT, which "gets less scrutiny than ETS, because ACT is not in the East and because it has never made the same kinds of outrageous claims for its tests that ETS and the College Board have for theirs."[3]

Today, highly selective colleges and universities accept both the ACT and the SAT, although many guidance counselors in traditionally SAT areas mistakenly think otherwise. The ACT offers an attractive alternative to the SAT. College-bound students should explore it thoroughly before settling on a standardized testing strategy.

[1] Lindquist's speech was entitled "The Nature of the Problem of Improving Scholarship and College Entrance Examinations." He delivered it on November 1, 1958, at the ETS Invitational Conference on Testing Problems.

[2] See *The Big Test: The Secret History of the American Meritocracy* by Nicholas Lemann, p. 94 (New York: Farrar, Straus and Giroux, 2000).

[3] Comment included in an e-mail to the author, August 25, 2004.

in style. I find ACT essay questions much more direct and concrete than SAT essay questions. An ACT writing prompt, for example, could ask a student to take a position on whether or not high schools should adopt dress codes (a real-world issue that relates to student life), while an SAT writing prompt might ask the writer to address whether people are motivated to achieve by personal satisfaction or by money and fame (an abstract issue that relates to human psychology).[15] Students who prefer theoretical questions to practical ones and who have no trouble composing their thoughts on paper quickly will likely feel comfortable with the SAT writing prompt, while those who would rather respond to a practical question than to an abstract one and who need every minute they can get to write should look closely at the ACT.

In addition to the intangible factors (academic profile and learning style) we have already discussed, three concrete details can help you ascertain if one test stands out as an obvious choice over the other for your child. (See "Test Results" section of worksheet.)

The SAT Reasoning Test

- The SAT lasts 3 hours and 20 minutes.

- It contains three sections: Critical Reading, Mathematics, and Writing, including a required 25-minute essay.

- A student can earn a maximum of 800 points on each of the three sections for a possible total of 2400.

- Incorrect answers result in lost points.

- Immediate cancellation can prevent scores from becoming a permanent part of a student's ETS score report.

- ETS does not offer "Score Choice." Colleges and universities see all scores except those a student has canceled, no matter what.

- A student may see his test questions, his answers, the correct answers, and a raw score conversion chart through a supplementary service called Question and Answer Service (QAS).

The Origins of the SAT Reasoning Test

The SAT Reasoning Test has gone through several iterations since its development in the 1920s. Originally called the Scholastic Aptitude Test, the SAT was designed to measure a person's innate intelligence—his natural brainpower—rather than what he had learned in school. Ironically, SAT creator Carl Brigham eventually lost faith in his own test and came to see SAT scores as a "composite including schooling, background, familiarity with English and everything else," rather than as a pure measure of aptitude. His growing opposition to use of the SAT as a criterion for college admission delayed its adoption on a large scale until after his untimely death, in 1943.[1] It did not take long after that, though, for the College Board (which owns the SAT) and the Educational Testing Service (ETS, which develops, administers, and scores the test) to promote use of the SAT as a criterion for admission to selective colleges and universities around the country.

The College Board insisted for decades that test takers could not increase their scores by studying, since the SAT gauged a person's natural aptitude. Stanley Kaplan proved that position wrong, though, and, over the past twenty years or so, the College Board has changed both the name of the SAT and its claim that the test measures innate ability. What began as the Scholastic Aptitude Test evolved briefly into the Scholastic Assessment Test, then the SAT I Reasoning Test (with the acronym no longer representing anything), and, most recently, the SAT Reasoning Test. Now, the College Board itself sells test-preparation materials that it promotes as the only ones "created by the test maker."[2]

The SAT has provoked vehement criticism over time from scholars, investigative journalists, and advocacy groups alike. David Owen, author of a meticulously documented, scathing indictment of ETS called *None of the Above: The Truth Behind the SATs*, thinks that the College Board and ETS have fostered this criticism by exaggerating the power and value of the test. Former Albert Einstein associate Banesh Hoffman's objections to the SAT inspired him to write a full-length work, *The Tyranny of Testing*, published in 1964. Nicholas Lemann, a highly respected journalist and author like David Owen, in 1999 wrote *The Big Test: The Secret History of the American Meritocracy*, yet another volume

[1] See *The Big Test: The Secret History of the American Meritocracy* by Nicholas Lemann, pp. 34 and 41 (New York: Farrar, Straus and Giroux, 2000).
[2] See www.collegeboard.com for additional information on College Board SAT preparation materials.

that critically examined the College Board and ETS. The National Center for Fair and Open Testing (FairTest) has done more than criticize the College Board: in 1993, FairTest filed a complaint with the Office for Civil Rights that charged both organizations with illegally assisting gender bias. The settlement required changes in the format of the PSAT.

For all the controversy surrounding the SAT, the introduction of standardized testing marked a shift in college admissions at the most elite institutions in the country. Stanley Kaplan, founder of the first major SAT test-preparation company in the country, credits standardized testing with opening the doors to the Ivy League. I met Kaplan once and recall his insistence that tests like the SAT enabled public school students with no wealth or family connections to study for an examination, do well on it, and get into colleges and universities that, in his day, had only welcomed children of privilege. Former Yale University Dean of Undergraduate Admissions Worth David, who spent more than twenty years in his position, agrees. According to David, the limitations of the test notwithstanding,

> The SAT played a major role in opening up elite, private institutions after WW II. Strong scores made it difficult to overlook talented, prospective students, many of them urban Catholics and Jews. Moreover, the test scores could validate the strength of applications from schools and areas relatively unknown to college admissions offices.

The SAT has clearly made its mark in higher education and will continue to play a significant role in admissions at selective institutions for the foreseeable future.

- First, have your child sit for the PSAT and a practice ACT and look at how these scores compare to the middle 50 percent range at colleges and universities that interest him. (You can find median or middle 50 percent scores in college guides and on college and university Web sites.) Encourage your child to explore whether switching to the other test could improve his scores if they fall toward the bottom of or below this range.

- Second, take note of whether your child has already performed measurably better on one test than on the other, for example, if he took the PSAT and then took a practice ACT.

- Third, discuss with your child whether he feels significantly more comfortable with one test than with the other.

One of my recent clients who had already taken the PSAT and planned to continue with the SAT found that he preferred the ACT when he tried a practice test on my recommendation. He favored the ACT so strongly that he traveled to Philadelphia to sit for the examination on a date on which ACT, Inc., was not administering its test in New York.

Your child does not have to register for actual tests to get this comparative information. Both companies, ACT, Inc., and the College Board, make practice questions available on their Web sites and sell books or pamphlets with additional tests, complete with scoring guides. Test-preparation companies in major urban areas frequently offer "mock" ACT and SAT examinations (sometimes for free and sometimes for a fee), which they score as if your child has taken a real one. Academic profile and learning style questions can provide initial insight into which test might better suit your child. Nothing that I can think of, however, beats having your child try practice questions for each test in order to make a fully informed decision.

Last but not least, make sure to consider some brass tacks issues for each of these two standardized tests, such as the length of each test and the order in which the sections appear. For students who do not need to take the essay, the ACT runs slightly less than three hours—thirty minutes less than the SAT. The SAT also places the essay—one of the most anxiety-provoking sections of the test—first, which can unnerve for the duration of the examination those students who feel they did poorly on it. (The essay comes last on the ACT.) Students lose points for incorrect answers on the SAT; they do not on the ACT. ACT, Inc., offers an attractive "Score Choice" option, which means that your child only reports to colleges and universities the scores that he designates. The College Board requires students to report all SAT scores except those that a student cancels within the allowable window, in which case the student does not see them either. These differences could affect the strength of your child's standardized testing profile and, for that reason, warrant examination and discussion.

HELPING YOUR CHILD DECIDE WHETHER OR NOT TO TAKE SAT SUBJECT TESTS

So much emphasis tends to be placed on the ACT and/or SAT, that Subject Tests (formerly known as SAT II Tests and, before that, Achievement Tests) stand out in my mind as the forgotten stepchild of college admissions testing. Students squeeze them in almost as an afterthought, as they put together their college lists and see that some of the institutions at which they are looking ask for them. In fact, numerous top-tier institutions require or recommend that applicants take Subject Tests, which means that they require the same careful consideration and preparation that the ACT and SAT do.

The College Board introduced Subject Tests in 1937 as a way to "measure how much a student knows about a particular academic subject such as biology or American history."[16] Subject Tests last one hour each and ask multiple-choice questions. Scores range from a minimum of 200 to a maximum of 800 points. ETS does not offer Score Choice for Subject Tests, which means that the results appear on your child's permanent ETS record unless he cancels them within the allowable window of time after the test. The College Board permits test takers to complete up to three Subject Tests in a single sitting, although students may not take the SAT Reasoning Test and Subject Tests on the same day. Those who complete more than one Subject Test in a single sitting and want to cancel one of their scores must cancel all of them, according to College Board policy, a definite negative! (You can see the details of the College Board's score cancellation policy at www.collegeboard.com.)

Colleges and universities that require or recommend Subject Tests frequently do so because faculty members like them. I used to agree with that requirement but have grown increasingly frustrated with the uneven distribution and impractical nature of questions on these tests. A U.S. history examination that several of my clients took in May of their junior year, for example, heavily emphasized the post–World War II period, an era that few high school courses ever get to, let alone by May. One question asked them to identify the comedian who starred in the 1950s situation comedy *The Honeymooners*—a great popular culture question for Trivial Pursuit, but not necessarily one for a college entrance examination. Tim Levin, who has written test-preparation guides for Kaplan, Inc., cites similar examples from biology Subject

Tests, which he has seen arbitrarily emphasize one or two areas, such as plants or insects, out of an entire survey course curriculum.

The SAT Subject Tests

- The College Board and ETS offer SAT Subject Tests in over 20 areas.

- Each Subject Test lasts 1 hour and contains multiple-choice questions.

- A student can earn a minimum score of 200 and a maximum of 800 on a Subject Test.

- Some subjects offer multiple levels of difficulty, for example, Math Level 1 and Level 2.

- Subject Tests measure mastery of content that a student has learned in school, not his intelligence or aptitude.

- A student may cancel a score right after he takes the test, but does not have a Score Choice option later.

- A student may take up to three Subject Tests in one day, but may not combine SAT Reasoning and SAT Subject Tests in the same sitting.

- Some selective colleges require one or more Subject Test in addition to the SAT or ACT.

- Other colleges recommend but do not require them and many do not ask for them at all.

- Institutions that require Subject Tests sometimes exempt ACT takers from them.

While almost every selective college and university requires candidates to take either the ACT or the SAT, wide variation exists in Subject Test requirements. Although some exceptions do exist, I have found the following rules to hold true:

1. Programs with a special academic focus require applicants to take specific Subject Tests. For example, engineering

candidates at Tufts and Princeton have to take Math Level 1 or 2 and Physics or Chemistry.

2. Top 20 colleges and universities generally ask candidates to take two or three Subject Tests in addition to the ACT or SAT. For example, Harvard and Princeton both require the ACT or the SAT plus three Subject Tests. Dartmouth requires the ACT or SAT plus two Subject Tests.

3. Some of these institutions only require Subject Tests from prospective students who take the SAT and waive them for those taking the ACT. For example, Amherst, Brown, Duke, and Wesleyan require two Subject Tests if applicants take the SAT but none if they take the ACT.

4. Institutions outside of the Top 20 generally do not require Subject Tests, although they may recommend them or allow students to use them as an alternative to the SAT.

My advice on Subject Tests depends on the colleges and universities to which your child plans to apply, his academic profile, and his work ethic.

Use the worksheets on pages 98 and 99 to confirm whether or not your child needs these tests. If he has not yet started considering where to apply (for example, if he is a freshman or sophomore in high school), pick several institutions that you think might interest him (because he has friends who attended and were happy there or because you think they make a good fit for him). Try to stay realistic, like the mother who came to see me with her tenth-grade son several weeks ago. "He's a smart kid and I want him to go to the best place possible," she told me. "But we're not talking about Harvard."

High school seniors in the process of applying to college can use these worksheets to determine if an application to a particular institution really matters as much to them as they initially thought it did. A student who has taken the ACT with writing and wants to apply to Brown, Amherst, Wesleyan, Duke, and Georgetown, for example, will find that, of those choices, only Georgetown asks for Subject Tests in addition to the ACT. The others do not (although they require them from SAT takers). Georgetown would have to rank pretty high on my list for me to take three separate examinations, all of which call for rigorous preparation, that none of my other top choices demand.

Your child's current grade in school (circle one):   Below grade nine   Grade nine   Grade ten   Grade eleven   Grade twelve

Does Your Child Need to Take Subject Tests If He Takes the ACT?

Instructions: Fill in below the colleges and universities your child is considering. Go to each institution's Web site, click on the link for undergraduate admissions, and follow the Web site navigation to the standardized testing requirements for admission. Some colleges and universities list this information in a clearly labeled area called "Standardized Testing," others categorize it under "Requirements for Admission," and still others make you look for it, e.g., in the "Frequently Asked Questions" area. Answer the questions below based on what you find and then continue to the second page of this worksheet and complete the exact same steps for the SAT Reasoning Test.

Name of Institution	Does it require or recommend ACT?	Does it require ACT with writing?	Do applicants need to take Subject Tests in addition to the ACT? Please list below any specific tests that the college or university requests, e.g., Math Level 1. Please note if the tests are required or recommended.
Example: Stanford University	Yes	Yes	2 Subject Tests recommended - Math Level 2 preferred as one of them

If your child applies to all of the schools above, which tests will he have to take? Not all institutions require Subject Tests, so only use the second box below if necessary.

Scenario 1: ACT

Please check all that apply:

❑   ACT
❑   ACT optional writing component
❑   One additional Subject Test **OR**
❑   Two additional Subject Tests **OR**
❑   Three additional Subject Tests **OR**
❑   Four additional Subject Tests (several schools require 2–3 Subject Tests, but they all require different ones).

Total # of required tests:

Subject Test Requirements

Please check the specific Subject Tests that the institutions on your list require or recommend:

❑   Math Level 1
❑   Math Level 2
❑   Physics
❑   Chemistry
❑   Biology
❑   Other (please specify):

Total # of required Subject Tests:

Does Your Child Need to Take Subject Tests If He Takes the SAT?

Instructions: Fill in below the colleges and universities your child is considering. Go to each institution's Web site, click on the link for undergraduate admissions, and follow the Web site navigation to the standardized testing requirements for admission. Some colleges and universities list this information in a clearly labeled area called "Standardized Testing," others categorize it under "Requirements for Admission," and still others make you look for it, e.g., in the "Frequently Asked Questions" area. Answer the questions below based on what you find.

Name of Institution	Does it require or recommend SAT?	Do applicants need to take Subject Tests in addition to the SAT? Please list below any specific tests that the college or university requests, e.g., Math Level 1. Please note if the tests are required or recommended.
Example: Stanford University	Yes	2 Subject Tests recommended - Math Level 2 preferred as one of them

If your child applies to all of the schools above, which tests will he have to take? Not all institutions require Subject Tests, so only use the second box below if necessary.

Scenario 2: SAT

Please check all that apply:

☐ SAT
☐ One additional Subject Test **OR**
☐ Two additional Subject Tests **OR**
☐ Three additional Subject Tests **OR**
☐ Four additional Subject Tests (several schools require 2–3 Subject Tests, but they all require different ones).

Total # of required tests:

Subject Test Requirements

Please check the specific Subject Tests that the institutions on your list require or recommend:

☐ Math Level 1
☐ Math Level 2
☐ Physics
☐ Chemistry
☐ Biology
☐ Other (please specify): _____

Total # of required Subject Tests:

If you feel certain that your child will need Subject Tests—or if you just want to leave as many options open as possible for the moment—seriously consider whether or not he stands to do well on them. Remember, the institutions that generally require Subject Tests stand out as some of the best in the country, so doing well for an unhooked applicant means breaking 700 out of a possible 800, sometimes even better. Students need to know the material like the back of their hand *and* need to review for the tests with consistency and rigor. The worksheet on page 101 helps you to determine your child's Subject Test outlook.

Passionate learners generally do extremely well on Subject Tests in areas that inspire them. (See "Academic Profile" section of worksheet.) My client Jake, whom I mentioned in Chapter One, has a passion for U.S. history and politics and sometimes reads a book a week in those areas. He earned a 780 on the U.S. history Subject Test. My cousin—the one who convinced his mom to let him work as a mechanic when she wanted him to work in a laboratory—eats, sleeps, and breathes physics. He scored 800 on the Subject Test. You should also consider how well your child performs in school in a particular area. Liking a subject a lot, getting B's in school, and completing some kind of review may help a child break 600 or even 650 on a Subject Test. Having a passion for a particular area, getting A's in school, and completing a review program will push that score to the next level.

Doing well on Subject Tests in most cases necessitates consistent and rigorous review over eight to twelve weeks. (See "Work Ethic" section of worksheet.) Simply enrolling your child in a formal program does not suffice, as completing homework assignments matters just as much as attending the class sessions. Maximizing the benefits of test preparation means consistently completing homework assignments. If your child cannot do this in a self-motivated way, he may want to think carefully before registering for Subject Tests.

Reviewing for Subject Tests requires a substantial time commitment, as the previous paragraph suggests. You and your child need to look closely at how much test preparation he can handle, given that these tests usually fall right around the time that students also take either the ACT or the SAT. (See "ACT/SAT" section of worksheet.) Lizzie, a client of mine who desperately needed to raise her SAT scores when she took them in May of her junior year, was planning to take two Subject Tests one month later, in June. I explained

Your child's current grade in school (circle one):   Below grade nine   Grade nine   Grade ten   Grade eleven   Grade twelve

Determining Whether Your Child Should Take SAT Subject Tests

	Strongly Agree		Agree		Somewhat Agree		Disagree		Strongly Disagree	
Academic Profile: My child is a passionate learner (see Chapter One).	10	9	8	7	6	5	4	3	2	1	0
Academic Profile: My child has a particular passion for the areas in which he is considering taking Subject Tests.	10	9	8	7	6	5	4	3	2	1	0
Academic Profile: My child consistently receives A's in the areas in which he is considering taking Subject Tests.	10	9	8	7	6	5	4	3	2	1	0
Work Ethic: My child is self-motivated and would/does consistently complete his test-preparation assignments on time.	10	9	8	7	6	5	4	3	2	1	0
Work Ethic: My child is willing to put in eight to twelve weeks of consistent and rigorous study for each Subject Test that he takes.	10	9	8	7	6	5	4	3	2	1	0
ACT/SAT: My child has achieved his goals on the ACT or SAT and will not be overloaded by studying for additional standardized tests.	10	9	8	7	6	5	4	3	2	1	0
Colleges of Interest: My child plans to apply to specialized programs that require Subject Tests, e.g., engineering.	10	9	8	7	6	5	4	3	2	1	0
Colleges of Interest: My child plans to apply to more than one college or university that requires Subject Tests.	10	9	8	7	6	5	4	3	2	1	0
Colleges of Interest: Those institutions still require Subject Tests, even if my child takes the ACT rather than the SAT.	10	9	8	7	6	5	4	3	2	1	0

to her and her parents that sitting for multiple tests in such close proximity to each other would leave her with poor to mediocre scores in all of them and prove self-defeating in the long run. She took my advice, directed her full attention to the SAT preparation program that I had laid out for her, raised her scores by 100 points in each section, and decided to skip Subject Tests altogether. Think about Lizzie's scenario and whether or not it applies to your child as you and he discuss whether and when he should take Subject Tests.

The process of determining whether or not Subject Tests look like an appropriate option for your child could double as the first step in thinking about suitable places for him to apply. (See "Colleges of Interest" section of worksheet.) I would have misgivings about encouraging a student who does not qualify as a passionate learner in any area, who is not self-motivated, and who is still struggling with the ACT or the SAT to focus on Harvard. At the same time, clients of mine have taken three Subject Tests just to apply to that one dream school to which they have an infinitesimal chance of getting accepted. One young man poignantly shared with me his understanding that he most likely would not get into Georgetown but that, if he did not try, he would always wonder. Several strategic tips can help maximize your child's results in instances such as these.

Young people who do not stand out as strong candidates to take Subject Tests but who want to do so anyway should strongly consider taking Math Level 1 and English Literature, both of which overlap significantly with the ACT and the SAT. Those who study rigorously for an April or May sitting of the ACT or the SAT have accomplished much of the preparation they need to take either of these two Subject Tests in June (although I would still recommend using the intervening four weeks to continue studying). By the same token, these students should avoid Math Level 2, chemistry, physics, and languages with listening, areas that attract high-octane students against whom other test takers must then compete for a percentile ranking. (An English Literature score of 700, for example, puts a student in the 85th percentile, while a physics score of 700 only places a student in the 65th percentile.[17]) As a general rule, only native speakers or those who have lived and functioned using a language overseas should take a language Subject Test with listening and only those with a nearly perfect mathematics score on the PSAT or first round of the ACT or SAT should register for an advanced mathematics or science examination.

FREQUENTLY ASKED QUESTIONS

Instead of going through a tedious decision process about which test to take, the ACT or the SAT, an increasing number of students at my child's high school are taking both and then just submitting the stronger score to colleges. Why not just simplify the process and take this approach?

Two key reasons would lead me to advise against this strategy. First, the more time your child spends on testing, the less time he has for other aspects of his high school experience, such as schoolwork, extracurricular activities, etc. Overloading on standardized testing diverts young people's attention away from other areas of interest and possible opportunities. Second, colleges will automatically see an SAT score if your child also has to submit Subject Test scores, even if he would prefer that they consider only his ACT score, as Subject Tests and the SAT appear on the same score report. Students should take advantage of the ample opportunity they have to try practice tests for both the ACT and the SAT and then concentrate on the test that suits them better of the two.

We live on the East Coast and our child's guidance counselor insists that colleges and universities want students from our area to take the SAT, not the ACT. Is the counselor correct in her belief that taking the ACT will hurt our daughter's chances for admission?

I hate to say this, but your daughter's counselor is dead wrong. Two misconceptions about the ACT circulate frequently: first, that colleges and universities expect East Coast students to take the SAT and not the ACT, and, second, that East Coast institutions prefer to see the SAT from all their applicants. Both are patently untrue. Selective colleges and universities around the country, including the most elite East Coast institutions, accept either test no matter where you live.

Deans of admission whom I interviewed for this book made that point emphatically when I spoke to them: Every one of them, without exception, felt equally comfortable with both the ACT and the SAT. Some wondered aloud why more students do not take the ACT, given the tangible advantages that it offers over the SAT. One called both tests "helpful," but noted that, in making an admissions decision, "I would probably be more comfortable with the ACT alone, than with the SAT alone. I just don't feel that the SAT by itself is enough. The ACT has much more breadth as a test than the SAT." When asked if a lone student taking the ACT at an SAT high school would be putting himself at a disadvantage, these deans of admission gave quite the opposite response. Arlene Cash, Vice President for Enrollment Management at Spelman College, went so far as to call such a student "brave" and noted that independent behavior like that would impress her.

The 2005 revisions to the SAT have also precipitated a backlash from high schools around the country, including elite independents. "We have already started to shift to the ACT," a highly regarded college counselor at one of those high schools shared with me. "A year from now, many of our students will be taking it and we will be an ACT testing center." The trend seems to be moving toward the ACT rather than away from it, at many levels. That being said, colleges usually outline standardized testing requirements on their Web sites. Check online or place calls to admissions offices at several colleges or universities that your child has identified to ask about their acceptance of the ACT. Hearing directly from them that the ACT puts your child at no disadvantage will hopefully allay any fears you might have.

My son is a sophomore in high school and has no idea where he wants to apply to college. He is taking an AP class this year and his teacher is encouraging him to take the Subject Test as well. Is there any disadvantage to his just taking it and seeing how he does? If he ends up applying to institutions that do not require it, he will not have done himself any harm anyway, right, given that they do not consider those scores?

Complete the worksheet in this chapter called "Determining Whether Your Child Should Take SAT Subject Tests." Then ask yourself if your child has a passion for this subject, if he is getting A's in the class, and if he is willing to put in the necessary time to study for the Subject Test in addition to the AP examination, which he will need to do. If you can answer all of these questions with a resounding yes, then taking this Subject Test might serve your child well. Keep in mind, though, that unless he cancels the score within the allowable window following the test, it will automatically and indelibly show up on his score report. Not doing well weakens his overall standardized testing profile, even for colleges and universities that do not require Subject Tests, as they see the entire score report.

A few of the college Web sites I've looked at say that they will accept AP or IB scores in lieu of the ACT or SAT. What are these tests and do they represent an appropriate alternative to the ACT and SAT for my child?

As we discussed in Chapters One through Three, AP and IB programs give high school students the opportunity through high-level examinations to demonstrate advanced academic achievement, earn college credit, and/or place-out of required college courses.[18] Students usually take these courses and corresponding examinations in their junior and/or senior year. In a limited number of instances, admissions offices will use the results of these examinations in lieu of ACT or SAT scores.

An AP test generally follows an intensive one-year academic course that provides rigorous preparation. Students may sign up for AP tests without having taken a formal course; however, I would only recommend that option for passionate learners with the discipline to pursue independent study of an AP curriculum over an entire academic year, preferably with ongoing support from a teacher. (See the account in Chapter One of the single instance in my almost ten-year teaching career in which I recommended this option to a student.) Your child does not have to report his scores to colleges and may exercise Score Choice if he wishes to report some but not others. ETS keeps AP and SAT score reports separate from each other.

Unlike the College Board and ETS, the International Baccalaureate Organization (IBO) does not allow your child to pick and choose the individual IB courses that he takes. His high school must offer an approved IB program that requires him to follow an organized sequence of courses in six subject areas. Successful completion of that sequence (and the accompanying examinations) leads to a specially designated "IB diploma."

AP scores range from a minimum of 1 to a maximum of 5, IB from 1 to 7. Colleges and universities consider successful AP and IB results in the admissions process if students have taken any of these examinations prior to senior year, sometimes in place of other standardized tests. The definition of a successful score depends on the institution: Top 20 colleges and universities are generally looking for scores of 4 or 5 on the AP and 6 or 7 on the IB. To figure out exactly what score would make a favorable impression on admissions officers at a particular place, go to the Web site, enter the terms "AP" or "IB" in the search field (depending on which one interests you), and browse through your search results. You will sometimes find general guidelines on the institution's policies for granting course credit or course waivers for AP and IB scores. You may also see specific departmental guidelines for individual examination results, such as for biology or chemistry. I would recommend reporting AP or IB scores that fall at or above an institution's cutoff point for granting course credit or course waivers.

AP and IB courses and examinations can provide a challenging academic experience for your child as long as he feels prepared for and committed to a highly demanding workload. You should not consider them a direct substitute for either the ACT or the SAT, as preparing for AP or IB examinations requires significantly more time and effort than preparing for the ACT or SAT and only a handful of institutions accept AP or IB scores as substitutes for the ACT or SAT anyway. Encourage your child to take AP or IB classes and/or examinations if your assessment of him, his high school, and his course selection options all point to AP or IB courses and examinations as appropriate options for him—not because you or he thinks they will look good for college. I've said it before, and I'll say it again: struggling and doing poorly in higher level courses not only shortchange your child, but can also look bad in the admissions folder.

STEP-BY-STEP CHECKLIST:
DECIDING WHICH STANDARDIZED TESTS TO TAKE

❑ Make sure your child takes the PSAT at every point at which his high school offers it (in both grades ten and eleven, if possible).

❑ Analyze PSAT scores to determine whether or not your child should look at the ACT as an alternative to the SAT.

❑ Use PSAT results to identify the areas that most need to improve and on what ACT or SAT test preparation should focus.

❑ Compare your child's PSAT scores to the middle 50 percent range of SAT scores for admitted applicants at colleges and universities that interest him. If he falls at the bottom of or below that range, pay special attention to his test-preparation program and to whether or not taking Subject Tests will stretch him too thin.

❑ Ask your child to try practice questions for both the ACT and SAT before he makes a final decision about which test to take.

❑ Use practice test results and an analysis of your child's academic profile and learning style to select the test that makes the most sense for him, the ACT or the SAT. (You can use the worksheet "Determining Whether Your Child Should Take the ACT or the SAT" to help make that determination.)

❑ Concentrate fully on that test (as opposed to having your child prepare for and take both the ACT and the SAT).

❑ Conduct some preliminary research on standardized testing requirements for colleges and universities that interest your child or that represent the type of institution to which you see him applying.

❑ Complete the worksheets "Does Your Child Need to Take Subject Tests If He Takes the ACT?" and "Does Your Child Need to Take Subject Tests If He Takes the SAT?" to determine whether or not these tests have relevance for your child.

❑ Use the worksheet "Determining Whether Your Child Should Take SAT Subject Tests" to gauge his prospects for doing well on these examinations.

❑ Map out a test-taking calendar based on what you conclude after you fill out the worksheets.

Preparing for Standardized Tests (the ACT, the SAT, and Subject Tests)

Families generally devote more time, energy, and financial resources to standardized testing than they do to any other area of the college admissions process—far more than they need to. Those with the means to spend $5,000 on an international summer community service adventure for their child in Costa Rica or Hungary can also expend up to six or seven times as much on ACT or SAT preparation. Parents who lack these kinds of resources sometimes fear that they are not fulfilling their responsibility to their children. The mother and father of one young man with whom I am working both began looking for second jobs in their son's sophomore year, not to pay for college but to finance his test preparation! Yes, your child likely needs formal preparation for required college admissions tests, but no, you do not need to spend thousands of dollars on it.

This chapter helps you understand which students especially need formal test preparation and then walks you through a series of steps to help you determine the optimal approach for your child, based on her academic profile, learning style, and study habits. In my own private practice, I have come up with a standardized testing preparation program that has brought significant score improvements to those of my clients who have used it. I share that program with you here, especially since it offers a cost-effective option that you can implement no matter where you live.

DETERMINING THE EXTENT TO WHICH YOUR CHILD NEEDS FORMAL PREPARATION FOR THE ACT OR SAT

Almost any student can benefit from ACT or SAT preparation. Calibrating how much test preparation your child needs depends largely on who she is and how her scores compare with those of her peers applying to similar colleges and universities. (When I say "peers," I mean classmates who come from a similar demographic background, rather than all other test takers across the country.) Standardized test scores vary significantly across groups. Statistics show that suburban students typically outperform their urban and rural peers, for example, white and Asian students' scores generally surpass those of blacks and Hispanics, and boys historically get better results than girls (even though girls tend to earn better grades in college than boys do). Experienced admissions officers know that they cannot use standardized tests to compare a student from an affluent, professional community to one from an economically depressed, rural area. Instead, they look at the high school a candidate attends, the environment in which she lives, family income level, whether or not parents attended college, and more. They then use standardized test scores as one way to distinguish between applicants from the same or similar groups.

The more homogeneous a high school looks, the more standardized test scores can help admissions officers as they evaluate its applicant pool. You may remember from the discussion of GPA and class rank in Chapter Three that many high schools, especially those in suburban communities, have responded to political pressure from parents, who feel that a top ranking will help their children get into college. Every student with a GPA at or above a certain point, therefore, gets ranked number one. "Schools force us to look at standardized testing when they have 330 students and 38 valedictorians, every one of whom has a GPA of 4.0," Swarthmore College Dean of Admissions Jim Bock points out. "Standardized testing helps differentiate between them." Similarly, a solid transcript from a student at a poor urban or rural high school means much more to admissions officers than it otherwise would if it comes with above-average standardized test scores that demonstrate that she has the ability to survive academically at a selective college or university.

How Much ACT/SAT Prep Does Your Child Need?

- Compare your child's grade-eleven PSAT or mock ACT or SAT results to the average scores for her high school.

- Account for demographic variations by factoring in the relevant characteristics that appear in the next box.

- Then compare her scores to the middle 50 percent range for incoming freshmen at colleges and universities that interest her.

- If, relative to her peer group, your child appears competitive for a college or university in every way except her test scores, ACT or SAT preparation should rank high on your list of priorities.

- If, relative to her peer group, your child's preliminary test scores appear competitive for a particular institution, balance test preparation against other ways in which she could strengthen her application, such as raising her grades or taking on leadership roles in extracurricular activities.

Figuring out where your child falls on her high school's test score curve can help you gauge how much test preparation she needs, if any, for the specific colleges and universities to which she plans to apply. You can start by comparing her eleventh-grade PSAT or mock ACT or SAT scores from the same year to the average scores for her high school, figures that you can usually obtain from the college guidance office.[19] (We will talk later in this chapter about why it makes sense to hold off on test preparation until your child reaches grade eleven, in case you are thinking that you want her to start sooner than that.) Scores that fall above the mean suggest that your child is starting out ahead of the game compared with her high school peer group; below the mean implies the reverse. Now you need to drill down further, to any subpopulations into which your child falls based on income, race, gender, etc., to determine the true value of her test scores.

As I mentioned earlier, research has established that certain demographic characteristics correlate with higher or lower test scores. SAT scores rise, for example, with family income and with parent level of education. A student who falls into a higher-scoring demographic category needs to have test results that match that specific peer group.

Let's look at a concrete example—a young person at a high school in an affluent suburb of New York City who wants to attend a Top 20 college or university. Coming from a high income home with parents who both obtained advanced degrees means that this applicant, statistically speaking, has a greater chance of doing well on standardized tests than those from households without these characteristics; admissions officers at Top 20 colleges and universities will hold her to that standard and look for ACT or SAT scores well above both her high school mean *and* the institution's middle 50 percent range for incoming freshmen. A candidate who attends this same affluent, suburban high school but has non-college-educated parents, on the other hand, can remain competitive in the eyes of admissions officers from Top 20 institutions, even with test scores that fall closer to the high school mean than the student described above and within the middle 50 percent range for incoming freshmen. Hooked students— such as those from underrepresented racial and ethnic groups, recruited athletes, and children of alumni—can also afford to have slightly lower standardized test scores than their unhooked peers.

The Demographics of Standardized Test Scores
(based on annual College Board analysis of SAT takers)

- Test scores rise with family income level.

- Test scores rise with parent level of education.

- Suburban test takers typically outperform their urban and rural counterparts.

- White and Asian students generally earn higher scores than African American and Latino students.

- Boys tend to score higher than girls.

The last piece of the puzzle in determining how much test preparation your child needs lies in looking critically at the rest of her profile, relative to the colleges and universities to which she plans to apply. If, compared with her peer group, your child's preliminary test scores appear competitive for a particular institution, balance test preparation against other ways in which she could strengthen her application, such as raising her grades or taking on leadership roles in extracurricular activities. If, on the other hand, your child appears competitive for a college or university in every way except her test scores, ACT or SAT preparation should rank high on your list of priorities. Two of my clients this year, Jake and Lizzie, illustrate this point well: Jake took his ACT once and received a composite score of 32, comfortably at the top of or slightly above the middle 50 percent range at the institutions to which he planned to apply. He wanted to take the test again, but I persuaded him to hold off on doing so until he had studied for the two Subject Tests he was taking and strengthened his extracurricular activities. Lizzie, with many outstanding extracurriculars, however, received abysmal PSAT scores relative to her peer group. Strengthening her profile for the colleges and universities that interested her had to include rigorous SAT preparation.

Following the steps that I have laid out thus far will help you gauge the degree to which your child should concentrate on standardized test preparation, compared to raising her grades, for example, or taking on leadership roles in extracurricular activities. If panic is setting in because senior year is approaching and you think that your child needs an intensive makeover in all three areas—academics, extracurriculars, and standardized testing—reexamine the colleges and universities on her list. (We will return, in the next chapter, to a discussion on putting together an appropriate combination of reach, target, and safety schools.) Simultaneously stepping up the pressure and intensity in three such critical areas of your child's life could stretch her too thin and prove counterproductive, especially during junior and senior year. Committing time and energy to test preparation should not lead to significant opportunity cost in other key areas if you have helped your child set appropriate goals and weigh the importance of her standardized test scores in the context of her entire admissions folder. Yes, those applicants who beat the statistical norm for their demographic group at a particular institution stand out, while those from traditionally high-scoring populations who fall short of their peers offer admissions officers an easy reason to eliminate them from consideration. Standardized test results alone, however, do not guarantee admission, especially if other important components of the folder do not hold up to scrutiny.

SELECTING THE RIGHT FORM OF TEST PREPARATION FOR YOUR CHILD[20]

Studying for the ACT or SAT can significantly raise your child's scores, as long as she uses a method that matches her academic profile, learning style, and study habits. The most commonly used approaches to test preparation fall into three different categories:

1. Do-it-yourself (your child studies independently from a book, software program, and/or online course);

2. Kaplan, Princeton Review, and other classroom options (your child participates in a structured class with ten to twenty other students); and

3. Semiprivate/private tutoring (small group or one-on-one sessions from an instructor who works for himself, as a junior tutor for another established instructor, or for a large company).

I have seen students successfully use all three of these options. The "Selecting the Right Form of Test Preparation for Your Child" worksheet and the discussion that follows will help you determine which one looks like the right choice for your child.

Your child's academic profile can rule out certain test-prep options right off the bat (see "Academic Profile" section of the worksheet). Solid students and passionate learners can potentially thrive in several different learning environments. The next several questions will help narrow down which ones look ideal for your child if she falls into either of these two categories. Underachievers and struggling students, however, have already shown through their day-to-day academic performance that do-it-yourself and classroom alternatives probably do not meet their needs. Do-it-yourself strategies do not provide enough structure, while traditional classroom settings have already proved problematic for them, either because they get bored (underachievers) or because they cannot keep pace with the rest of the class (struggling students). In both of these cases, I strongly recommend either semiprivate or private tutoring.

The next several questions on learning style can help you determine if your solid student or passionate learner would do well in a classroom setting. Although your child's success to date in a tradi-

Your child's current grade in school (circle one):   Below grade nine   Grade nine   Grade ten   Grade eleven   Grade twelve

Selecting the Right Form of Test Preparation for Your Child

	Strongly Agree		Agree		Somewhat Agree		Disagree		Strongly Disagree		
Academic Profile: My child is a solid student. (See Chapter One.)	10	9	8	7	6	5	4	3	2	1	0
Academic Profile: My child is a passionate learner. (See Chapter One.)	10	9	8	7	6	5	4	3	2	1	0
Academic Profile: My child is an underachiever. (See Chapter One.)	10	9	8	7	6	5	4	3	2	1	0
Academic Profile: My child is a struggling student. (See Chapter One.)	10	9	8	7	6	5	4	3	2	1	0
Learning Style: My child thrives in a traditional classroom setting and does not need individualized instruction to master new content.	10	9	8	7	6	5	4	3	2	1	0
Learning Style: My child feels comfortable asking questions in class if she does not understand something.	10	9	8	7	6	5	4	3	2	1	0
Learning Style: My child feels comfortable seeking help from teachers outside of class if she does not understand something.	10	9	8	7	6	5	4	3	2	1	0
Learning Style: My child feels comfortable working with her peers in a study group.	10	9	8	7	6	5	4	3	2	1	0
Learning Style: My child sometimes needs to learn multiple approaches to solving a problem in order to understand it.	10	9	8	7	6	5	4	3	2	1	0
Study Habits: My child is a self-starter, i.e., she does not need the discipline and structure of a classroom or tutor to complete assignments.	10	9	8	7	6	5	4	3	2	1	0
Study Habits: If given a schedule of assignments, my child will complete them at the designated intervals rather than cram them all in at the end.	10	9	8	7	6	5	4	3	2	1	0
Practical Considerations: My child has access to the necessary resources to complete the test-preparation program we are considering for her, e.g., a high-speed Internet connection for an online course, a quiet place to study, etc.	10	9	8	7	6	5	4	3	2	1	0
Practical Considerations: We can comfortably afford the test-preparation program we are considering.	10	9	8	7	6	5	4	3	2	1	0

tional classroom setting bodes well for an organized test-preparation course, you also need to know whether she will feel comfortable asking questions in class and seeking extra help from the instructor outside of class if necessary. She may feel more at ease at her own school, with students and teachers whom she knows, than she does in a class with an unknown instructor and completely new faces sitting next to her. Ask your child about these issues, as well as about whether or not she sometimes needs to learn multiple approaches to solving a problem in order to understand it. Kaplan and Princeton Review—the classroom-based options that test-preparation expert Tim Levin recommends—train their staff to teach according to a specific method. Instructors coach students to follow a defined set of steps to do well on the test. The learning experience does not address individual student strengths and/or weaknesses and may not work for somebody who needs to examine problems in different ways, according to Levin.

Not all solid students or passionate learners qualify as self-starters, an essential characteristic for those who want to use a do-it-yourself solution. (See "Study Habits" section of worksheet.) I studied for the SAT in 1981 and was probably part of the last generation of high school students to prepare for it with a study guide and nothing else. I still remember how much I hated going to my room every evening and completing mind-numbing practice problems and tests. The strategy worked for me, probably as much due to the watchful eye of my mother as anything else. You need to ask yourself, though, if your child will complete do-it-yourself studying without your nagging or threatening punishment, as you do not want to set yourself up for an ongoing series of frustrating confrontations with your child.

Succeeding through both do-it-yourself and structured classroom approaches requires that your child study regularly and not skip assignments or save them until the last minute. Unprepared students can hide in a classroom, but not from a tutor in a small group or private session. Tutors can also work with your child several times a week (more frequently than test-preparation classes generally meet), if your child needs face-to-face encounters to motivate her to complete her assignments regularly. Consider semiprivate or private tutoring if your child—even a solid student or a passionate learner—tends to procrastinate and if you can afford this option.

Affordability stands out as one of several practical considerations in selecting a test-preparation program for your child (see "Practical Considerations" section of worksheet). If you are struggling with cost, determine a budget for what you can spend on test preparation first and then see which options fit into that overall number, rather than the other way around. You might also want to try the system that my own mother used when money was tight or if I asked for something discretionary, such as a 35-millimeter camera so that I could take photography to fulfill my high school art requirement: she matched every dollar that I earned. You'd better believe that I took photography much more seriously than I would have if I had not invested in it myself. (It became a lifelong hobby.) My contribution also allowed her to offer me something that she otherwise could not have afforded. Inquire at your child's high school or local community center about free tutoring through volunteers or through a corporate-sponsored program, and do not hesitate to ask private test-preparation companies about scholarships or reduced rates based on need. Make sure from a practical perspective that you can provide everything your child needs to complete a test-preparation program successfully, such as a high-speed Internet connection in a quiet part of the house if she will be participating in an online course.

SELECTING THE HIGHEST QUALITY
TEST-PREPARATION RESOURCES AVAILABLE

Once you and your child have selected the appropriate test-preparation program for her, you need to insure that she gets access to the best resources available. A do-it-yourself program with a poorly written book or a classroom course with an ineffective teacher will get her nowhere. The following tips will help you recognize quality in each of the test-preparation areas we have discussed.

Do-it-yourself students can choose from a wide array of books, software programs, and online courses. Start by consulting the ACT or College Board Web site, each of which makes free practice questions available and sells high-quality review materials. Tim Levin calls the study guides that the two companies publish "indispensable" and uses them in his own test-prep sessions (*The Official SAT Study Guide: For the New SAT* and *The Real ACT Prep Guide,* respectively). Students in search of additional practice tests may want to purchase Kaplan and/or Princeton Review books as well (in that order, as Kaplan tends to update its books more frequently than Princeton Review does). Both companies have large staffs that work on the books, according to Levin, who also advises students to avoid "chatty" study guides that talk about the test without providing enough actual practice questions. Practice questions engage students in "active studying," and stand out, above all test-taking strategies and tips, as *the key* to effective test preparation.

Essential Resources for Do-It-Yourself ACT or SAT Test Preparation

• Visit the ACT or College Board Web site and complete the available online practice questions.

• Use additional test-prep resources that ACT or the College Board produce as your primary source of practice tests.

• Use a Kaplan and/or Princeton Review study guide and/or software program for additional practice tests.

Other software and online programs exist—too many to mention—but, if you are considering another manufacturer's product, compare the price with what the test manufacturers themselves offer and then look for a review. (See, for example, www.gzkidzone.com or www. childrenssoftware.com.) Kaplan and Princeton Review software programs consistently get strong reviews and are reasonably priced. Their online courses, on the other hand, run hundreds of dollars, far more than what the test manufacturers themselves charge. You should not have to spend more than $100–$150 to purchase everything your child needs to pursue an effective do-it-yourself ACT or SAT preparation program.

Selecting a Classroom Program for ACT or SAT Test Preparation

• Check out Kaplan or Princeton Review.

• Research small, independent test-preparation companies that are not part of a national chain. (Research includes getting referrals!)

• In all cases, ask around for names of particularly effective and popular instructors—they are your child's key to success on the test.

If you and your child have settled on a classroom-based program, check out your local Kaplan or Princeton Review. These companies both teach students good methods for working through the ACT and the SAT, according to Tim Levin. Standardized tests in general and the SAT in particular "by their very structure, lend themselves to tricks and gimmicks," Levin explains. "Tests are beatable!" Major test-prep companies provide your child with a structured, scheduled way to get through the materials that she needs to study. Even if your child "knows the math, knows the verbal, has the writing skills—the structured assignments each week guide her through the preparation process and give her a sense of security."

Small, independent test-preparation companies have also opened in many locations.[21] The key to identifying the best possible fit for your child lies in talking to people, especially trusted guidance counselors and parents whose children have already gone through this experience. Find out which companies satisfied their customers and, just as importantly, the teachers within those companies whom educators and past students recommend.

Tim Levin's Questions to Ask a Private Tutor

- Have you worked for a test-preparation company? If not, what experience with and/or exposure to the test do you have?

- When was the last time you took the test yourself? How frequently do you retake it?

- How familiar are you with the retail study guides and which ones do you recommend?

- How much tutoring do you think my child needs?

- Do you have multiple strategies for teaching the same material that you can use depending on my child's learning style?

- Do you work with students in small groups? If so, how does such an arrangement affect your rates?

You need to perform similar due diligence in seeking a private tutor for your child. Levin, a sought-after New York City tutor himself, advises parents to look for a professional who either has test-preparation experience with a place like Kaplan or Princeton Review and is now operating independently, or has taken the time to develop his own expertise with the ACT or SAT. The tutor must know both his subject matter and the test well enough to coach and counsel your child. Especially proactive tutors take the test with their students and, in the case of the SAT, can then answer questions within the cancellation period to help your child decide whether or not to keep the score. A number of top-shelf private tutoring companies in Manhattan reduce their hourly rates by 30 to 60 percent when they work with students in small groups as opposed to individually, so consider collaborating with like-minded friends whose children may want to form a small group with yours.

Whichever test-preparation solution you choose, remember to keep this part of the admissions process in perspective. Responsible tutors and admissions officers alike bemoan the common misperception that the ACT or SAT matters most of all and that, if your child does well on the test, she will get to go wherever she wants. "That is not the case," Levin cautions. "There's much more to your child than her SAT score. Do not overvalue the test."

THE SECRET TO STANDARDIZED TESTING SUCCESS

My career in education has spanned roughly twenty years and, along the way, I have identified some professional heroes. Professor Uri Treisman, formerly of the University of California, Berkeley, stands out as one of them. As a graduate student and mathematics instructor at Berkeley in the 1970s, Treisman wanted to figure out why some students succeeded at calculus and others did not. He moved into the student dormitories and learned from his observations that the differing outcomes grew out of divergent approaches to studying: All of the subjects for Treisman's study spent roughly the same amount of time reviewing for tests on their own. Those who succeeded, however, came together in study groups to learn from each other after they had gotten as far as they could individually. Treisman used the results of this research to devise a new approach to teaching calculus that included the study group element, among other things. The same students who had been lagging behind in a traditional calculus class improved dramatically with the new program.[22]

I have borrowed from Treisman's research, both in my own classroom while I was still teaching and in advising families on test preparation, and the results have spoken for themselves. Once you and your child have determined the ideal test-preparation format for her, identify two or three other students interested in the same approach and arrange for the small group to participate together in whatever program the families select. The group can use any of the methods and resources we have already discussed, as long as students consistently perform two steps in between class sessions, online modules, or study guide chapters: get as far as they can on practice problems individually and then meet as a study group to learn from each other and help each other get "unstuck." The young people with whom I have worked who have followed these recommendations have seen their test scores rise significantly, and I would expect similar results for your child.

PREPARING FOR AND TAKING SUBJECT TESTS

Your child can use the same approach to prepare for Subject Tests that she implements for the ACT or SAT, although a few tips specific to those examinations apply. Subject Tests correlate directly to an area that your child is studying in school, either in a cumulative subject (mathematics, language, etc.) or in a one-year course (U.S. history, biology, etc.). Subject Tests that correlate to a one-year course should come at the end of the academic year in which your child has completed that curriculum. Those in cumulative subjects can come at different points in the school year, as long as the relevant coursework is ongoing. I do not recommend finishing a one-year course or the final year in a cumulative series of courses in June, reviewing for the Subject Test over the summer, and then taking it in the fall. Other obligations distract even those young people with the best intentions and preparing for a Subject Test in an area that they are no longer studying in school falls easily to the wayside.

Each Subject Test that your child takes requires the same rigorous preparation as the ACT or SAT, such as a formal review course, semi-private or private tutoring, a study group, etc. Unlike with the ACT or SAT, though, which most students take more than once, your child should plan to take each Subject Test only one time. Extenuating circumstances sometimes arise, such as the young woman who spilled water on her calculator just before the Math Level 1 examination and spent the first ten minutes of the test trying to get it to work. In such a scenario, I would advise a student to cancel the score so that, when she takes the test again, it looks on her score report like she sat for it only once.

Preparing For and Taking Subject Tests

• Schedule Subject Tests that correlate with a one-year course, such as physics or biology, for the end of the academic year in which your child is taking that course.

• With cumulative subjects, schedule the Subject Test while your child is still enrolled in a course in that area.

• Encourage your child to prepare for Subject Tests with the same rigor with which she prepares for the ACT or SAT.

• Go through the same method of selecting an appropriate form of test preparation for Subject Tests that you did for the ACT or SAT.

• Have your child aim to take each Subject Test only once, rather than multiple times.

• Have your child register for only one Subject Test on a given test date.

The possibility that your child may need to cancel a Subject Test score makes it highly advisable that she schedule only one Subject Test per test date. The College Board offers test takers an "all or nothing" Subject Test cancellation policy: students either cancel all examinations that they took on the same test date or they cancel none. Spreading out these tests across multiple dates will protect your child from having to choose between keeping a possibly damaging score or canceling a potentially strong one.

FREQUENTLY ASKED QUESTIONS

How many times do you think my child should take the ACT or SAT?

You can use your child's PSAT or mock ACT or SAT scores to make this determination. Some students stand out as naturally strong standardized test takers, either all around or in a particular subject, such as mathematics. If your child's preliminary results fall within 50 points of her target score for each section of the SAT (3 to 4 points on the ACT) *and* if she does not seem like the type to panic or freeze up on the day of the real thing, she may very well be able to study as needed the first time around and take the ACT or SAT just once.

Many students, though, have a tendency to freeze and underperform on standardized tests, in part because they have internalized the idea that they are "bad test takers." These young people typically study intensively for their first round of the test, walk in with jitters because the real thing never feels quite like the PSAT or mock tests, and wind up with disappointing results that give them an additional reason to think that they will never escape the "bad test taker" label ("I studied so hard and my scores still did not go up!"). If this description fits your child, I recommend that she follow the strategy below, one that comes from years of observing anxious students:

1. Take the ACT or SAT once with no preparation whatsoever.

2. Order TIR or QAS (the option that provides the test questions, correct answers, your child's answers, and the scoring conversion key) to pinpoint exactly which types of questions her test preparation should emphasize.

3. Engage in rigorous test preparation as outlined in this chapter.

4. Take the test a second time.

Knowing that the first round of scores will not count eliminates much of the anxiety that nervous test takers would otherwise feel. They walk into their second round of testing having seen the examination once before and knowing that they have mastered what they got wrong that first time around. The resulting boost in self-confidence alone can effectively add points to their score.

You may be wondering how a first score does not count, especially on the SAT, since the College Board does not offer Score Choice. Admissions officers take for granted these days that students take the ACT or SAT more than once. Their eye instinctively goes to the highest scores on the report and they see significant improvement between two sets of scores as a reflection of hard work and commitment, if anything. Some institutions, such as MIT and Pitzer, feed test scores into their computer system and generate their own score reports that include the best results and delete the rest. No admissions office will penalize a candidate for taking the ACT or SAT twice.

Continuing to prepare and repeatedly test beyond that point, however, will likely eke out minimal gains that make no positive difference in the admissions process and could have an unintended negative consequence. Somebody who has taken the ACT or SAT "three, four, five times in junior and senior year, begins to make you question her judgment," Rice's Julie Browning warns. Mount Holyoke's Jane Brown cautioned that repeat testing, when the college was still asking students to submit ACT or SAT scores, "in some ways would color our thinking about the student." The attempt to get scores up to a certain level can look in the extreme like what Clark University's Harold Wingood calls a "meat-grinder experience," something that admissions officers view as "almost always futile" and to which I do not recommend that you subject your child.

I know of some families who start their children's ACT or SAT preparation program in grade nine. When should my child begin studying for the ACT?

Placing a disproportionate emphasis on the ACT or SAT takes time and energy away from schoolwork and extracurricular activities, other critical aspects of your child's application and high school experience. A student can achieve optimal ACT or SAT results by working intensively for four to six months on the areas that need improvement. Doing anything more than that dramatically overstates the value of the test in the admissions process. As Mount Holyoke's Jane Brown would say, "Oh gosh, what a waste of valuable time!" I agree.

Make sure that, prior to beginning her test-preparation program, your child studies how to use her calculator. Test takers with detailed knowledge of how their calculators work have a considerable advantage over those who do not. Spending a little bit of extra time on that makes sense and doing it prior to the start of formal test preparation means that your child gets a few months of practice in the context of test-taking situations.

Are there any practical considerations to keep in mind in selecting a test center?

I strongly advise my clients to select a university, local private school, or suburban test center, in that order. Check with older students to find out where they tested and if they had a good experience. Numerous students have described proctoring conditions that unquestionably affected their scores, such as a proctor's failure to read directions or keep time (some students rely on periodic time checks, even if they wear a watch). One client recounted to me that a proctor and student screamed at each other for fifteen minutes while the others in the room were supposed to continue testing. Help your child plan how she will get to the test center and insure that she has everything she needs to feel confident and comfortable, such as a working calculator, accurate timepiece, sharpened pencils, etc. Keep in mind that the earlier your child registers for the test, the greater her likelihood of getting her first-choice location.

Consider lobbying your child's high school to become a test center if your child is taking the ACT or the SAT in a geographic region in which it has not traditionally been offered in the past and you cannot find a convenient testing location. Alternatively, contact the media relations office at either company (ACT or the College Board) to let them know that an increasing number of students in your area want to take their test but cannot find a convenient location at which to do so. I know of at least one instance in which an educator placed a call like this and, by the end of the day, the company had made arrangements for a conveniently located testing center for her students.

Last but not least, make sure your child knows not to select any score reporting when she registers for her test. The testing companies include a certain number of score reports to colleges and universities as part of your registration cost if you identify them when you sign up for the test. Selecting them at a later date requires that you pay an ancillary fee. Forgo the free service (reporting scores later costs only a nominal amount) and wait until your child's results come back before reporting them. A student with poor SAT scores may decide to switch over to the ACT and not need to submit an SAT score report at all. Your child needs to see her results before colleges and universities do in order to make the best decisions possible, even if that means spending a few extra dollars per school to send score reports after the fact. (The cost of reporting scores rises if you select an express delivery option.)

My son has been diagnosed with Attention Deficit Disorder (ADD) and his guidance counselor has advised us to apply for him to take his tests with "extended time." What exactly does this mean and how do we go about making this application?

Both ACT and the College Board make special provisions for students to receive extra time when they take their standardized tests if they can document that they have a medical or cognitive condition that impairs their test-taking ability. Not all applications for "extended time" get approved, however, so it helps that your child has the support of his high school guidance counselor. I would suggest searching on each of the company Web sites, where you will find details and contact information to help you proceed with the application.

STEP-BY-STEP CHECKLIST: PREPARING FOR THE ACT, SAT, AND SUBJECT TESTS

❏ Compare your child's grade-eleven PSAT or mock ACT or SAT results to the average scores for her high school.

❏ Account for demographic variations by factoring in the relevant characteristics mentioned in this chapter.

❏ Compare your child's scores to the middle 50 percent range for incoming freshmen at colleges and universities that interest her.

❏ Make ACT or SAT test preparation a top priority if, relative to her peer group, your child appears competitive for a college or university in every way except her test scores.

❏ Consider de-emphasizing test preparation and focusing instead on other ways in which your child could strengthen her application, such as raising her grades or taking on leadership roles in extracurricular activities, if, relative to her peer group, her preliminary test scores appear competitive at the institutions that interest her.

❏ Complete the worksheet "Selecting the Right Form of Test Preparation for Your Child" to determine if your child should rely on a do-it-yourself, classroom, or semiprivate/private tutoring program.

❏ Map out a test-taking and test-preparation calendar.

❏ For do-it-yourself students, start with the test-preparation materials that each of the two testing companies distributes and supplement them with Kaplan and Princeton Review products (in that order).

❏ For students pursuing a classroom-based approach, check out Kaplan, Princeton Review, and any independent test-preparation companies that educators and parents in your community recommend.

❏ Get recommendations for specific teachers within those companies.

❏ If you are seeking a private tutor, go through Tim Levin's list of recommended questions that appear in this chapter.

❏ Collaborate with several other families to enroll your children together in whatever form of test preparation you select and help the children form a test-prep study group.

❏ Schedule Subject Tests that correlate with a one-year course, such as physics or biology, for the end of the academic year in which your child is taking that curriculum.

❏ With cumulative subjects, schedule the Subject Test while your child is still enrolled in a course in that area.

❏ Encourage your child to prepare for Subject Tests with the same rigor with which she prepares for the ACT or SAT.

❏ Go through the same method of selecting an appropriate form of test preparation for Subject Tests that you do for the ACT or SAT.

❏ Have your child aim to take each Subject Test only once, rather than multiple times, unless extenuating circumstances disrupt her testing, in which case she should cancel the score.

❏ Have your child register for only one Subject Test on a given test date, in case she needs to cancel a score.

❏ Select test centers in university, private school, or suburban settings.

❏ Suggest to your child that she forward scores to colleges and universities only after she has seen them, rather than designating institutions to receive the score report when she registers to take the test.

❏ Make sure your child's test preparation includes (preferably at the beginning) information on how to use her calculator so that she has a detailed understanding of how it works and can maximize its utility when she takes her tests.

❏ Create conditions in your home that allow your child to get ample sleep and eat well for several days prior to the test date (not just the night before).

SEVEN

Deciding Where to Apply

Helping families put together a list of colleges and universities to look at stands out as one of the things that I most enjoy doing with clients. This part of the process, which ideally begins in the spring of junior year, feels to me like an adventure. The more flexibility a student expresses about the type of school he would consider, the more fun I have as we sit together in my office, each flipping simultaneously through copies of the same college guide. I factor into my suggestions the preferences, likes, and dislikes that a student has expressed to me and combine those with some back-of-the-envelope calculations that designate schools as reaches, targets, or safeties. Families leave my office with a concrete set of assignments to help them narrow the list to roughly fifteen choices (sometimes from as many as forty). They then complete a final round of research, including some campus visits, to come up with the final seven to which I recommend that candidates apply.

The first order of business entails sitting down with your child and defining what matters most in a school and what kind of learning and living environments will make him happy and comfortable for the next four years. Those criteria form the basis of his potentially long list of preliminary choices that you flag as reaches, targets, and safeties. You then work with your child over a period of time to compile a list of seven colleges and universities to which your child will apply.

UNDERSTANDING YOUR CHILD'S PREFERENCES

The very first round of research on where your child might want to apply has to start with him. Understanding his preferences and deal-breakers can help you focus and go through this winnowing process in a much more methodical and efficient way than you otherwise might. First, sit down with your child and fill out the "Helping Your Child Determine Where to Apply" worksheet. Set aside a couple of hours one evening to spread yourselves and your guidebooks out on the living room floor and go through the questions together. Sometimes broaching college can cause tension, especially if the two of you are already butting heads over it. If so, take a crack at this worksheet on your own and use your conclusions to make suggestions to your child as openings to do so come along.

You may have already purchased a college guide or two. If not, I recommend going to a bookstore and picking several off the shelf. Make sure that at least one of them comprehensively covers colleges and universities around the country, such as the one I use in my office with clients—*The Insider's Guide to the Colleges* (New York: St. Martin's Griffin, updated annually)—and then feel free to purchase one or two others that focus on specific themes, such as Loren Pope's *Colleges That Change Lives* (New York: Penguin, 2005), a book that parents especially have told me that they find helpful. Use the guides to look up examples of different kinds of colleges and universities, if necessary, as you and/or your child responds to the worksheet questions.

Each of the four categories that the worksheet covers will have its own level of importance for your child depending on his preferences and priorities. I have seen just about every possible permutation over the years, both with my students when I was teaching and with my private clients. One young man with whom I worked, for example, maintained throughout the process his desire for a strong political science department and a clean-cut campus that did not emphasize partying and drinking. These two criteria influenced more than anything else his final decision on where to attend. Conversely, a female client of mine named Brittany, whom you may remember my mentioning earlier in the book, told me that she wanted a Division III campus, in an urban area, with strong psychology and fine arts departments, and support for learning disabled students. She later dropped all but the first criterion. Completing this worksheet marks

Your child's current grade in school (circle one):   Below grade nine   Grade nine   Grade ten   Grade eleven   Grade twelve

Helping Your Child Determine Where to Apply

In each of the boxes below, please check all options that apply to your child.

Location/Setting

❑ My child would consider/prefer to attend a college/university no more than four to six hours away by car.

❑ My child would consider/prefer to attend a college/university in another part of the country (that requires plane travel).

❑ My child would consider/prefer an urban campus with city streets running through or immediately surrounding it.

❑ My child would consider/prefer a suburban campus that lies no more than 50–60 minutes by car from a city.

❑ My child would consider/prefer a campus in a small town setting.

❑ My child would consider/prefer a campus in a rural setting.

❑ Other: _____

Student/Campus Life

❑ My child would consider/prefer a small college/university ($\leq$3,000 students).

❑ My child would consider/prefer a mid-sized institution (5,000–8,000 students).

❑ My child would consider/prefer a large university ($\geq$10,000 students).

❑ My child would consider/prefer an institution that caters to a particular community, e.g., Historically Black College or University, single sex, etc.

❑ My child has special considerations to take into account, e.g., kosher dining, wheelchair access, support services for learning disabilities, etc.

❑ My child would consider/prefer an institution that guarantees on-campus housing all four years.

❑ My child would consider/prefer an institution with strong fraternities/sororities.

❑ Other: _____

Academic Resources and Requirements

❑ My child would consider/prefer a specialized program of study, e.g., engineering, fine arts, hospitality, etc.

❑ My child would consider/prefer a liberal arts education.

❑ Within a liberal arts context, my child plans to concentrate his studies in particular departments that need to be strong, e.g., history, literature, mathematics, etc.

❑ My child would consider/prefer a core curriculum that mandates specific courses.

❑ My child would consider/prefer general distributional requirements rather than specific required courses.

❑ My child prefers complete flexibility in selecting his courses.

❑ Other: _____

Extracurricular Activities

❑ The college/university my child attends must have a strong athletic program.

❑ The college/university my child attends must have a strong theater program.

❑ The college/university my child attends must have a strong job internship program.

❑ The college/university my child attends must have numerous publications for which my child could write.

❑ The college/university my child attends must permit students to study abroad and offer multiple programs in this area.

❑ Other: _____

❑ Other: _____

❑ Other: _____

the beginning of a dynamic process, as Brittany's experience illustrates; try to go through it in that spirit.

"Location, location, location" matters just as much in college admissions as it does in real estate. (See "Location/Setting" section of worksheet.) I cannot urge you and your child strongly enough to consider colleges and universities outside of your own region. Your willingness to do so could mean his getting into a significantly more selective academic institution than he might if he only applies to places close to home, as most colleges and universities that consider themselves national institutions put extra effort into attracting students from underrepresented areas (in admissions jargon, your child would have a "geographic hook"). Trying another part of the country could also help your child grow in unanticipated ways. Laura Clark, Director of College Counseling at New York's Fieldston School, loves exposing families to campuses across the country. "It took me years to get kids to think beyond the Northeast," Clark noted. "This past year, we sent almost 50 percent of our graduating class to other regions."[23] Widening their geographic scope has expanded both her students' perspective on college and the opportunities available to them.

Discussing the other aspect of location and setting with students— urban, suburban, small town, or rural campus—always makes me smile, as most teenagers do not have a clear sense of what these terms mean. Brittany, who specified her preference for an urban campus, realized only after her first round of college visits that she had mistakenly equated "urban" with the affluent Upper East Side Manhattan neighborhood in which she had grown up and attended high school. Read descriptions of institutions in each of these settings (urban, suburban, small town, rural) to see how they differ from each other; even those that technically fall into the same category can feel dissimilar depending on campus layout and surrounding neighborhood. New York City streets run through Columbia University and New York University in Manhattan, for example, while Rice University in Houston (also a major city) feels idyllic and self-contained when you walk the campus. Encourage your child to consider as many different settings as possible until, after reading campus descriptions and making several visits, he consistently expresses strong preferences. I help my clients keep their options open by including in my recommendations a few colleges and universities that lie outside the locations and settings they have designated; on multiple occasions, one of these "outlier" schools has caught a student's attention, sometimes quite unexpectedly.

Specific aspects of student and campus life sometimes factor into student preferences. (See "Student/Campus Life" section of worksheet.) Young people tend to have well-defined ideas on the size of the institution they would like to attend. Those who have attended small high schools, for example, sometimes want to move on to a mid-sized or large university rather than a small liberal arts college. Once again, try to make it possible for your child to visit at least one or two campuses that offer an alternative to his stated preference. If you are touring Occidental College in Los Angeles (a small liberal arts institution), for example, add to your itinerary a quick stop at UCLA (a large state university) as a point of comparison. You do not have to make these additional stops on every college trip that you take, but doing it once or twice could help expand your child's options and, by extension, opportunities for college admission.

Students sometimes need special encouragement to consider colleges and universitites that serve specific populations, such as Historically Black Colleges and Universities (HBCUs) or single-sex institutions. Make sure not to overlook these possibilities if they apply to your child, as they can offer invaluable opportunities that do not exist elsewhere. African American students know, for example, that, at an HBCU, "the criticism they receive, the praise they receive, the way they are seen as students stems from their intellectual abilities," Spelman College's Arlene Cash points out, a first for some who may have stood out before college as one of the only African Americans in the classroom. Similarly, students at women's colleges do "not face the kinds of stereotypes that they might in coeducational classrooms," according to Mount Holyoke's Jane Brown. "You have more women here studying traditionally male subjects, such as economics or chemistry, than you do at coeducational institutions." Both HBCUs and women's colleges have a higher proportion of faculty members that look like the populations that they serve than other institutions do, a circumstance that provides students with strong role models. While no single environment works for everybody, do not miss out on a potentially strong fit for your child because you overlooked these types of institutions.

Discuss with your child special needs that he wants to take into account or that you think he should consider, whether individual or community. Strong Jewish life, for example, means different things depending on the individual—a Hillel organization on campus, a kosher kitchen under the supervision of an Orthodox rabbi, a Jewish studies department, etc. Help your child identify areas that matter to him and then define his specific preferences. Encourage him to consider factors that he might otherwise ignore, such as fraternities and sororities, and how their presence or absence might affect his college experience. Student and campus life can sometimes have an even greater influence than academics on a young person's state of mind and satisfaction level, so make sure to give them the weight they deserve as you and your child discuss his preferences.

Some students have identified the presence or lack of strong academic and/or extracurricular resources in specific areas as deal-breakers. (See "Academic Resources and Requirements" and "Extracurricular Activities" sections of worksheet.) Your child could benefit from ongoing discussion with you or his counselor as he sorts through how much these criteria really matter to him, as I have seen many young people change their minds here. A client of mine who devotes every waking moment outside of school to theater, voice, and dance, for example, thought at one point that she wanted to attend Juilliard; she decided upon further reflection, however, that she would prefer a liberal arts institution to a conservatory. Young people also sometimes do not want to follow a core curriculum that requires specific courses, especially if they perceive themselves as weak in a subject that they would prefer to discontinue in college. Athletes have to decide if they want to target institutions at which they will likely play or those where they will warm the bench. Revisit these issues over time if you feel that your child is struggling with any of them and/ or would benefit from ongoing discussion. Students who have not identified academic or extracurricular deal-breakers can generally put together an initial college list based on the criteria in the top two boxes of the worksheet and then use the information in the bottom two boxes to narrow their options from there.

Remember to leave your child room to change his mind. The preferences he indicates on this worksheet represent parameters for an initial list. Expect them to evolve over time and let your child know that you welcome that possibility.

IDENTIFYING SPECIFIC COLLEGES AND UNIVERSITIES FOR YOUR CHILD

A strong guidance counselor stands out as the best possible source of suggestions on specific colleges and universities that your child should consider. (See the discussion in Chapter Two on how to identify a competent guidance counselor, if you have not already read it.) Those at the top of their field, like Fieldston's Laura Clark, know both your child *and* the college landscape well and can give you a helpful head start on the search process. You typically hear from your child's college counselor for the first time in the early winter or spring of his junior year when most high schools sponsor a college night for parents at which counselors and, sometimes, invited experts share information. Counselors at high schools with sufficient resources, such as affluent suburban and independent schools, will also likely set up individual family meetings as a follow-up to college night. There they will ask you and your child some of the very questions that we just walked through together, so your having completed that worksheet in advance of the appointment will add valuable focus to the discussion. A preliminary list of colleges and universities usually follows a few weeks after the individual meeting. Pay close attention to suggestions from a counselor with a solid track record, as her input reflects the caliber of schools at which she thinks your child has a competitive chance *and* where she will actively support your child's application.

Counselors have varying levels of resources at their disposal and possess a range of skills and experience with the college admissions process. Those in the public school system, for example, have not generally visited as many out-of-state campuses as some of their independent school counterparts have. Fieldston's Laura Clark, who worked in admissions at Princeton before she went into college counseling, observed that many public school counselors focused on state schools: "They knew the parameters and they knew they could get kids in there. Sometimes their schools even had budgetary incentives," such as California in the 1980s, where schools received extra funding for students whom they sent to the state system. Ask your child's counselor about the campuses she has visited and the basis for her recommendations to ascertain how much confidence you can place in them. A college counselor who knows both your child and the higher education world will be able to explain in detail why she has selected the colleges and universities that she has for your child.

I have observed over the years that mothers and fathers want to get involved in identifying possible matches for their children, but that they approach the process differently. Mothers tend to find a few books that they like and in which they then immerse themselves. They read voraciously and draw conclusions based on overall, qualitative impressions. Fathers, on the other hand, generally use a more quantitative and less holistic approach than mothers do. Dads seem to prefer ranked lists to general descriptions and they sometimes translate the information that they gather into their own database. I have seen them enter my office with everything from handwritten, annotated lists to computer-generated spreadsheets. Use whatever approach works for you and try to have fun with it, the same way that you would if you were leafing through travel books to plan a vacation. Err on the side of including too many colleges and universities rather than too few at this point, as your child will have plenty of opportunity to narrow his list as the process continues.

If you would like to have at least a few parameters to guide you as you begin your search, consult the list of college acceptances at your child's high school from the previous year. (Virtually every high school compiles one of these at the end of each school year.) Young people frequently have a sense of their academic and extracurricular peers. Sit down with your child and identify where students with profiles that resemble his have matriculated. Request the most recent college acceptance list from other high schools in your local area as well (or find them on each high school's Web site), as these lists will give you an indication of the colleges and universities that already have some familiarity with your community and the high schools in it.

I sometimes use the Internet in my ongoing search for new colleges and universities to recommend to my clients, especially when I am looking for small, liberal arts institutions in other parts of the country. My strategy entails visiting the Web site of a respected independent high school in another part of the country and checking the college acceptance list for names of institutions that I do not recognize. I then read guidebook descriptions of these colleges and universities and visit their Web sites. This approach has turned up some interesting alternatives for my adventurous clients that I might not have uncovered otherwise. I also check Web sites like *U.S. News &*

World Report, not so much for their overall rankings but for institutions that have strengths in particular areas, such as engineering. Consider the process of putting together your list as an ongoing cycle of checks and cross-checks of information that you get from multiple sources, including your child's college counselor, other families, other local high schools, the Internet, college guidebooks, and, if necessary, a private consultant.

Identifying potential matches for your child, by definition, means gauging his chances of getting into the places that interest him—in other words, classifying institutions appropriately as reaches, targets, or safeties based on his profile. A reach means exactly what it sounds like: a college or university that, according to the statistical odds, lies outside your child's likely range, but to which he may have a shot (albeit a small one) at gaining admission. A target represents an institution to which your child has a reasonable statistical chance of getting accepted, but no guarantees. A safety gives your child a college option if all else fails: objective criteria suggest that he will get into this college or university, even with his eyes closed and his hands tied behind his back. Some institutions, such as Harvard, Yale, or Princeton, qualify as a reach for anyone, as they are so competitive that nobody can feel confident that he has a reasonable statistical chance of admission. Generally, though, one person's reach is another person's target: your child's chance of acceptance to a given college or university depends on how his profile compares with the rest of the applicant pool in his geographic area and demographic group.

Determining your child's odds at different types of institutions means taking a well-balanced, grounded, and objective look at him, rather than an emotionally driven one. This approach may seem difficult at first—after all, he is your child; however, if my mother (the woman who urged me in college to apply for a Rhodes scholarship because I was "such a good person") could do it, anybody can. I still remember the evening at the dinner table when she asked me how my college applications were going. I had just applied early action to my first choice and so I did not understand her question. "Well, you weren't planning to wait for your early action results before you filled out more applications, were you?" she asked, somewhat puzzled. "What if you don't get in or if you get deferred? You will have a grand total of two weeks to complete all your other applications." I had been floating along in a blissful early-action haze and my mother's firm, clear reality check brought me back down to earth. You need to play that same role for your child and you can only do that if you work with the facts in front of you.

When I do my "back-of-the-envelope calculations," I assess several variables simultaneously. First, I get a qualitative sense of who a young person is. Second, I compare his academic transcript and test scores with the averages for an institution's most recent entering class. (You can frequently find this information in the admissions area of a college or university's Web site.) Third, I consider any possible hooks that a student has at a particular institution. Fourth, I look at the percentage of its applicant pool that a college or university accepts. Given the years of experience and familiarity with different schools that I have under my belt, I make these calculations at almost lightning speed. A few detailed examples can help you understand how to walk through these same steps yourself.

Christopher, a young Brit who came to the United States via Singapore and then France, brought an international perspective to engineering by virtue of his having lived in four countries on three separate continents. He had earned straight A's in the most challenging classes at his high school. His standardized test scores—800s in everything related to mathematics and sciences plus a nice 750 in writing—complemented his transcript and topped the charts of every college and university to which he was applying. He also captained at least two teams and had taken on multiple other leadership roles at his school. These accomplishments, combined with his genuinely likable and engaging personality, had made Christopher a hero at his high school and translated into strong letters of recommendation from his teachers and counselor.

Even with these credentials, however, Christopher—an unhooked applicant at his top choices—had to consider all three of them as reaches: each accepted only 11 to 15 percent of its undergraduate applicant pool and had a surplus of engineering candidates with solid 800s on their standardized tests. In other words, in a room of ten students, Christopher's reaches were going to select fewer than two from a group of applicants, many with grades and test scores similar to his. Christopher had no way of knowing if he would catch their attention. His targets, on the other hand, accepted 24 to 29 percent of their prospective undergraduates (two or three candidates from that room of ten) and, in certain cases, were actively seeking strong New York City students, a geographic hook for Christopher. Two of his reaches wait-listed Christopher and he chose to attend the third. Every other place accepted him.

Annie came across as an earnest, hardworking, solid student. Her academic diligence and involvement in her high school commanded the respect of her teachers and headmaster, who offered to lend his personal support to her early-decision candidacy at his Ivy League alma mater. As an unhooked applicant from the most competitive territory in the country, though, Annie needed more than A's and B's with standardized test scores that barely broke 650 in each area. Remember, in that room of ten students, from whom an Ivy League institution would only select one, she would have been competing with at least several students like Christopher, not to mention other candidates with their own compelling profiles. Annie should have been looking for her reaches instead at places that accepted 25 to 35 percent of their applicant pools, where her test scores would have fallen right smack in the middle of their middle 50 percent range, not very competitive for an unhooked New York City kid. (See Chapter Six for a discussion of how admissions officers take a student's profile and background into account in interpreting test scores.) Her targets needed to accept 36 to 50 percent of their applicants. Anything beyond that represented a safety for her.

Annie ended up attending a college that normally would have represented a reach for her (it accepted only 21 percent of its applicant pool) but where she had two hooks. First, the college was actively seeking to diversify its campus and Annie was part Vietnamese. Second, her brother was entering his junior year at the same place and had done well there. (The weight that admissions offices give to sibling connections varies depending on the institution, but you should not overlook this factor, as it can work in a student's favor.) Last but not least, this college did not require standardized test scores, a plus for Annie, as her test scores fell below the middle 50 percent range for those students in the most recent entering class who did report them. When all was said and done, Annie had applied to four reaches (of which she got into one), two targets (of which she also got into one), and one safety. Reconfiguring that list to include two reaches, four targets, and a safety would have resulted in at least one or two additional acceptances for Annie, a scenario that would have made her feel better about herself than she did at the end of this process.

I want to counter Annie's situation with a final example of a student who had weaker credentials than she, but who put together a more appropriate list for himself than she did and thereby ended up with an attractive set of options. Seth attended a weaker high school than Annie, where he earned solid B's (as opposed to Annie's mix of A's and B's). He took college courses when he had the opportunity, both over the summer and through a dual enrollment program that his high school offered with a nearby university, but never distinguished himself academically beyond that. His Subject Test scores averaged below 600 and he received a 24, out of a possible 36, on his ACT. In spite of his unremarkable, albeit solid, academic record and test scores, Seth stood out as one of the most upstanding, dependable, and ethical young people in a high school overflowing with what seemed like exactly the opposite. He committed remarkable amounts of time and energy to extracurricular activities, where he took on significant leadership roles in school and made the most of interesting opportunities outside of school. Seth, in his own way, had made himself a star at his high school.

Seth put together a smart list of seven colleges and universities. His two reaches admitted 37 and 40 percent of their candidates, respectively. His ACT score fell comfortably into the middle 50 percent range at the first and just below that range at the second. The first also offered Seth a geographic hook. Each of his three targets accepted roughly 50 to 60 percent of its applicants and, at all three, his ACT score fell, once again, within the middle 50 percent range of the most recent entering class. One of his targets was actively recruiting East Coast students (in its literature, the school proudly highlighted that 50 percent of the student body came from outside the state), a factor that translated into a geographic hook. Both of Seth's safeties had admit rates of 70 to 80 percent and thereby offered him a comfortable margin of security. One of the two was actively recruiting male students to correct a gender imbalance and so Seth had a hook there, too. (Seth looked at the male-to-female ratio and figured this one out on his own.) Seth put his list together almost entirely on his own, with minimal input from me, his parents, or his college counselor. He applied first and foremost to places that interested him, but also seemed to understand intuitively the value of all kinds of hooks, including gender and geography. He felt like a rock star when his decision letters arrived in April; having been accepted to all seven institutions, he spent almost the entire month deliberating carefully over where to attend.

These three stories impart several valuable lessons about flagging colleges and universities as reaches, targets, and safeties and eventually deciding where to apply. Christopher's experience illustrates that certain institutions qualify as a reach for anybody, especially somebody unhooked, even with impressive and objectively competitive credentials. Annie's results demonstrate the importance of calibrating reaches, targets, and safeties realistically, as her failure to do so left her with only three choices at the end of the admissions process (versus the five or six that she could have had if she had put together an appropriate list). Seth's experience shows how creating a strategic list can result in an average student having his pick of a number of fine schools and making the best of the process. All three stories highlight the significance of identifying, if possible, colleges and universities where you have a hook: Annie's ethnic background and her brother's presence on campus made her a highly desirable applicant at a college that otherwise may not have accepted her. Christopher and Seth both used geography to their advantage and Seth used gender as well.

Flagging colleges and universities as reaches, targets, and safeties should not overshadow how your child feels about the places on his preliminary list. After a client and I put together this list in my office, I ask him to take the first set of options that we write down and research every single one. To me, research means reading a complete description of each college or university in at least one guidebook, preferably more than that, and taking a thorough tour of every Web site. Students should look at academic requirements, take a virtual tour of the campus, and soak up as much as they can about studying and living there. The next time we meet, they can then explain to me not only which places appealed to them and which ones did not, but, more importantly, why they came to the conclusions that they did. These details make it possible for me to use a much more clearly defined set of preferences than they could give me at the beginning of the process to tailor any subsequent versions of the list. After your child completes this homework assignment, you may want to run through the questions on the worksheet a second time, as your child's preferences may have changed or solidified as a result of his research.

If you do not feel qualified or if you lack the time to do the in-depth research that the steps above outline, find a qualified independent college counselor and pay for one or two sessions to get this information from an expert. Remember to check the credentials of the consultant and to walk away immediately from anybody who claims to have connections that will help your child get into a particular college or university. Following these steps with your child, either on your own or with outside help, increases the likelihood that your child will have an array of high-quality choices when decision letters arrive.

NARROWING THE LIST: CAMPUS VISITS

In my experience, students who take their research assignment seriously can cut their preliminary list of colleges and universities by one third to one half. They still need to make it ideally down to seven, though—that is, one or two reaches, four or five targets, and one safety—about which they feel equally enthusiastic. Campus visits can go a long way toward helping your child decide whether to keep or eliminate a college or university that he likes on paper, and they hold special importance for students applying to places outside of their geographic region. Your child does not have to visit every campus that he is considering, but I would recommend at least three or four within driving distance and/or one long-distance trip for students applying to places far from home. Make sure also to include at least one safety on your travel itinerary, as it is important to treat safeties as seriously as targets and reaches throughout this process. Fall airfare sales can make a long-distance visit affordable and you can always send a mature and independent student on his own to stay in the dormitories, an arrangement that college admissions offices will make for you as a courtesy and for which they charge nothing.

Typically, students take a "college trip" together with their parents or their peers to a city or region where they are looking at several colleges and universities. College visits with peers include school- or nonprofit-sponsored tours that usually occur in the spring of junior year. Trips with parents generally take place over the summer just before or over an extended fall weekend during senior year. Both types of visit afford your child a helpful vantage point from which to assess a campus.

The college trip that you and your child take together will likely include a formal tour and a group information session in the admissions office. I would suggest adding to it an informal walk around the town or city that hosts the college campus (or a drive in a rural area) and possibly an interview, depending on the institution's policy. Each of these elements of a visit can provide you and your child with helpful information that may have more of an impact if you see or hear it for yourself than if you read somebody else's interpretation of it.

Important Questions to Ask on a Campus Tour

- How does the campus change at night (gates locking, pedestrian traffic, etc.)?

- Does the university provide an escort service to walk students from place to place on campus at night?

- Do male and female students share dormitories and/or bathrooms?

- Where do most students eat their meals freshman year? After that?

- Do most students continue to live on campus after freshman year?

Formal tours give you a glimpse of campus layout and resources, such as libraries, laboratories, and athletic complexes. They also allow you to gauge how your child would get around campus, how the institution approaches student safety, and whether or not the campus has an overall look and feel that appeal to your child. You will learn more about life on campus if you visit when classes are in session, in which case your child might enjoy attending one with a student host (admissions offices can make these arrangements for you). Even without students there, however, you should take advantage of the opportunity to ask questions and benefit from those that others ask as well.

Group information sessions follow a standard format and usually just precede or follow a tour so that you can schedule both together easily. In an information session, an admissions officer makes a short presentation to a group of parents and students, all of whom, like you and your child, are embarking on a college search. Members of the audience can ask questions following the presentation and the admissions officer usually hangs around for a little while at the end to respond to individual inquiries. The availability of information online makes it possible for you to find answers to many of your questions before you even visit a campus. I would suggest spending time on an institution's Web site to see if anything there helps you formulate questions, the answers to which you could not find online. Admissions offices also routinely have an officer on call for the day, so you can follow up easily by telephone with additional inquiries. You may find that looking around the room to see who else is attending the information session and then listening to what they ask provides you with valuable information in and of itself.

Make sure to take an informal walk around the area that surrounds the campus. Walk a few blocks away from campus in several directions to see what the neighborhood feels like. Ask how the environment changes at night. Urban campuses, for example, frequently lock gates that remain open during the day.

Particularly independent students may want to visit colleges on their own and/or spend a night in the dormitories and attend classes. Admissions offices routinely arrange for undergraduates to host visiting high school seniors, both during application season in the fall and decision season in the spring. Colleges generally do not offer overnight accommodations over the weekend or during examination periods. Spending a night in the dormitories on a Thursday can give visitors a preview of weekend social life, if your child wants that experience. I strongly recommend an overnight stay for students considering an early application to a particular college or university. Otherwise, I would limit overnight visits in the fall to a couple of top choices at most and save the bulk of them for the final round of decision making in the spring, as they take up a lot of time that could interfere with your child's already overburdened schedule in the fall of his senior year. You can stay in a hotel just down the road if it makes you feel comfortable, regardless of when the overnight visit takes place. Keep in mind that hotels book well in advance if a special event, such as homecoming, is taking place on campus.

> **Important Questions to Ask in an Information Session**
>
> - Do you see all ACT/SAT scores or does your computer only input the highest ones?
>
> - Do you use a formula or numerical scale to evaluate applications? If so, what components does the formula or scale include and how much weight does each one carry?
>
> - When could a supplementary letter of recommendation help a student and when could it hurt?
>
> - Do you advise students to submit supplementary materials, such as artwork or recordings? Why or why not?

FALLING IN LOVE: EARLY ACTION OR EARLY DECISION

Every year my schedule becomes crazed as November early-admission deadlines approach. Many students and their families find the temptation to apply early hard to resist and I understand why: in exchange for submitting his application a couple of months before the regular deadline, your child could find out six weeks later that the college or university of his dreams accepted him, that he does not have to submit any other college applications, and that the pressure and stress of the college admissions process have ended for him in December or January rather than in April. I find early-admission programs tempting for two additional reasons: research has shown that (1) a higher percentage of students get in from the early-applicant pool than from the regular applicant pool and (2) students who apply early and get deferred have a statistically better chance of getting accepted in April than students who apply regular decision. In other words, applying early can increase your child's chances of getting admitted. With these facts in front of you, hearing that early admission might not work in your child's best interests may sound counterintuitive; however, these programs have definite trade-offs and could actually prove disadvantageous to your child, depending on his circumstances. Helping your child make a good decision about whether or not to apply early means knowing what he stands to gain or lose either way.

Colleges and universities use early-admission programs to improve their yield rate. In admissions jargon, the term "yield" refers to the percentage of students that an institution admits who actually accept the offer, as opposed to going somewhere else. Admissions offices get competitive about their yield rate: they want their college or university to appeal more to students than the competition does, in the same way that Honda hopes that people buy more Hondas than Toyotas. The more candidates a college or university can lock into attending through an early-admission program, the better its yield rate.

Should My Child Apply Early?

Consider early-admission programs if you answer "true" to all five statements below. Otherwise, think carefully about whether these programs present an appropriate option for your child.

- The college or university to which he would apply stands out as his clear first choice.

- He has an academic transcript through the end of his junior year that can stand on its own.

- He will have comfortably completed all standardized tests by October of his senior year.

- He can get two strong letters of recommendation from junior-year teachers, without having to rely on teachers from senior year.

- You are not applying for financial aid or can afford to take whatever package a college or university offers, without comparing it with others.

Colleges and universities offer a variety of early-admission programs, among which "early decision" and "early action" crop up most frequently of all. Both options require your child to submit his application by an early deadline (usually some time in November, but some schools offer a second early deadline in December or January). In return, the college or university notifies your child of its decision, in many cases, within four to six weeks. *Early decision* usually requires that you apply early to only one place, while restrictions on *early action* candidates vary with the institution.

Getting accepted early decision means that your child must withdraw his applications at all other colleges and universities and make a binding decision to attend the institution that admitted him early. Early action, on the other hand, lets him know his admissions status early without his having to make a commitment to the college or university. In fact, he may apply elsewhere, see if other institutions accept him, and wait until May of his senior year to notify the college or university that accepted him early action about whether or not he will attend.

Both early-decision and early-action applicants may receive a "deferral" letter. Deferral means that the admissions office does not feel comfortable admitting a student before it sees the full crop of candidates for that year. Your child's application goes back into the general pool and he receives a final decision in April, with everyone else.

I look for several criteria to determine whether or not a client stands out as a strong candidate for an early-admission program. First and foremost, a student has to have a clear, unequivocal first choice. Even in nonbinding early-action situations, the momentum of applying early and getting in can make it hard for an exhausted, overburdened high school senior to submit additional applications, a decision he may regret later if he had reservations that he did not express about the college or university to which he applied early. Next, I look closely at any trend that the high school transcript shows. A student whose grades have improved steadily over time may want colleges to see that progress continue into his senior year, a possibility that applying early eliminates since the first marking term of the year has usually not ended by the early-application deadline. Similarly, I look at whether or not a student needs additional time in his senior year to complete his standardized testing, as the last test date that students can use for an early application falls in October (as opposed to the January or February test dates that students applying regular decision may schedule). All of these criteria add up to one overall bottom line: your child's application, based on the information available by the end of his junior year, should look as strong as it is going to get; any evidence that his profile will improve in the first half of his senior year should make you think long and hard before encouraging him to apply somewhere early.

Families applying for financial aid have an additional factor to consider. Colleges award final financial-aid packages in the spring, not the fall. The financial-aid estimate that comes with a fall acceptance letter is not binding and could change. Applying somewhere early decision, therefore, means committing to a college or university before you receive a final award letter. It also means forgoing the opportunity to compare the aid package that one college or university is offering you with what others might have put on the table.

Early-admission options can offer wonderful advantages, as long as you and your child have thought through all the details and determined that an early-action or early-decision program represents an appropriate choice for him. Remember also that colleges and universities take early-decision commitments seriously. Applying early decision, getting accepted, and then deciding not to attend will reflect badly on your child, his guidance counselor, and his high school and could hurt the chances of other students from his school who apply to that same college or university in the future.

FREQUENTLY ASKED QUESTIONS

Our daughter wants to submit between fifteen and twenty applications. She says that the Common Application™ eliminates a lot of the work and so the number of places to which she applies does not matter. This number still sounds excessive to us. Does she need to apply to this many schools?

Applying to as many as twenty places sounds excessive to me, too, even with the Common Application™. Many colleges and universities that accept the Common Application™ ask for a "supplement" that pertains just to them, usually an additional essay or series of one-paragraph responses. You can take a look at individual college supplements yourself at www.commonapp.org to see the kind of additional work they require—definitely nothing to sneeze at, especially if we are talking about possibly up to twenty of them! Churning out that many applications and accompanying essays could detract from the time that your daughter can put into them and, as a result, from their overall quality. You should also consider cost. Application fees routinely run as much as $50 each these days. Submitting them to twenty institutions could add up to $1,000!

Some high schools limit the number of colleges and universities to which they allow seniors to apply for these very reasons. They want to protect parents and students from the panic and hysteria that can accompany the college admissions process and lead to irrational decisions. They also want to insulate their teachers and counselors from the excessive paperwork burden that each student applying to twenty schools would cause for them.

I recommend that students apply to seven schools: one or two reaches, four or five targets, and one safety. These numbers balance practical concerns—for example, the time and money necessary to complete applications—with every family's desire to maximize a young person's chances for success. I have no objection to shifting the numbers a bit so that they include maybe three targets and two safeties, if that modification makes a family comfortable. I also understand when the Christophers of the world decide they want to go for three reaches instead of two. In most cases, though, investing the time to put together a strong, well-researched list makes more than seven or eight applications superfluous.

What should my son be looking for in a safety?

I always tell my clients that they should get just as excited about their safety schools as they do about the other places on their list. People frequently put all of their time into selecting and visiting their targets and reaches. At the last minute they add on a less selective college or university than their other choices and call it a safety. This approach misses the whole point: you want your child to have one college or university that he would feel excited about attending *and* that looks 99 percent likely to admit him.

I used one of my recent clients, Seth, as an example in this chapter of a student who effectively flagged institutions as reaches, targets, and safeties, and who almost single-handedly put together a masterful college list for himself. Seth got into all seven of his schools and, even then, liked his safety so much that it took him a week to cross it off his list. You and your child can find a safety that fits this bill, too. Doing so stands out as an essential part of putting together a good college list.

Should we consider our financial situation and cost of tuition, room, and board as criteria in where our child applies?

Folks who have worked in admissions and financial aid for any length of time all say that, in their experience, high-need families have a tendency to underestimate the financial aid they will receive. Combine that common misperception with the fact that some of the most expensive colleges and universities in the country also stand out as some of the most generous with financial aid awards and you can see why I tread very carefully in counseling people on when and how to consider cost. The answer to this question depends on many variables, some highly personal in nature, including the degree to which you have already planned and set aside funds to pay for your child's college education, the amount you wish to allocate regardless of your ability to pay, competing financial demands on your family, and more.

Financial aid packages generally combine the following, in varying amounts depending on a family's need:

- a grant from the institution;

- access to low-interest student loans;

- an expected contribution from the student's employment on campus and/or over the summer;

- an expected contribution from the student's saved assets; and

- an expected contribution from the family.

How you and your child feel about his accruing debt and working while he attends college comes down to highly personal decisions. I did both so that I could pay my way through Yale and do not regret a moment of it. Spelman College's Arlene Cash advises parents to "consider a college education an investment—one of the few expenditures that will appreciate over time," as a student's employment opportunities increase with every year of college he completes. Compare that value to "a brand-new car—you drive it off the lot, bring it back in an hour, and it's worth $10,000 less."

If you really want to play things safe financially, I suggest following the advice of Ron Inniss, an extraordinary guidance counselor in the Boston Public Schools and financial-aid advisor at www.college broadband.com. Inniss, who works primarily with low- and middle-income families, counsels parents to develop a contingency plan in the event (however unlikely) that they receive no financial aid whatsoever. This scenario may eliminate the possibility of college altogether, as even resident tuition at a state school may exceed your financial limitations. Inniss urges families in that position to come up with a noncollege alternative for the following year, just in case. No financial aid at all might mean that your child has to attend a local institution so that he can live at home and thereby eliminate room and board expenses. Alternatively, a no-aid scenario could mean leaving the college list as-is and taking on an additional job (you and/or your spouse), not giving holiday gifts, and/or eliminating family vacations. Financial decision-making for college can get complex and emotionally charged, so, no matter what you decide, take the time to think about these issues and, when necessary, to discuss them openly with your child.

Our daughter is finishing her junior year but still refuses to discuss college. She has already accompanied her older siblings on college visits in previous years. Now that it's her turn, though, she refuses to talk about where she might like to apply or even visit. We are not sure what to do.

A young person's reluctance to initiate the college search process could stem from several different factors. I have seen in my office parents who unwittingly dominate the discussion and even speak on behalf of their children. Not surprisingly, teenagers frequently shut down in response and an unhealthy communication pattern begins. Parents insist that the child refuses to take initiative, get involved, or express his preferences about college while the child does not perceive any opening or opportunity to do so. Try to take a step back and examine your own behaviors when you broach the subject of college with your child. Ask yourself if you are dominating the discussion and possibly even crowding out your child's ability to express herself. Consider not talking about college at all with your child for several weeks to see what happens. At the very least, a temporary moratorium on the topic could allow any existing tension between the two of you to dissipate.

If this scenario does not sound like it applies to your family, consider the possibility that your child is equating the college search process with the first step in leaving home, a daunting prospect for some young people. Allow discussions about college to flow at your child's pace rather than yours. Remember that many institutions accept both applications and standardized test scores as late as February of your child's senior year. A child can begin the college admissions process in September of his senior year and still have five full months to complete everything that it requires. Some young people may find this late start date necessary in order to begin contemplating leaving home.

STEP-BY-STEP CHECKLIST:
DECIDING WHERE TO APPLY

❏ Attend college night and/or college fairs at your child's high school (usually in the winter or early spring of your child's junior year).

❏ Purchase at least one or two comprehensive college guides that provide you with summaries of and basic facts about colleges and universities around the country.

❏ Complete the worksheet "Helping Your Child Determine Where to Apply," with your child if he is ready to go through this exercise, and preferably before meeting with your child's guidance counselor.

❏ Schedule a family meeting with your child's guidance counselor if she has not contacted you about one herself by March of your child's junior year.

❏ Ask the counselor if she will be providing your child with a list of suggested colleges and universities to research and/or visit.

❏ If so, once you receive the list, ask her how and why she selected the colleges and universities on it for your child.

❏ Consult multiple sources of information—such as college guides, college acceptance lists for high schools in your area, college acceptance lists for well-respected high schools in other parts of the country—as you help your child construct a preliminary list of colleges and universities, either as a supplement to or substitute for a list from his counselor.

❏ Help your child flag colleges and universities as reaches, targets, or safeties if his college counselor does not do this for him.

❏ Once your child has his initial list (which could include as many as thirty to forty colleges and universities), encourage him to read about each institution thoroughly in college guides, visit each one's Web site, and eliminate those that no longer appeal to him upon further examination.

❑ If your child's counselor cannot help you with the above steps and if you do not feel comfortable taking them on by yourself, schedule one or two sessions with a well-respected independent college counselor in your area for assistance with putting together a preliminary list.

❑ Begin scheduling college visits for the summer before and/or the fall of your child's senior year.

❑ Evaluate with your child and, if possible, with his counselor whether or not an early-admission program makes sense for your child.

EIGHT

The College Interview

College interviews arise as a postscript when I am working with clients. Most interviews have little to no bearing on admissions decisions, although those that do can matter a lot. You and your child need to know how to identify the interviews that count and then prepare for them accordingly. As a parent, you may also find it helpful to learn that, contrary to what you might think, few if any of the pre-interview battles with your child that you might be envisioning (what to wear, hairstyle, etc.) merit the time it would take to have them. In this one area of the college admissions process, your child can relax and, quite literally, let her hair down.

THE KINDS OF INTERVIEWS AVAILABLE AND HOW ADMISSIONS OFFICERS WEIGH THEM

Colleges and universities generally make at least one of the following three types of admissions interviews available to prospective students:

1. An on-campus interview at the admissions office that can take place even before your child decides whether or not to apply to that institution;

2. A meeting with an admissions officer who, on the fall travel circuit, is visiting high schools in your local area (this type of interview can also take place before your child decides whether or not to apply to that institution); and

3. An interview with an alumni representative of the college or university who lives in your local area and who sets up an appointment with your child, usually within a month or so of her having submitted her application.

Most colleges and universities treat the interview in either one of two ways: they call it optional (students may take advantage of it if they wish) or they describe it as "recommended but not required." A small number of them mandate or strongly recommend an interview for all applicants.

The few colleges and universities that weigh the interview heavily, such as MIT and Pitzer, make this position clear on their Web sites. MIT describes the interview as "strongly recommended." A fifty-year policy of mandating alumni interviews ended only recently (out of concern that the policy was overloading interviewers) and the admissions office plans to reinstitute it as soon as possible, according to Marilee Jones. MIT takes alumni interviews so seriously that it trains interviewers on conducting and writing up the sessions and then scores the quality of their interview reports. Pitzer College's Arnaldo Rodriguez also "strongly recommends" that applicants schedule an interview, as "it does have some impact." Colleges and universities that feel as strongly as MIT and Pitzer do about interviews generally work hard to make them available and accessible to candidates. Pitzer applicants, for example, can interview on campus, with admissions representatives who travel around the country to visit high schools, and even by telephone.

Those institutions that do not factor the interview into their decision, such as Carleton College and Lehigh University, call it optional or sometimes do not mention it on their Web sites at all. Call the admissions office and ask to speak to the officer on call for the day if you want to confirm your impression that the interview does not count. I checked in with the deans of admission at Carleton and Lehigh just to see if their comments matched what appears on the Web sites of their respective institutions. Carleton's Paul Thiboutot called a student's choice not to interview "absolutely okay," and Lehigh's Eric Kaplan described the interview as "much more of an information exchange than an evaluation. It's not something that will influence an admissions decision." Institutions that say they do not count the interview mean it and you can take them at their word.

Many colleges and universities describe interviews as "recommended but not required," a characterization that sounds less clear than the other two that we just discussed and that leaves many students wondering about what to do. Institutions that recommend but do not require an interview generally do not penalize your child if she decides not to have one; however, as Rice University's Julie Browning explains, if an interview report shows up in the folder, "we talk about it." An exception to this rule sometimes comes up when students who live near a campus do not take the time to interview. Both Swarthmore's Jim Bock and Grinnell's Jim Sumner advise those applicants to make a special effort to do so, as they question the level of interest of local applicants who do not. If your child plans to apply to a nearby college or university that recommends but does not require interviews, she may want to call the admissions office and ask if they expect her to make an appointment. She should assume in most other "recommended but not required" cases, though, that an interview report that goes into her folder will factor into the admissions decision but that she will not suffer a penalty if she chooses not to interview at all.

WHAT TO EXPECT IN THE INTERVIEW

In anticipating college interviews, many students work up the level of dread that I did in my junior year of high school when somebody spread a rumor that admissions officers on one campus assessed how interviewees reacted under pressure by asking them to open a window that somebody had previously nailed shut. I was not applying to that particular college, but the story made me fear what my own interviews held in store for me. Years later, as I conducted admissions interviews myself at Yale, I learned just how little foundation that story had. Knowing what to expect in college interviews (and what not to expect!) can eliminate needless anxiety for your child.

It may encourage your child to know that most students do well in college interviews, according to deans of admission at colleges and universities around the country. Clark University's Harold Wingood can "think of only one instance in roughly twenty years in which an interview ruled out a student who was otherwise qualified. He was so obnoxious, so rude, that we could not imagine his being part of our community." MIT's Marilee Jones agrees that the interview "only rarely hurts applicants. Students who have the interview are far more likely to be admitted to MIT than not." Rice's Julie Browning has observed over the years that students who do not fare well in the college interview frequently entered into it either unprepared or because their parents forced them to do it. Let your child know that she should only interview if she wants to and that, if she does, with a little preparation she will do just fine.

Campus and alumni interviews both focus on (1) the college or university to which your child is applying, (2) your child's interests and activities, and (3) any overlap between the two. Interviewers generally ask benign and, in some cases, predictable questions, such as "Explain what makes this college a good fit for you," "Describe your academic interests," "Discuss how you spend your time outside of school," etc. Your child should go to an interview with some knowledge of the college or university, prepared to carry on a comfortable conversation about her own interests and activities, and able to explain what has sparked her interest in that particular institution.

Admissions officers sometimes conduct campus interviews themselves over the summer. They travel in the fall, though, and, while their itinerary may permit them to interview your child when they pass through your hometown, others will conduct sessions on campus in their absence. Those others include various members of the college or university community, such as faculty spouses, students, or recent graduates who work part-time for the admissions office.

Alumni interviews take place in your local area, frequently in the office of a graduate of the college or university to which your child is applying. Alumni conduct interviews on a volunteer basis and span all ages, from recent graduates to seasoned professionals who finished college decades ago. Most institutions do not provide ongoing training to their alumni interviewers and, as with any volunteer enterprise, quality and tone can vary dramatically. My clients' experiences have run the gamut, from formal to informal, stiff to relaxed, and more. Minimal preparation should insure that everything runs smoothly and that your child comes out of the alumni interview feeling like it went well.

PREPARING FOR THE COLLEGE INTERVIEW

Your child has covered most of the preparation for her interviews if she completed the homework assignment on researching colleges that

I outlined in Chapter Seven. At most, she may need to refresh her memory a bit on a particular institution and formulate a few questions in advance. A few practice sessions with you or another adult can help her collect her thoughts and get comfortable talking about herself, something that not everyone can do with ease. After that, she should be good to go!

Young people sometimes make the mistake of thinking that acing an interview means coming across as exotic or in possession of superhero-like characteristics. In fact, interviewers want to know what interests your child, what gets her excited about and involved in the academics and activities that she pursues. Her actual interests matter less than the motivations behind them. Help your child think through and explain to you which subjects she enjoys in school, why she has taken on the responsibility of captaining the girls' soccer team, for example, or why she decided to work at the local delicatessen over the summer instead of going to summer camp with her friends. The ability to put those thoughts into words will serve her well in an interview.

Preparing for a College Interview

- Encourage your child to complete the research assignment on colleges if she has not already done so. (See Chapter Seven.)

- Help her formulate several questions in advance that build facts about the college or university into them.

- Explain to your child that she should avoid questions that call for quick factual responses that she could have easily looked up online.

- Assist your child in formulating at least one open-ended question to ask the interviewer that could lead to substantive discussion.

- Let your child practice talking to you about her interests and her accomplishments, so that she can get comfortable with what she wants to highlight about herself in the interview.

The online and college guide research that your child completed as she put together her list of colleges and universities will help her articulate why a particular institution appeals to her. She should also prepare several questions about the institution for her interviewer. Inquiries that reflect prior knowledge leave a favorable impression, as they suggest that your child has done her homework. A client of mine who wanted strong theater and business programs only applied to universities that offered both. In her interviews, she asked if, as an undergraduate, she could enroll in graduate business courses and, if so, whether or not the university placed a cap on the number she could take. This question demonstrated to her interviewers that (1) specific features of the academic program had drawn her to the university, and (2) she had done her homework prior to the interview. Steer your child away from quick, factual questions, the answers to which she could have looked up easily online. Encourage her to pose at least one open-ended question that could lead to substantive discussion, such as "How do you think your alma mater differs today from when you went to school there?"

Mock interviews can improve your child's presentation skills and lessen anxiety about the interview situation in general. You, another relative, or a family friend can use the following questions to help your child do a trial run:

1. Tell me about your interests, both academic and extracurricular.

2. Why have you decided to apply to this college?

3. Do you see yourself taking advantage of specific resources on campus and, if so, which ones?

4. How would you add to academic and extracurricular life on campus?

5. Do you have any questions for me?

Mock interviews can take on greater importance for some students than for others, such as shy students or those who come from a culture that equates talking about personal accomplishments with undesirable boasting. If either of these descriptions or a similar one applies to your child, help her identify in advance ways to talk about herself that do not make her feel awkward, as well as particular topics about which she can speak with enthusiasm and energy, such as courses or activities that she enjoys. Encourage your child to let the interviewer know up front that discussing her achievements with others makes her uncomfortable because she is shy or because her culture discourages it. Interviewers will usually gladly shift the focus of the conversation to help a student feel at ease.

PRACTICAL CONSIDERATIONS FOR THE INTERVIEW

You want your child to look neat, clean, healthy, and well rested when she arrives at the admissions or alumni interviewer's office on the day of her interview. Getting lost and arriving late or having her feel out of place in the waiting room because she is the only one in a midriff top can derail an interview before it even begins. You can help your child have a successful experience by addressing in advance practical considerations that can eliminate unnecessary problems.

I always pick out my wardrobe for media appearances several days in advance, both to eliminate stress the day of the event itself and to make sure I have time to attend to any last-minute details. It makes sense for you and your child to do the same thing. Young people should wear what feels comfortable to them as a formal outfit. For some that may mean a blouse and a pair of slacks and for others it could mean a suit. As long as she looks clean, neat, and well rested, your child's comfort in her own skin matters more than almost anything else in this situation, as she does not want to appear stiff and uncomfortable because of what she is wearing. By the same token, she should not use the college interview to express her individuality through her wardrobe. Specific items to avoid include tee shirts, jeans, baggy or drooping pants, sneakers, short skirts, plunging necklines, clingy tops, and stiletto heels (traditional garb, like saris, is fine).

Hair also needs to look neat and clean but does not otherwise need to conform to a particular style. Your child does not have to take out braids, cut her locks, or dye hair back to its natural color. Once again, her comfort level in her own skin matters a lot. Looking like herself will help her act like herself, the scenario that lends itself best of all to a successful interview.

Plan wisely any travel taking place on the day of the interview itself. If you are driving a significant distance, such as from San Francisco to Los Angeles, listen to traffic reports early in the day and add time, as needed. Always build an extra hour into your travel time, even if traffic advisories do not indicate it is necessary. Avoid covering too much distance on the day of your appointment if at all possible, as you want to minimize the chance of problems, like getting a flat tire, running into traffic, losing your way, or just showing up plain exhausted.

Practical Considerations for the Interview

- Select the interview outfit with your child several days in advance.

- Allow ample travel time so as not to arrive late or flustered.

- Remind your child to leave electronic devices with you and to spit out her gum before she enters the building.

- Instruct your child to ask the interviewer for his card or to ask the receptionist for his name and contact information.

- Bring a preposted thank-you note with you so that your child can fill it out and send it immediately following the interview.

- Try to schedule appointments so that your child interviews at her first choice only after she has had one or two appointments at other colleges or universities on her list.

Remind your child to turn off her cell phone and/or beeper and spit out her gum as she enters the building. Better yet, suggest that she leave all electronic devices in the car or with you. Let her know that she can convey self-confidence by extending a firm handshake to the interviewer, both at the beginning and end of the interview, and by maintaining eye contact during the conversation. She should also thank the person with whom she met at the end of the session and request his card. If he does not have one, she can ask the receptionist in the outer office to write down his name. She should then send a thank-you note immediately. You can even bring one with you and have her fill it out and mail it as soon as you leave the admissions office.

One last practical consideration concerns the scheduling of interviews. I always prefer students to have at least one other interview experience prior to the one at their first-choice college or university. Try scheduling appointments so that your child gets a few warm-ups at other colleges and universities on her list prior to the one that matters to her most of all. Doing so will eliminate some of her anxiety and build confidence as the process continues.

FREQUENTLY ASKED QUESTIONS

My son's admissions office interview at his first-choice college lasted thirty minutes but his classmate's lasted an hour. Why would one applicant get more time than another?

On-campus interviews generally last about thirty minutes. They sometimes run longer than that for any number of reasons, such as last-minute cancellations. I know of at least one instance, albeit a rare one, in which an on-campus interview lasted two hours. The student's high school counselor recommended that he interview over the summer with the admissions officer whose territory included that high school. The counselor knew that admissions officer loved to chat and predicted correctly that, schedule permitting, he might talk with the student indefinitely. Circumstances such as these occur by chance. Take advantage of them when they come your way but do not worry when they do not.

Our daughter, a talented musician, returned frustrated from her first college interview. The interviewer knew nothing about music and did not understand any of our daughter's technical references. How should she handle this situation going forward?

Interviewers will find your daughter's passion for music and her motivation for studying it much more interesting than any technical details she can recount. I would advise her to skip the technicalities and focus on why she loves music. She will engage her interviewer more than it sounds like she has thus far. The information that you say the interviewer did not understand sounds appropriate for the materials that accompany the performance tape that your daughter sends to the music department for evaluation, which she should look into doing if she has not already.

My daughter went for an alumni interview and felt very uncomfortable with the person conducting it. The other applicants from her high school had a similar experience. They all walked away from the alumni interview with far less enthusiasm for that particular college than they had had before. What can we do to rectify the situation?

Alumni conduct interviews for their alma maters on a volunteer basis. The quality of these interviews and of the resulting reports that go into student folders varies dramatically as a result. As an admissions officer at Yale, I found some alumni interview reports helpful and others not. I also heard a range of feedback from guidance counselors on the alumni who had interviewed their students, including at least one story that sounded similar to your daughter's. You may want to counsel your daughter against evaluating an entire college or university based on a single individual, as well as suggest that she mention the experience to her college counselor. If he has a relationship with the admissions officer who handles your territory at the institution in question, he would be doing that person a favor if he places a call and tactfully explains that multiple students at his high school felt uncomfortable with the same alumni interviewer. The admissions officer can then send that feedback through the appropriate channels (without attaching the counselor's name to it) and perhaps avoid a recurrence of a similar situation next year.

Our son insists that he wants to go to his college interviews alone but all the other parents we know are accompanying their children. What should we do?

It sounds like you have a particularly independent son who wants to manage the college application process on his own. I would start by compromising where possible and not insisting that one policy has to govern every case. You may not mind, for example, if your son travels by himself to a local campus or to one a short bus or train ride away, whereas you may feel differently about a trip that requires a long car ride or a plane flight. Try to create at least one situation in which you can live with your son traveling on his own; allowing him some freedom will signal that you have confidence in him and respect his decisions. Let him know at the same time, though, that you do want to accompany him on at least a few occasions. I would also take this experience with the interview as an indicator that your son may not want you to get involved with other parts of the college application process either, such as giving him feedback on his essay. Prepare yourself now for his asking you to stay out of things and do not take it personally.

STEP-BY-STEP CHECKLIST:
THE COLLEGE INTERVIEW

❏ Determine whether each college and university that your child wants to visit makes interviews optional, requires them, or recommends them without requiring them.

❏ Encourage your child to complete the research assignment on colleges (see Chapter Seven) if she has not already done so.

❏ Help your child formulate several questions in advance that build facts about the college or university into them.

❏ Explain to your child that she should avoid questions that call for quick factual responses that she could have easily looked up online.

❏ Assist your child in formulating at least one open-ended question to ask the interviewer that could lead to substantive discussion.

❏ Let your child practice talking to you about her interests and her accomplishments, so that she can get comfortable with what she wants to highlight about herself in the interview.

❏ Offer to conduct a formal mock interview with her.

❏ Select the interview outfit with your child several days in advance.

❏ Allow ample travel time so as not to arrive late or flustered.

❏ Remind your child to leave electronic devices with you and to spit out her gum before she enters the building.

❏ Instruct your child to ask the interviewer for his card or to ask the receptionist for his name and contact information.

❏ Bring a preposted thank-you note with you so that she can fill it out and send it immediately following the interview.

❏ Try to schedule appointments so that your child interviews at her first choice only after she has had one or two appointments at other colleges or universities on her list.

NINE

Letters of Recommendation

Strong, well-written letters of recommendation stopped me in my tracks when I worked in admissions at Yale, no matter how many applications I had read that day. I loved seeing a student through another person's eyes and learning what made him shine, both academically and personally. Ted Spencer at the University of Michigan calls letters of recommendation "wonderful pieces" of the application. Most selective colleges and universities require at least one from a teacher (sometimes two), plus one from the guidance counselor. Families frequently do not know, however, whom to approach for teacher letters of recommendation, what kind of information to provide teachers and counselors so that they write the strongest letters possible, and whether or not to solicit supplementary letters of recommendation from other parties. Understanding how admissions officers, teachers, and counselors view these letters may help you make some of these determinations. Following a few simple tips, in addition, could significantly strengthen the letters people write for your child and, by extension, his college applications.

WHAT ADMISSIONS OFFICERS LOOK FOR IN LETTERS OF RECOMMENDATION

Admissions officers read tens of applications in a day, sometimes more than one thousand in a single admissions cycle. Well-written letters of recommendation bring students off the page and into the room with the admissions officer reading the folder. They tell stories—

"We love stories!" MIT's Marilee Jones emphasized when we spoke—and capture the reader's attention.

Letters from teachers should focus on your child's strengths in the classroom. Anybody can write about a young person's friendliness or good nature, but teachers have the unique ability to talk about the student's academic strengths and abilities—"about preparation, ingenuity, creativity," as Pitzer's Arnaldo Rodriguez explains. Stories should focus on things that happened in the classroom, such as a student's "willingness to ask for extra help, willingness to help others, work style, ability to persist through difficult problems," Clark's Harold Wingood points out. Specific examples that illustrate those points maximize the effectiveness of anecdotes.

What Admissions Officers Look For in Letters of Recommendation

- Letters of recommendation should tell stories that include specific examples.

- Teacher recommendations especially should focus on a young person's academic strengths in the classroom.

- Personality traits, interests, etc., should arise in the context of student performance and life in the classroom.

- Counselor letters should explain relevant school policies, such as GPA and class rank calculation.

- Counselors should clarify how a student has used the resources available to him and has contributed to his school and/or community.

- Counselor recommendations stand out as the best place to explain extenuating circumstances that have interfered with student achievement.

Teacher recommenders sometimes restate information, such as test scores or extracurricular activities, that appears elsewhere in a student's folder. Admissions officers do not find that kind of repetition helpful. Instead, Rice's Julie Browning wants to know what makes "a student's face light up when he is learning. What is it about him that makes the teacher look forward to grading his papers?" Teachers who write effective letters frequently do mention a young person's personality traits, but in the context of his life as a student in the classroom. "Johnny's papers in my class always combined cutting-edge analysis with his trademark energy and wit" gives admissions officers far more helpful details than simply stating, "Johnny's sense of humor makes everybody laugh." Worth David, my former boss and Dean of Undergraduate Admissions at Yale for more than twenty years, always said, "We want to know who the kids are that the teachers really want to teach."

Admissions officers understand that counselors, especially those in large public high schools, have a far greater number of letters to write than teachers do. Counselors also do not see students with the frequency or in the academic setting that teachers do. Rice's Julie Browning looks, therefore, for three specific staple pieces of information from counselors:

1. An explanation of school policies, such as grading, class rank, and curriculum;

2. An understanding of how a student has used the resources available to him at his high school; and

3. Insight into how a student has contributed to his school and community.

Admissions officers also look to counselors as the logical source of information about personal hardships that a student has endured and, hopefully, overcome. One of my clients explained to me that her transcript showed a dramatic decline in her junior year because of a medical condition. Her academic performance picked up within six weeks of her having begun treatment, but her condition had persisted undiagnosed long enough so that her grades never fully recovered. This young woman fortunately had a close relationship with her guidance counselor, who helped her get back on track academically; he included an explanation of her academic decline and then of her self-motivated turnaround in his letter of recommendation, a far more effective way to convey the information than if she had tried to do so herself.

Comparative references from teachers and counselors resonate well with admissions officers, especially if an educator has spent significant time in the classroom or in schools, and can identify a young person as one of the top that she has taught in her career. Admissions officers who have handled the same territory over time recognize the teachers and counselors who write helpful and illustrative letters year after year and who use superlative language sparingly. Those educators have earned credibility as recommenders so that, when they do identify somebody as one of their best ever, experienced admissions officers take notice. Teachers and counselors who routinely use this kind of language can also bring themselves to the attention of admissions officers—in a negative way. They risk doing a long-term disservice to their students and to their school, as they can discredit themselves as reliable sources.

Every so often, teachers or counselors who have detailed knowledge of a college or university explain why a particular student and institution would suit each other well. These statements, in order to have value, must point to specifics rather than to generalities. Clark University, for example, has "been cited as an example of how a college should interact with its community. We take that very seriously," Harold Wingood points out. "We look for qualities that will help students succeed in that environment," such as a clearly demonstrated commitment to public service. An especially effective teacher or counselor letter might highlight the kinds of characteristics that Clark is seeking and point out the resulting good fit between student and institution.

SOLICITING EFFECTIVE TEACHER RECOMMENDATIONS

Your child can increase his chances of getting strong letters of recommendation if he selects his recommenders well and if he makes their task as easy as possible. Accomplishing these two objectives requires you to consider multiple variables, which the "Soliciting Effective Teacher Recommendations" worksheet outlines for you. You can complete a separate worksheet for each teacher your child is considering and then compare the results to select the one or two strongest of all.

Parents and students sometimes focus disproportionately on the teachers they are considering as recommenders when, in fact, they should be looking first and foremost at the young person himself (see "Student Performance" criteria in the first box). Ideally your child has earned one of his strongest grades of all (A's or B's, if possible) from any teacher he is considering. Other factors matter just as much if not more than grades, though, such as the effort your child put into a class and the enjoyment he derived from it—intangibles that I was always able to sense when I was teaching. Students for whom an A lies out of reach in a particular course can still convey passion and commitment. "Some of the letters that I have enjoyed reading the most are about kids who are not as competitive as others," University of Michigan's Ted Spencer agrees. "You can still say good things about a young person who is not the most competitive," but who diligently seeks extra help, offers to assist his peers, or demonstrates that he is working hard even if he does not earn an A. Think about the classes in which your child has demonstrated any of these characteristics—the more items your child can check in this first box, the more he should consider the teacher of that class as a possible recommender.

You want to look for specific characteristics in the teacher, herself, as well as in your child (see "Teacher Characteristics" criteria in the next box). A teacher's poor writing ability has torpedoed many worthy applications—as a colleague from another Ivy League institution reinforced when he ruefully remarked to me once that a compelling applicant "wrote better than his recommenders did." Look at a teacher's comments on your child's corrected tests and papers to get a sense of how well she writes—those who enjoy writing generally include more comments on student work than those who do not, if only because they cannot resist the temptation to do so. Stay focused on teachers who had your child as a student in grades eleven or twelve, if at all possible, as they have generally taught him in more advanced classes than the teachers who had him in grades nine and ten did. (Some colleges and universities require that recommendations come only from grade eleven or twelve teachers.) If your child needs more than one teacher recommendation, try to solicit them from people in different academic departments. Colleges and universities that request two have generally done so at least in part so that they can hear about your child as a student from multiple perspectives. Keep an eye out for passionate and experienced teachers among those you are considering, as these qualities come through in letters and can add valuable strength and substance to an educator's discussion of your child.

Your child can make the letter-writing task as easy as possible for his recommenders by putting together for them the same packet that I suggest to my clients (see the worksheet's suggestions for "Making the Task Easy"). The first piece in the packet, a successful test or pa-

Your child's current grade in school (circle one):   Below grade nine   Grade nine   Grade ten   Grade eleven   Grade twelve

Soliciting Effective Teacher Recommendations

In each of the boxes below, please check all options that apply.

Student Performance

❑ My child earned an A or B for the year in this teacher's class.

❑ My child put effort into this teacher's class and the teacher knew it.

❑ My child enjoyed this teacher's class, as well as the subject in general, and the teacher knew it.

❑ My child wrote strong papers in this teacher's class.

❑ My child participated in class discussion.

❑ My child earned strong test scores in this teacher's class.

❑ My child and this teacher have a good rapport (this teacher has a sense of my child beyond simply his papers and test scores).

❑ Other: _____

Teacher Characteristics

❑ Comments on my child's tests and papers suggest that this teacher writes well.

❑ My child took a class with this teacher in grade eleven or twelve.

❑ In instances in which my child needs to submit two teacher recommendations, he has selected recommenders who taught him in different subject areas, e.g., English and science.

❑ This teacher appears to have a passion for her work.

❑ This teacher has spent at least five years in the classroom.

❑ Other: _____

Making the Task Easy

❑ My child has at least one major paper and/or test with teacher comments on it that he could give her when he asks her to write the recommendation.

❑ For each of the colleges and universities to which he is applying, my child can provide the teacher with one or two sentences that explain why the institution suits him well.

❑ My child will provide the teacher with a self-addressed, stamped envelope and a separate recommendation form for each college or university to which he is applying.

❑ The teacher will receive all of the above from my child at least six to eight weeks before the application deadlines.

❑ Other: _____

Additional Considerations

❑ My child is soliciting recommendations from three teachers and his guidance counselor will select the two strongest of the three.

❑ My child's guidance counselor agrees with my child's choices of teacher recommenders.

❑ In instances in which a teacher has left the school, my child has sought out her updated contact information.

❑ Other: _____

per that your child completed for the teacher and that has her comments on it, could refresh the instructor's memory about specific academic strengths that your child displayed in her class. Remember that admissions officers prefer specific examples to general statements; a graded assignment can provide a recommender with a few of those details on paper right in front of her (or inspire her to think of others). The second item in the packet—for each of the institutions to which your child is applying, one or two sentences that explain why the institution suits him well—could give a recommender what she needs to tailor a letter to a particular college or university. If your child feels uncomfortable asking her to do this for seven different institutions, at least encourage him to make the request for his top two or three choices. Self-addressed, stamped envelopes and a separate recommendation form for each college or university to which your child is applying should all look impeccably neat and clean, with every area that your child had to complete in advance typed rather than handwritten; maintaining a high standard with even the small details conveys your child's seriousness about the process. Getting these materials to recommenders in a timely fashion reinforces this message and may motivate them to complete your child's letters before the last-minute rush.

Helpful guidance counselors can also steer students in selecting appropriate recommenders. Those with experience in a school have read letters by many teachers over the years and have some knowledge of which ones write well and put effort into their recommendations. If multiple teachers look like potentially strong recommenders, your child may want to request three letters and ask his guidance counselor to select the two strongest of all. Your child's counselor can also help him locate a teacher whom he wants to ask for a recommendation but who has left the high school, a perfectly acceptable scenario from an admissions perspective. Encourage your child to enlist his counselor's support on all of these fronts, if the counselor is willing and able to offer it. (See Chapter Two's discussion on how to determine a guidance counselor's competence, if you have not already read it.)

STRENGTHENING YOUR CHILD'S GUIDANCE COUNSELOR RECOMMENDATION

Unlike with his teachers, your child does not get to choose who writes his guidance counselor recommendation. High schools use their own, self-defined criteria to assign students to counselors, generally with little or no input from families. That person writes your child's recommendation—regardless of how well the two know each other—and acts as your child's liaison with the colleges and universities to which he is applying. Getting to know his counselor and following any instructions that his counselor gives him stand out as the most important steps your child can take toward strengthening his guidance counselor recommendation. The ideal way in which to take those steps depends on the type of high school he attends and the resources it offers.

Dropping in for periodic informal chats with his guidance counselor can benefit your child regardless of the type of high school he attends. Counselors like Fieldston's Laura Clark who try in their recommendations "to make the admissions officer feel that she is sitting in the room with the student" write as if they are "composing a character sketch or developing a character in a novel" and are always looking for supporting details. Boston Public Schools guidance counselor Ron Inniss, who at points in his career has had responsibility for almost two hundred graduating seniors in a single year, relies on his motivated counselees not to wait for formal appointments. He remembers one recent student who learned of his regular 6:00 A.M. arrival at work and who used to drop in a couple of times a week at 6:30 A.M. to "shoot the breeze." Those conversations proved invaluable in Inniss's writing the young man a powerful recommendation.[24] Students at large high schools may have to work a little harder than their counterparts elsewhere to get face time with their guidance counselor, but putting in that kind of effort could make a substantive difference in the letter of recommendation they receive.

Clark incorporates into her letter quotations from teachers who are not writing for the student but who may have a unique perspective on him. Your child's counselor, especially if she has the kind of student load that Inniss does, may not solicit that type of input from teachers in the building. Your child, however, can cull specific comments from graded assignments and put them together for his counselor. I recommend making copies of the pages with the comments

Excerpts from Ron Inniss's Brag Sheet

PERSONAL DATA

1. Tell us about yourself! Please comment on your values, personality, and character traits, and any unusual circumstances in your life that you feel are important. This is important information for your guidance counselor to have in order to write your college recommendation.

2. Please list your interests, talents, special abilities, and hobbies.

3. Please describe an experience or activity that has had a significant impact on you and why.

4. Are there any special considerations or unusual circumstances regarding your background that should be highlighted? Are there any obstacles you are struggling with or have overcome?

5. If you could take a year and do anything you wanted to do, what would you do? Why?

6. List five adjectives that you think best describe you.

7. What do you think are your academic, social, and personal strengths?

ACTIVITIES, WORK EXPERIENCE, HONORS, AND AWARDS: Please fill in each of the tables on an attached sheet with the following information.

1. School activities (student and/or class government, class activities, clubs and organizations, sports, and/or other school-related activities)—indicate year(s) of participation, special leadership role(s), and/or office(s) held.

2. Out-of-school activities (community service, church or synagogue activities, sports, and/or volunteer work)—indicate year(s) of participation, special leadership role(s), and/or office(s) held.

3. Work experience (summer, part-time, and/or academic year)—indicate year(s) of participation, special leadership role(s), and/or office(s) held.

4. Honors and awards (academic achievement awards, Honor Roll, National Honor Society, recognition in athletics/performing arts, community awards, etc.)—for each award, honor, or recognition listed, indicate year received.

on them, which your child can then attach to an accompanying cover sheet. The cover sheet should include each comment, the instructor's name, the class she taught, and the grade in which your child took the course. Taking this type of initiative will catch a counselor's attention, independent of what the teacher comments themselves say.

Your child's guidance counselor may have distributed what Inniss calls a "brag sheet." Inniss's version contains a series of questions that he has tweaked over the years to solicit information from students that he can use in writing their letters of recommendation. (See "Excerpts from Ron Inniss's Brag Sheet.") He has found over the years that the effort that a student invests in answering these questions has a direct impact on the strength of the letter he can write for that young person. Your child can compose answers to Inniss's questions and give the information to his own counselor if she does not distribute something similar of her own. For each of the colleges and universities to which your child is applying, he should, of course, also give his guidance counselor the same one or two sentences that he gave his teacher recommenders that explain his interest in the institution.

If your child has a skilled and experienced counselor like Clark or Inniss, avoid taking steps that interfere with the work that his counselor is doing with him. Inniss can recount specific instances in which counselees resisted his advice and chose to rely instead on poorly qualified independent or volunteer college counselors. Clark and her colleagues at Fieldston get to know their counselees and develop an ability to represent them accurately to colleges and universities in part through supporting them as they draft their college essays. Fieldston students who turn to a consultant for help with the essay instead of to their counselor could find that doing so "impedes them in the college process here in the end."

SUPPLEMENTARY LETTERS OF RECOMMENDATION

A supplementary letter of recommendation—one that someone has written and submitted to a college or university on your child's behalf, above and beyond the required teacher and counselor recommendations—has the potential to strengthen your child's folder, *under certain circumstances.* I hold my clients to strict criteria when they ask me about forwarding this kind of unsolicited material to colleges and universities, as it also has the power to weaken an application. You can use the same criteria that I give my clients to determine whether or not this optional step in the admissions process looks like a good fit for your child. (See the following worksheet.)

"The thicker the file, the thicker the kid," several deans of admission replied when I asked them about supplementary letters. (See "Author of the Letter" section on the worksheet.) One additional letter might work well, depending on whether or not it meets the rest of the criteria that follow, but a "bulky" folder filled with extra letters that lack relevance "can actually hurt you," according to Jim Sumner at Grinnell College. Students who submit numerous outside letters frequently end up with a collection of them that all say the same thing, "a waste of everybody's time," Rice's Julie Browning asserts. Consider a supplementary letter if you can think of one person who stands head and shoulders above the crowd as the clear choice to write it.

Knowing your child well should stand out as the key characteristic of somebody writing a supplementary letter for him. That person should have worked with your child in some capacity and have the ability to narrate a significant and relevant story about him. I suggested to one of my clients, who had volunteered tirelessly on behalf of her church, but always in an informal capacity, that she ask her priest for a recommendation. This young woman had earned no titles, formal leadership roles, or membership in an official organization, yet she had helped raise thousands of dollars for community service projects on behalf of her parish. The priest gladly agreed.

Some families actively seek what Cornell's Doris Davis dubs "'designer' letters of recommendation," the ones with "the state senate seal or a celebrity's signature" that they think will impress readers. Admissions officers generally find these letters thin on content and stiff in tone—"worthless," according to MIT's Marilee Jones. Davis, a former colleague from Yale who has worked in admissions at

Determining Whether Your Child Should Submit a Supplementary Letter of Recommendation

	Strongly Agree			Agree		Somewhat Agree		Disagree		Strongly Disagree
Author of the Letter: One person clearly stands out in my mind as the appropriate author of a supplementary letter of recommendation for my child.	10	9	8	7	6	5	4	3	2	1	0
Author of the Letter: I am focusing on this person because s/he knows my child well, not because of her/his name value.	10	9	8	7	6	5	4	3	2	1	0
Letter of Recommendation: This person's letter would provide new and relevant information about my child that readers would not get from other parts of the application.	10	9	8	7	6	5	4	3	2	1	0
Letter of Recommendation: The supplementary letter would emphasize positive aspects of my child's profile, rather than explain negative ones.	10	9	8	7	6	5	4	3	2	1	0
My Child: My child feels comfortable asking this person to write a letter on his behalf.	10	9	8	7	6	5	4	3	2	1	0
My Child: For each of the colleges and universities to which he is applying, my child is prepared to provide this recommender with one or two sentences that explain his interest in the institution.	10	9	8	7	6	5	4	3	2	1	0

several highly selective institutions, remembers reading three identical letters—"VERBATIM"—from a world-renowned religious figure for three different students in the same applicant pool. She also recalls a letter from a former U.S. Secretary of State recommending the grandchild of a high-ranking foreign dignitary. The Secretary of State had clearly never met the student and, even more distracting to Davis, misspelled the applicant's name! She cautions against the errors that can take place when students stray outside their normal range of relationships to get an individual to write a letter on their behalf. The individual feels obligated, for whatever reason, to comply with the request, but doing so frequently adds little, if anything, to the folder.

Supplementary letters that make a positive difference do so because they add new and relevant information that readers are not already getting from other parts of the application. (See "Letter of Recommendation" section of worksheet.) I cannot emphasize this point enough, as most of the unsolicited letters that I read in admissions at Yale simply repeated what I had already seen and added nothing of value, even if the writer made clear that he knew the applicant well. The priest who wrote on behalf of the client whom I mentioned earlier pulled together in his letter a summary of all of the activities that the young woman had undertaken on behalf of the church. The large number of them (many involved short-term projects, such as food drives, walks for hunger, etc.) had led the young woman to group them together on her list of extracurricular activities under the umbrella category of "community service." The priest's letter provided the elaboration that readers needed to understand and appreciate them.

Helpful and relevant information can come from an employer, a coach, a therapist, a parent, even the student himself! Laura Clark, who worked in admissions at Princeton before she moved into college guidance, used to appreciate letters from students at resource-constrained high schools that painted realistic portraits of their environment that their guidance counselor recommendations may not have. Students attempting to gain admission to a selective college or university while they work under adverse conditions at their high schools should especially consider soliciting an additional letter of recommendation from somebody who can comment on their academic strengths, such as an instructor in an academic enrichment program like Upward Bound, GEAR UP, or Urban Scholars. Grinnell's Jim Sumner has observed that these students' teachers at school may just not express themselves well in writing. A supplementary letter that speaks specifically to academics would have added value in that context.

I frequently encounter families who want to use supplementary letters to shed light on what they see as a negative aspect of the student's profile. One high school junior wanted a dean to write a special letter of explanation for a low grade the previous year that the student felt had resulted from a personality conflict with the teacher. These types of letters can backfire and send up a red flag to admissions officers. "We seem to find that the weaker the grades, the weaker the test scores, the more labored the explanations of these things," Ted Spencer at the University of Michigan noted, whereas a line or two in the context of a letter that emphasizes the positive may provide useful information. An orchestra conductor writing about a student's musical talent, for example, would assist admissions officers by mentioning that the student had played in a concert at Carnegie Hall the night before her SATs. Note the difference, however, between this brief, one-line clarification in an overall positive context versus an entire letter that focuses on why the student did not perform well on her SATs.

Lastly, your child must feel comfortable asking somebody to write a letter on his behalf. (See "My Child" section of worksheet.) He must also be willing to provide the recommender with the same one or two sentences on each college or university to which he is applying that he gave his teachers and guidance counselor. Your child's lack of comfort approaching the individual or his unwillingness to do what it takes to make the recommender's task as easy as possible could reflect that you and/or he has selected the wrong person for this task, or that your child would prefer not to submit a supplementary letter at all. Either scenario merits a full discussion between the two of you, before you ask somebody to perform a favor on your behalf and before you add unsolicited information to an already chock-full folder.

FREQUENTLY ASKED QUESTIONS

My daughter does not want to sign away her right to read her letters of recommendation but her guidance counselor is advising her to do so. Does it matter one way or the other?

Your daughter may not have a choice. Some teachers and counselors refuse to write letters of recommendation unless students sign the waiver statement on the first page of the form that relinquishes their right to read the contents. I would suggest that your daughter sign the waiver as a courtesy, so as not to experience any potentially uncomfortable moments with her recommenders. Some may give her a copy of the letter for her files anyway. (I always did with my students.)

One of my son's teacher recommenders has asked him for a list of his extracurricular activities, test scores, and other information that appear elsewhere in the application. Should we take this request as a sign that the recommendation will include a lot of extraneous information that admissions officers do not want to see?

You really have no way of knowing either way. Many teachers and counselors ask students for a list or description of how they spend their time outside of the classroom. Some simply regurgitate the information, laundry-list style. Others integrate select details seamlessly into the recommendation in a way that adds texture and substance. You have no way of knowing how this teacher plans to incorporate the material that she is requesting. Keep in mind that your child can give his teacher an annotated list that highlights activities and achievements that relate to her subject area. He can note for a mathematics teacher, for example, that participation on the chess team or in the philosophy club picks up on his passion for problem solving.

My daughter has a passion for art and would like her fine arts senior seminar instructor to write one of her teacher recommendations. Could this kind of letter weaken her application since not everybody sees art as a serious academic pursuit?

Some of the most selective institutions in the country, including Yale and Harvard, grant degrees in the visual arts. Admissions officers will find a letter from your daughter's fine arts instructor helpful if the rest of her application reflects her passion for art and if the teacher's description of his own class and the work your daughter has done in it indicate some degree of academic rigor. An applicant who expresses a passion for chemistry, on the other hand, and whose folder does not suggest any interest in art may provoke questions if he solicits a required letter of reference from a fine arts instructor. Encourage your daughter to confirm whether or not a college or university that she is exploring grants a degree in visual arts. She may want to call the admissions offices at any that do not to confirm whether or not a letter from her fine arts instructor satisfies the teacher recommendation requirement or whether she needs to submit it as a supplementary piece of information.

Our son attends a small magnet high school that has a teaching staff of fewer than ten people. Not one of them has been teaching for more than five years. Does this circumstance automatically mean that his letters of recommendation will weaken his college applications?

Not necessarily. First of all, teachers at small, mission-driven schools like your son's generally have a lot of passion and enthusiasm for their work. They will likely bend over backwards to assist your child throughout the college admissions process. It would not hurt to inquire about the college guidance program they have set up, if you do not already have some familiarity with it. I would want to know how much experience the head counselor has had with college admissions, as opposed to the other areas that fall under the guidance counseling umbrella, as an experienced college counselor will sometimes give feedback to beginning teachers on writing effective recommendations. I would also ask whether or not the counselor attends annual meetings of organizations like the National Association of College Admission Counseling (NACAC) and the College Board. These annual meetings give counselors the opportunity to meet, network with, and cultivate relationships with admissions officers. (They also offer workshops on writing effective recommendations.)

STEP-BY-STEP CHECKLIST: LETTERS OF RECOMMENDATION

❑ Complete the worksheet "Soliciting Effective Teacher Recommendations" for each instructor your child is considering as a recommender.

❑ Select the teacher(s) for whom you can check off the greatest number of criteria on the worksheet.

❑ Encourage your child to give his teacher recommender(s) a packet that contains the items that appear on the worksheet and that will facilitate the letter-writing task.

❑ If your child has a helpful guidance counselor, consult her for assistance with selecting teacher recommenders. (See the worksheet for additional details.)

❑ Suggest to your child that he drop in to see his guidance counselor informally from time to time.

❑ Help your child select strong teacher comments from graded assignments and put those remarks together on one typed page to give the counselor.

❑ Remind your child to fill out and return any "brag sheet" that his counselor distributed or to use the one in this chapter if his counselor did not give out one of her own.

❑ For each of the colleges and universities to which your child is applying, encourage him to give his guidance counselor the same one or two sentences that he gave his teacher recommenders that explain his interest in the institution.

❑ Complete the worksheet "Determining Whether Your Child Should Submit a Supplementary Letter of Recommendation" and use the criteria there to determine whether taking this additional step will benefit your child.

TEN

Completing the College Essay and Other Parts of the Application

I undertake the college essay and accompanying written parts of the application last of all when I work with my clients. Students may still be scheduling interviews, taking standardized tests, and putting together a list of colleges when we begin the essay. They have ideally begun addressing these other parts of the process by the end of junior year, some even earlier than that. The essay, though, needs to wait until some additional time has elapsed.

Writing an effective college essay requires that a young person take several steps back to think about herself and her experiences in a mature, reflective way. The months leading up to senior year—when your child has begun visiting college campuses and envisioning herself away from home—add to her life experiences and emotional development in ways that can enrich how she sees and writes about herself. A few students each year, usually those who have made significant progress with their other admissions requirements and are thinking about applying early, want to take the initiative and work on the essay over the summer. Everybody else with whom I work, though, typically waits until fall of senior year, a time frame that feels appropriate to me as well.

Helping students with the college essay challenges me more than assisting them with any other part of the process does, for one simple reason: I have to fight the constant urge to spoon-feed them topics and line-by-line revisions of their writing. As a result, I designed a college essay writing workshop that offers young people the opportunity to brainstorm together with me and their peers, present their work for repeated critique from all of us, and then withdraw to the privacy of their own thoughts to revise and refine for the next presentation. The workshop approach allows college applicants to write in their own voice and still get invaluable feedback on content and format. You can implement a similar program in your own community if you feel comfortable collaborating with other families, or you can encourage your child to put together her own writers workshop with friends at school who are also completing their application essays. Like me, you should work hard to limit the line-by-line feedback that you give your child on her writing. The application essay represents in some respects a rite of passage between high school and college. Getting through it as independently as possible could reward your child both on the college admissions front and in her journey to young adulthood.

ESSAYS THAT WORK

This chapter draws from examples of essays that have worked for me, both as an admissions officer and as someone who advises college applicants, because the writing has effectively brought me into that young person's world. These essays have told stories, complete with vivid examples, in a well-crafted and heartfelt way that caught my attention. In some cases they have made me laugh and, in others, they have literally brought tears to my eyes.

One client, a young man from a stereotypical suburban household with two parents, four children, and a dog, went to spend a month during the school year with an aunt and uncle in Queens, New York, who had ten children. This sociable teenager "envisioned a month of non-stop amusement, cousins left and right, and plenty of ice cream." He quickly learned, though, that life in a household of twelve people (he brought the number at the dinner table to thirteen) required a "unique discipline . . . a concerted effort of twelve devoted individuals." He took me with him from his rush to get ready for school in the morning (sleeping in one's school clothes at night shortened the morning trip from bed to school bus) to the dinner table in the evening (turning a juice container on its side when none remained prevented you from having to say "it's empty," over and over again). The essay read as if it were coming from him—a critical criterion for success, according to Cornell's Doris Davis—and as if it were providing me with a ticket to accompany him through this experience.

Another client of mine wrote about his introduction to Ryu Kyu Kempo, an Okinawan style of karate that he had studied for several years, initially at his father's instigation. Like the student who wrote about his month in Queens with his cousins, this young man used details that might have looked mundane on the surface, such as the discomfort of his uniform ("I swear to this day it is made of cardboard"), to transport the reader with him into the dojo (karate training hall). I could feel myself experiencing all the awkwardness of his first few years as a beginner and cheering for him as he toiled and stuck with the sport. This young man wrote from his heart, as he used his passion for karate to convey who he was and what he cared about.

Characteristics of College Application Essays That Work

- They tell a story.

- They provide vivid examples that allow the reader to put himself in the student's situation or mindset.

- They sound authentic, like they are coming from the student herself, rather than from a college-essay coach.

- The writer gets to the heart of what she wants to say, so that the essay reflects who she is and what she cares about.

For several years now, I have shown students these two essays in the first session of each workshop cycle. They never get written copies, as I do not want to encourage the notion that one correct formula or template for essay writing exists. Instead, I use a projector to display them while participants read, critique, and grade them. (See the following essay grading rubric.) My clients have found this exercise (what educators would call "modeling," that is, giving students an example of the type of final result they are aiming for themselves) extremely helpful. They absorb the important points about writing a successful essay—telling a story, using specific examples to illustrate it, and speaking in their own voice—without feeling that they must

Date: _____

College Application Essay Rubric

Step 1 – Introductory Paragraph: Main Idea (1 Paragraph - 20 Points)

❑ The reader can clearly see the one **main idea** around which the rest of the essay revolves (5).
❑ You can express your main idea in one sentence (5).
❑ The main idea reveals something about you, the way in which you think, etc. (5).
❑ The main idea does not just repeat biographical details (5).

Total Points – Introductory Paragraph: _____

Step 2 – Background Information (1 Paragraph - 20 Points)

You clearly identify for the reader any necessary background information and/or context that s/he needs to understand your essay, including

❑ Who the main characters are (5).
❑ What the significant events are (5).
❑ Where and when the significant events take place (5).
❑ You provide this information without giving unnecessary details that just take up space (5).

Total Points – Background Information: _____

Step 3 – Body Paragraphs: Illustrating Details/Examples (1–2 Par. - 15 Pts.)

❑ You have provided enough examples to help your reader put him/herself in the situation you are describing (5).
❑ All of your details/examples connect back to your main idea (5).
❑ You have included vivid details that let the reader hear, see, taste, touch, feel, and/or smell the people, events, experiences, locations, etc., about which you are writing (5).

Total Points – Body Paragraphs: _____

Step 4 – Concluding Paragraph (1 Paragraph - 10 Points)

❑ Your conclusion reflects your final thoughts on the topic of your essay, e.g., what you learned about yourself, how an event changed the way you think, a final statement you want to make, etc. (5).
❑ Your reader feels a sense of completion to your essay as a result of your conclusion, i.e., no loose ends are left undone (5).

Total Points – Concluding Paragraph: _____

Step 5 – Storytelling (20 Points)

❑ You have organized your paragraphs in a way that makes sense to your reader (5).
❑ The paragraphs flow smoothly from one to the other in a way that the reader can understand and follow (5).
❑ Your essay tells a story or presents a viewpoint that the reader clearly understands by the end (5).
❑ Your essay holds the reader's attention (s/he'd rather finish your essay than watch WWF, go to the mall, or surf the Internet) (5).

Total Points – Storytelling: _____

Step 6 – Proofreading: Mechanics Vocabulary & Tone (15 Points)

❑ You have used effective proofreading to eliminate typographical, spelling, and/or grammatical errors in your writing (5).
❑ Essay uses active voice wherever possible (5).
❑ Formatting includes indented paragraphs, same margins all the way around, same font and type size throughout (5).

Total Points – Proofreading: _____

Grading Scale

90-100: A. Outstanding!
80-89: B. Very good.
70-79: C. Fair. Needs some improvement.
60-69: D. Needs significant improvement.
 <60: F. Not yet—try again.

Three things I like about this essay include

1.

2.

3.

Point Total/Letter Grade/Performance Level

Intro. Paragraph: _____
Background Info: _____
Body ¶'s: _____
Concluding Par.: _____
Storytelling: _____
Proofreading: _____

Total Points: _____

Letter Grade: _____

follow a single recipe for success. The grading exercise also gets them used to editing based on workshop critique, a key part of the development of their final product. We can then move easily into the next phase of the workshop, selecting a topic.

SELECTING A TOPIC

Students generally have a much harder time coming up with an essay topic than they do with what follows. Sometimes they are starting with a completely blank slate, such as when they use the Common Application™ that allows them to choose their own topic.[25] Other times they have to make choices within certain parameters, such as: "Identify a person, living or dead, with whom you would have lunch if you could and explain your choice." Encourage your child to sit down with her writing workshop peers to brainstorm out loud and give each other feedback, a method that lessens the pressure that they would feel sitting at their computers, alone and frustrated. Most find the process far less painful than they had initially envisioned.

Selecting a Topic

- In a study group setting, your child can look at examples of essays that work and then brainstorm topics with her peers and an adult moderator.

- Encourage your child to select a topic about which she feels passionate.

- Whatever she decides to write about should allow her to keep the focus on herself, rather than on an issue, an event, or another person.

- The topic should answer the question asked, especially if your child is trying to use the same essay in multiple contexts.

The actual topic that your child selects, ironically, does not matter nearly as much as how she approaches it. As Mount Holyoke's Jane Brown says, "It's what you have to say about a subject that matters rather than what you choose to write about." Young people sometimes make the mistake of thinking that they have to focus on something sensational, like building latrines in an underdeveloped country. In fact, your child can select as a topic drawing and writing comics, watching movies, playing on the school golf team, performing in theater productions, working to improve at basketball, or enjoying her grandmother's cooking—all of which have come up in essays that my students have written and that have worked, without their sounding particularly exotic.

Young people who have come to me for help on the essay have frequently chosen to focus on experiences or activities about which they feel passionate, even if others would find those same experiences or activities mundane. This characteristic definitely sets apart the essays that I remember from my admissions experience at Yale, such as an applicant from my territory who wrote about his love for the theater and his heartfelt wish that his father (who would have preferred to see his son on the athletic field) would come to see him perform on stage. Although other parts of the young man's application reflected his strength as a candidate, his essay in particular motivated me to advocate for him in front of the committee, which voted him in.

Certain topics have a propensity to lead students away from focusing on themselves. A reader has to know more about the applicant at the end of the essay than he did at the beginning; otherwise, the essay has fallen short of the intended goal. The role model essay, for example, "gets students every time," Cornell's Doris Davis points out. "You wind up wanting to admit the role model and have learned nothing about the applicant." Applicants who write about issues, events, and other influences in their lives should take special care to keep the focus on themselves rather than on these external details.

On a practical note, an essay topic should always answer the question asked. Streamlining the process by writing one essay for every application works if your child is using the Common Application™. When each institution is asking its own individual question, though, your child must adjust her essay as needed to insure that it responds with equal relevance to every application. Cornell's Doris Davis also advises students to indicate the question they are answering at the top of the page if the application has given them a choice.

WRITING AND THEN REWRITING

Different teaching strategies bring out the best in a young person's writing, depending on her temperament, learning style, experiences in school, and more. I have always favored a structured approach initially, as many students fear the blank page. I step back from a defined framework for those who do not seem to need it or who, once they have gotten started, find themselves off and running. You can determine how much support your child needs with writing based on her enthusiasm for it, track record to date, and overall reaction to writing the college essay.

In session one of our six-part workshop, participants saw examples of essays that worked. They then brainstormed with each other and with me about their own possible topics. Everybody left with an initial topic around which to create a first draft and with a college application essay editing rubric that she had already used twice in critiquing the sample essays. The rubric gives those students who need it a well-defined sense of structure within which to create their essay. While using the rubric does not represent the only successful approach to writing a college application essay, I have found that it provides meaningful and significant support to those students who otherwise have difficulty.

The rubric lays out for students some of the key writing elements that characterize strong essays. First and foremost, the writer must state things "plainly and clearly," Spelman's Arlene Cash insists. The beginning of the essay stands out as an area in which plain and clear prose can prove critical to what follows. The writer must introduce decisively in the first paragraph a main idea that does more than simply restate biographical details; she may also briefly recap background information that the reader needs to understand the rest of the content. Some people choose to weave that background in throughout the body of the essay. Others include a background information paragraph right after the introduction (see "Background Information" section of rubric on page 188). Any of these methods can work, provided that explanatory details flow quickly and succinctly and do not dominate the body of the essay.

We have already gone over the importance that examples and supporting details have in the telling of a story. Reciting them like a laundry list adds little, though, especially if they bore the reader. One of my clients wanted to make the point that, like Lizzie Bennet in Jane

Austen's *Pride and Prejudice,* she had to break free of a domineering and somewhat ridiculous older female relative (in this case, a cousin) as part of her own journey to young adulthood. Initially, her examples sounded flat and uninteresting. They made the reader want to run away from her essay in the same way in which she had wanted to flee her cousin's company in the situation she was describing. We used the workshop discussion of her essay to explore what she was actually thinking and feeling when the situation she was discussing took place and discovered that, in speaking about them, she made us laugh. The young woman used the same examples in her next draft but recast them in a way that made the entire essay appear stronger and more compelling than it had in the previous session.

Essays that I have found particularly successful conclude with some kind of lesson learned. Ideally, the reader feels he has gleaned something significant about the writer. The writer demonstrating that she herself has taken something meaningful away from an experience or relationship can enhance that perception. Touching on these kinds of points runs the risk of sounding trite or, as my students would say, "corny." In fact, the concluding paragraph never has to use words like "lesson," "learned," or "discovered," as my karate kid demonstrated:

> Now as a black belt in my sixth year, I free my mind from thought, submit to my Sensei, and simply absorb all that he teaches. In the dojo my spirit is concentrated, allowing me to harness the full power of my chi [energy]. I fight passionately, clearly, and confidently. The wealth of karate lies in understanding—understanding of others, the world, oneself. Pursuing that understanding, both inside and outside the dojo, will always be a part of me.

The concluding paragraph makes clear that this young man's love of karate stems in part from the sport's continually pushing him to learn and grow. I have read this essay on countless occasions and, each time I arrive at this final paragraph, find myself wanting to hit the admit button at the committee table!

Smooth flow and clean presentation matter, as admissions officers want to see evidence of solid writing skills. Careful proofreading also stands out as a *must.* Students sometimes rely on word processing software packages that can overlook egregious errors. Nothing substitutes for the keen eye of an adult with strong proofreading skills. If your child asks you to take on that role, remember always to point out several positive aspects of the essay first, as positive feedback opens up any writer to hearing more of what you have to say. Beginning with criticism, no matter how constructive your intent, can shut somebody down and make it hard for her to absorb important points that could improve her writing.

I have referred throughout this chapter to the six sessions that my workshop comprises. After that first one in which we look at sample essays, we spend the remaining five reading, critiquing, and grading drafts of student essays—first drafts, second drafts, and sometimes even third drafts. Not all high school teachers emphasize the value of writing and then rewriting. The success of your child's college essay depends on her ability to write a draft; get feedback on it from you, a teacher, a counselor, her writers workshop, or another trusted source; put the draft down, look at it again later; and then take another stab at it. I have never met a student who completed a successful application essay on her first attempt. Students who rely on the rubric also watch their scores inch up with each successive draft.

COMPLETING THE REST OF THE COLLEGE APPLICATION

Applying to college means filling out forms, many of which ask for straightforward, factual information about your child, her academic record, standardized test scores, family background, activities, and more. Completing this part of the written application does not have to take much time, especially if your child is using the Common Application™, which over two hundred colleges and universities around the country accept. Do not worry about your child setting this paperwork aside until after she finishes her essay. (Regular admission deadlines begin as of January 1 and can run into February, sometimes even March.) When she does get to this portion of the application, though, encourage her to give it the time that it deserves so that she does not shortchange herself in the admissions process. Small variations in the way in which your child presents herself here can affect how admissions officers see her.

Personal Data

The personal data section, although straightforward where it asks for name, address, etc., also requests details about your child that require interpretation. Your child must always represent herself honestly and accurately in every area of her application and should never manipulate an answer to strengthen her chances for admission. At the same time, admissions officers need to know if she legitimately comes from a population that they consider in short supply and are actively seeking to increase on campus, so that they can make an informed decision. In that context, your child needs to present herself as fully and accurately as possible so as not to shortchange either herself or the college or university to which she is applying.

Possible areas of academic concentration, or what your child intends to major in, can sometimes give her an advantage in the admissions process. Predominantly male engineering programs, for instance, are always seeking qualified female candidates. Likewise, a female student expressing an interest in any non–biological science usually catches an admissions officer's attention, especially if she is applying to an institution like MIT that focuses on the sciences or engineering. Elementary education programs frequently seek male students. Keep in mind that admissions officers look for corroboration of a stated interest in other areas of the application, such as a strong Subject Test score in physics or chemistry, advanced level coursework, and/or a letter of recommendation from a teacher in those subjects. Indicating nuclear physics as an intended major will look out of place and have little value if nothing else in the application supports your child's interest and/or background in that area.

Languages, cultural influences at home, even ethnicity may also require extra thought from your child as she puts them down on paper, as underrepresented populations do get an advantage—or hook—in the admissions process. Many students come from multicultural or multilingual backgrounds, such as one of my clients with European, African American, and Cherokee background. This young man initially omitted "Native American" when he indicated his race/ethnicity because he had no official paperwork establishing his membership in the tribe. His father, however, could document a significant Cherokee presence in his family, enough so that it constituted part of his identity and a great source of pride. I generally advise students to indicate a particular ethnic or racial component of their background if it has influenced the way in which they see themselves, as it clearly did with this young man. Ask yourself how comfortable your child would feel discussing this part of her profile in an admissions interview or essay. Those applicants who do not feel comfortable enough to discuss how it has influenced them probably would not benefit from describing themselves that way in the Personal Data section.

Test Information

Make sure that your child reports in this area of the application only the standardized test scores that an institution requires, unless additional scores reflect well on her. A student who has taken the ACT and is applying to Yale or Swarthmore, for example, does not have to report Subject Test scores, even if she took those tests and is forwarding the results elsewhere. Your child may want to spend extra time completing multiple versions of this page so that each college or university receives only the test scores that it requires (unless, once again, additional scores strengthen her application, such as when they fall significantly above the mean score for a given institution).

Family

This area of the application offers students the opportunity to identify several additional hooks for admissions officers, primarily based on if and where parents attended college. Many institutions look at a "non-coll" applicant—somebody whose parents did not attend college themselves—as having a hook. At the other end of the spectrum, most selective institutions value what they call a "legacy" connection—a history of another family member attending the same institution—as some colleges and universities have documented that legacy students tend to donate more to their alma mater after graduation than those without that connection. Mount Holyoke's Jane Brown sees legacy connections as helping to develop "community. When you have sisters, mothers, and grandmothers who have all gone here, it creates a special element for us. Students really like that sense of tradition."

Extracurricular, Personal, and Volunteer Activities

The summary of extracurricular activities gives your child the chance to shine—to showcase her accomplishments in areas that interest her, areas in which she has chosen to get involved. Yet, your child could easily sell herself short if she does not think through her presentation of the information. Classic pitfalls include haphazard lists with either too much or too little detail, both of which can cause admissions officers to miss important highlights. Your input on this part of the application could have special importance, as few counselors review college applications to this level of detail. Try to keep two key words in mind as you help your child review her activities: highlight and consolidate.

Janine's Revised List of Extracurricular Activities

Activity	Grade Level	Hours per Week	Weeks per Year	Positions Held, Honors Won, Letters Earned
~~Film Club~~ (not significant)	9	1	20	
~~Television Club~~ (not significant)	9	.5	15	
~~Spanish Club~~ (not significant)	10	.5	10	
~~Food Drive~~ (consolidated under Church of the Holy Name below)	9–12	2.5	40	
Varsity Tennis	10–12	4–7	17	Varsity letter
Varsity Track	10–12	4–7	20	Varsity letter
~~Blood Drive~~ (consolidated under Church of the Holy Name below)	10–12	3	4	
~~Fund-raising Drive~~ (consolidated under Church of the Holy Name below)	11	3	10	
The Spectator (school newspaper)	10–12	3	30	Photography editor (12)
The Chronicle (school yearbook)	11–12	3	25	Layout editor (12)
Church of the Holy Name Community Service (Food, Blood, and Fund-Raising Drives)	9–12	3–6	35–40	Student organizer

The feedback I gave one of my recent clients illustrates both concepts. Janine had participated in roughly ten different activities throughout high school. The initial list she brought me itemized everything from Film Club in grade nine to three years of varsity tennis in grades ten through twelve. The sheer number of activities made it difficult for me to identify those to which she had devoted energy and time over several years as opposed to the ones in which she had participated for only a brief period. I also noticed that Janine had organized multiple charity drives, none of which had taken place as part of a formal initiative. Rather than waiting for a larger charitable entity to launch the campaigns, she had simply decided on her own at various points throughout high school to organize food collections, clothing drives, or other such events on behalf of her church. She then listed each separately, a strategy that made the initiatives look scattered, unconnected, and smaller than they would have if they all fell under one shared umbrella.

To streamline her list of extracurriculars, Janine and I first highlighted the activities that mattered. Remember that we discussed in Chapter Four the importance of demonstrating commitment and leadership. Janine's sustained involvement in several activities over time, such as tennis, school newspaper, and track, made it unnecessary to include extraneous one-semester experiments, such as Film Club in grade nine. We eliminated all activities in which she had been involved for only one year of high school, unless she had attained a leadership position. Right away, her list looked uncluttered and easy to read; examples of leadership and longevity now stood out.

Next, we consolidated. Janine had organized each of her charitable drives on behalf of her church. In some cases she accepted a leadership role in a campaign that the church itself had planned. In other cases, she came up with an idea, implemented it on her own, and then donated the proceeds to her church to distribute. With the permission and support of her priest, Janine and I grouped these separate initiatives under the heading "Church of the Holy Name Community Service" and gave her the title "Student organizer." Her priest, who characterized Janine's commitment as exceptional, also agreed to write a supplementary letter of recommendation for her. The resulting extracurricular profile (shown on page 196) emphasized Janine's strengths and unique contributions instead of conveying a candidate with scattered, halfhearted interests.

MEETING DEADLINES

Many aspects of the college admissions process have dates and deadlines attached to them. Only the actual completion of the written application, however, takes place within the confines of your home. Students take their standardized tests at a local high school or college with hundreds of their peers, solicit letters of recommendation at school, and interview at admissions offices or with alumni. Conversely, filling out the application generally occurs in isolation, without the socialization and peer interaction that the other parts of the process can bring. Following a proactive strategy can increase the chances that you become a valuable support and resource for your child as she completes this final step in the process and can lessen the odds that nagging, tension, and even conflict develop between the two of you.

As a first step, take a few minutes at the beginning of your child's senior year to make some time-frame calculations privately, before you initiate a discussion with her. You do not need to worry about this part of the process before then. In fact, many colleges and universities do not even distribute applications for the upcoming admissions cycle until around that time. Use the "College Application Calendar 1" to pinpoint when your child will have completed each of the other components of the process. Doing so will enable you to identify a window during which she can concentrate on the essay with few other distractions, such as the ACT, the SAT, etc.

An obvious time frame for completing applications may jump out at you. If your child is finishing her standardized testing in October of her senior year, for example, you do not want to start discussing the essay and application with her before then. Regular admission deadlines begin in January and, depending on the institution, can roll into March. She has plenty of time to get everything done if she holds off on the application until November. The combined pressure of testing and completing the application simultaneously could backfire and result in her doing well on neither one. Students applying through an early-admission program, on the other hand, operate on a shortened time frame, as deadlines begin in November. These young people have made a decision to complete the process in an accelerated way, however, and have either gotten a head start on it (by completing standardized testing the year before) or possess the drive to get everything done without relying on your supervision or involvement.

Date: _____

College Application Calendar 1

Standardized Testing

Test	Date completed
SAT Reasoning Test (first time, if applicable)	
SAT Reasoning Test (second time, if applicable)	
ACT (first time, if applicable)	
ACT (second time, if applicable)	
SAT Subject Test #1 (if applicable)	
SAT Subject Test #2 (if applicable)	
SAT Subject Test #3 (if applicable)	
Other (please specify):	
Other (please specify):	
Date by which all standardized testing completed	

Campus Visits

Campus Visit	Date completed
Campus visit #1	
Campus visit #2	
Campus visit #3	
Campus visit #4	
Other (please specify):	
Other (please specify):	
Date by which all campus visits completed	

Extracurricular Activities

Activity	Date completed
Completed game tape, performance tape, portfolio, etc. (if submitting evidence of a special talent)	
Contacted scouts, coaches, department chairs, et al. (if submitting evidence of a special talent)	
Other (please specify):	
Other (please specify):	
Date by which all extracurricular materials accompanying application completed	

Letters of Recommendation

Recommender	Date completed
Prepared packet for and gave it to teacher #1	
Prepared packet for and gave it to teacher #2 (if applicable)	
Prepared packet for and gave it to teacher #3 (if applicable)	
Prepared packet for and gave it to guidance counselor	
Prepared packet for and gave it to additional recommender (if applicable)	
Other (please specify):	
Other (please specify):	
Date by which all letter of recommendation packets distributed	

Once you have completed this preliminary calendar, sit down with your child and show it to her. Ask her if tackling the application come November sounds good to her since she will have finished her testing the previous month. She may say yes or she may remind you that she has the lead in the school play, which is going up in early December. Look at her application deadlines together and discuss if putting things off until after the play will give her enough time. If she is focusing on colleges and universities with January 15 and February 1 deadlines and has completed everything else, turning to the written application in December should work fine.

This preliminary conversation sets the stage for you and your child to develop a timeline for completion of her written application. As the "College Application Calendar 2" illustrates, you need to know at this point exactly what your child has to accomplish and by when. Specifically, either she or you need to verify whether or not each of the colleges and universities to which she is applying accepts the Common Application™, whether or not those that do accept the Common Application™ require a supplement (additional essay questions just for them), and when applications have to arrive at the admissions office. You can ask your child to commit to her own personal deadline date for each college or university application that you then add to this calendar and post on the refrigerator.

I would also take this opportunity to ask your child how you can help her through this challenging set of tasks. Some young people want to complete the application independently or with support from school personnel, but may still appreciate periodic check-ins from you. Others want to enroll in a course that takes them through the process, or hire a private tutor and not hear anything from you at all. Most young people with whom I have worked want to feel ownership over this part of the college admissions process and, therefore, establish at least minimal boundaries that they ask their parents not to cross. Those boundaries vary with each individual. You will find that the first half of your child's senior year goes by much more peacefully than it otherwise would if you identify your child's boundaries sooner rather than later and put in the effort that it takes to respect them.

Respecting boundaries does not mean withholding encouragement or support. Consider acknowledging your child in some small way each time she crosses a milestone in the college admissions process. If she loves a particular coffeehouse or ice cream parlor, get her a

Date: _____

College Application Calendar 2

Name of College or University	Postmark Deadline	Targeted Completion Date	Targeted Mailing Date	Date Put in the Mail

small gift certificate to the place and leave it on her pillow the day she goes to take a standardized test. Consider releasing her from household chores during the couple of weeks that the two of you have designated for her to write the college essay. Continue to offer your child signs of support throughout the fall of her senior year, as the pressure on her will definitely be mounting until she gets those applications in the mail. Once she has made it past this ultimate deadline, I would suggest offering her either a dinner out at a restaurant of her choice or her favorite home-cooked meal to celebrate. Most young people appreciate the thought that such a personalized gesture reflects, even if some do not want to admit it.

FREQUENTLY ASKED QUESTIONS

Every time I bring up the subject of college, our son gets angry and upset and says that I am pressuring him. He has almost finished his junior year and I cannot broach a discussion with him about where he wants to apply, let alone talk about scheduling and deadlines. I do not know what to do.

In the throes of the college admissions process, one parent sometimes takes on the role of scheduler and enforcer, even if inadvertently. The time may have come for your spouse to assume the primary role of communicating with your son about college. One of my favorite families went through a similar experience last year. The young man accused his mother of nagging him whenever she talked with him about college but responded fine when his father raised the topic. It turned out that his mother normally took on the "bad cop" role about homework, household chores, and other responsibilities, while his father frequently traveled for work. I advised the mother to let her husband take over the informal college guidance job at home and the family's dynamics around the entire issue improved dramatically (as did the mother's day-to-day relationship with her son).

If your son responds with equal frustration and hostility to both of you (a scenario that would surprise me based on what I have seen over the years), you may want to check in with his counselor to see if he can run interference for you. You clearly have a right to know the colleges and universities to which he plans to apply, *especially if he expects you to pay for it.* See if you can schedule an appointment with your son, your spouse, and the counselor in which you discuss some of these issues on neutral territory and then lay out the parameters for what you expect him to inform you about moving forward.

I would like to help my son put together the type of college essay writing workshop that you describe in this chapter. He and I both agree that the group would benefit from having an adult facilitator. Whom should I approach to take on this role?

You can approach several different people to see if they would take on the responsibility. I would go first to a college counselor at a top-notch independent school in your area and see if he has an interest in taking on the work for a fee. Independent school counselors have sometimes worked in college admissions themselves and certainly have experience helping students write effective essays. This person may also be able to recommend somebody if he cannot do it himself.

If you have no luck in the counseling office, I would go next either to a well-regarded English teacher at a top-notch independent school or to a graduate student at a local university who has experience teaching writing. I would only approach an independent college consultant on the recommendation of the college counselor whom I mentioned above. I cannot emphasize enough how many people hang their shingles as independent college counselors who lack the skill, experience, and/or ethics to do the job in a credible way.

Our daughter worked hard on her essay, with help from an English teacher at school, but my wife and I agree that it still needs a lot of work. What should we do to help her get to that final, polished draft?

The answer to this question depends on whether or not the essay that your daughter has written accurately represents both her writing ability and who she is. I see a full range of essays in my interactions with students and not all of them captivate me the way the two that I mentioned earlier in this chapter did. They all, however, represent the best work that the individual author could produce. I push a student as hard as I can to write and rewrite as many times as it takes for her to produce *her* best final draft possible. The point at which she has arrived at that best final product usually makes itself pretty clear. My continuing to press beyond that point means that I am in fact writing the essay, rather than the student, a circumstance that will not serve her well in the college admissions process.

Admissions officers want your daughter's voice to sound authentic— like her, rather than like you or another adult coaching her on her writing. If the current version of your daughter's essay does not do *her* justice, then you might want to raise the issue with her to see if she can put in some additional work on it. If the current version of your daughter's essay does not do *you* justice, I would leave things alone and allow her to represent herself with her own voice.

Our son, who is going into his senior year, has a tendency to try activities for a brief period of time and then go on to new things. This pattern means that his list of activities on the application will not demonstrate leadership or commitment. Should he still include them or is there no point to doing so because they do not look impressive?

Students who have not chosen to focus on leadership and commitment but instead have taken your son's approach and have used high school to try various activities should by all means delineate the areas in which they have spent their time. Your son may want to speak with his guidance counselor about his curiosity and ongoing desire to try new activities, in order to eliminate the misperception that he moves aimlessly from activity to activity. He may also want to emphasize the activities that he has tried, has enjoyed, and plans to continue in college. Keep in mind that not everybody can take on a leadership role. Reliable foot soldiers play an important role in student activities as well.

STEP-BY-STEP CHECKLIST: COMPLETING THE COLLEGE APPLICATION ESSAY AND OTHER PARTS OF THE WRITTEN APPLICATION

❑ Use the "College Application Calendar 1" to identify the ideal window during which your child can concentrate on her admissions essay and other parts of the written application.

❑ Use the "College Application Calendar 2" as a springboard for discussion with your child about application deadlines.

❑ Post a completed version of the "College Application Calendar 2" on the refrigerator after you and your child fill it out together.

❑ Ask your child how you can best help her with the written application.

❑ Collaborate with other families to put together a college essay-writing workshop if your child would like to participate in one.

❑ Contact the college counseling office at a well-respected independent high school in your area to get a referral for a workshop facilitator.

❑ Provide the facilitator with a copy of the "College Application Essay Rubric."

❑ Encourage your child to seek ongoing workshop feedback and rewrite her essay repeatedly.

❑ Review with your child the way in which she plans to present herself in the Personal Data, Testing, and Family information portions of the written application.

❑ Review with your child the way in which she plans to present her extracurricular activities in the written application.

❑ Offer your child continuous small acknowledgments and gestures of support as she crosses major milestones in the college admissions process.

ELEVEN

Waiting for Decision Letters and Finalizing Where to Attend

B y January or February of your child's senior year (sooner than that for early-decision/early-action applicants), college applications have gone in and you must now wait to receive decision letters. Several concerns remain on the table for many families during this waiting period—namely applying for financial aid and searching for scholarships. This chapter will guide you through that process, as well as through the different scenarios a family can encounter when decision letters arrive.

APPLYING FOR FINANCIAL AID

Families applying for financial aid must fill out the Free Application for Federal Student Aid (FAFSA), the form that determines eligibility for federal grant, loan, and work-study dollars. Some selective colleges and universities ask families to complete additional paperwork, such as the College Scholarship Service/Financial Aid Profile (CSS Profile), to help them decide how to distribute their own financial-aid dollars. The ease with which you complete these forms will depend in part on how well you have organized your own financial records (tax returns, investment documents, etc.) and how carefully you read and follow the instructions. Ron Inniss, financial aid expert at www.collegebroadband.com, states emphatically that missed deadlines and sloppiness in filling out forms stand out as the major reasons that families lose out on financial-aid dollars.

Before you begin tackling either the FAFSA or the CSS Profile, you need to figure out the financial-aid application requirements for each college and university to which your child is applying. Your child put together a calendar of deadlines for his college applications and you now need to do the same thing for financial aid. (See the "Financial-Aid Calendar.") Continue to update this calendar as your child adds colleges and universities to his list. You can then turn to the CSS Profile as soon as you know that he is applying to even a single institution that requires it, as the College Board accepts it as early as October of your child's senior year.

You can access the CSS Profile in the parent section of the College Board Web site (www.collegeboard.com). Depending on your degree of computer and financial literacy, you may find the Web site frustrating at best and intimidating at worst (neither Ron Inniss nor I find it user-friendly). The College Board only accepts the CSS Profile online, so people who do not feel especially computer-literate and would prefer to work with a hard copy do not have that option. To make the process as painless as possible, I strongly recommend downloading the registration guide, printing it, and reading it thoroughly before you attempt to enter any data online. The CSS Profile asks you to submit detailed and comprehensive information, to an even greater degree than the FAFSA does. Jumping into it without adequate preparation may make completing the CSS Profile far more painful than it needs to be.

Keep in mind that you can save what you have entered online and return to it later. This feature allows you to complete the CSS Profile in installments, an option that may come as a relief once you get started, especially for divorced parents who must both enter information. The College Board has designed its software so that neither divorced parent can see the other's entries. This privacy-protecting feature may cause some initial confusion even for the most computer-literate users. The good news is that completing the CSS Profile first makes filling out the FAFSA feel easy.

The U.S. Department of Education has created an extremely helpful area on its Web site (www.fafsa.ed.gov) that gives you everything you need to fill out the FAFSA. "Before Filling Out the FAFSA" provides an overview of the documents you must have in front of you to complete the requested information and includes a "Pre-Application

Date: _____

Financial Aid Calendar

Name of College or University	FAFSA Deadline	CSS Profile Deadline (N/A if not required)	Comments and/or additional forms required

Worksheet" that previews the questions you will encounter on the FAFSA itself. You can move on to "Filling Out a FAFSA" when you feel ready to complete the actual form. The Web site even offers visitors a "FAFSA Follow-Up" section that outlines what happens once you have submitted your materials.

Applying for Financial Aid

- Complete a Financial Aid Calendar to determine which forms you have to submit and by when.

- Read the CSS/Financial Aid Profile registration guide, if applicable.

- Discuss with your accountant or financial planner whether or not you need to make any short-term changes to your portfolio, such as transferring accounts from your child's name to yours.

- Complete and submit the CSS/Financial Aid Profile in early October.

- Register for a PIN for you and your child on the FAFSA Web site no later than early October.

- Begin working on the FAFSA as soon thereafter as possible.

- Submit the FAFSA on January 1 or as soon thereafter as possible.

- Prepare and submit any additional materials that individual colleges and universities require as soon as possible.

- Use the "Mail/Call Financial Aid Worksheet" to follow up with each college and university and confirm receipt of your materials.

- Go to a Web site like www.act.org to check your Estimated Family Contribution (EFC).

It makes sense to do as much as you can on your FAFSA in the fall so that you can send it in as soon after January 1 as possible (the earliest date that the Department of Education will accept it). The Department of Education allows you to complete and transmit your information electronically or as a hard copy via postal mail. If you feel comfortable with electronic transmission, both you and your child should register at the FAFSA Web site in September or October for your personal identification numbers (PINs). These PINs allow you to "sign" your FAFSA electronically for online submission. A FAFSA that comes in via the Internet without a PIN goes into a holding pattern until the Department of Education receives a hard copy of a signature page from you. This holding pattern negates the instant receipt benefit of having sent it in online.

Any family with a fixed income that will not change in the new year, such as those on public assistance, can complete the entire FAFSA in the fall and send it in immediately on January 1. Those whose financial information will change from the previous year and who have to wait until after January 1 to enter it can still get a head start on the FAFSA by walking through the "Pre-Application Worksheet" in December to familiarize themselves with the format. Remember that timeliness matters: missing any of the financial-aid deadlines for the colleges and universities to which your child is applying means you may be giving money away. Institutions will have already begun allocating financial aid resources and fewer dollars will remain for you.

Colleges and universities may ask you to submit additional paperwork in support of your financia aid application, such as family income tax returns. Complete the CSS Profile and the FAFSA first and then move as quickly as possible through any remaining requirements. If you have not completed your tax return by the financial aid deadline, send the previous year's return and then update your file as soon as possible. Wait two to three weeks after the submission of your materials and then call each financial aid office to confirm receipt. Note the date and time of each call, as well as the name of the person with whom you speak, so that you can refer to this information in the future, if necessary. The "Mail/Call Financial Aid Worksheet" shown on page 212 can help you organize and track this part of the process. (Use a separate worksheet for each institution.)

Some families begin detailed financial planning for college well before their children reach high school (see "General Financial Planning Tips for College"). You can still make short-term inroads, though, even a couple of years before you have to start paying tuition (see "Financial Aid Road Map—Part I). A discussion with an accountant or financial planner prior to submitting your financial aid forms could reveal some quick and easy changes to your portfolio that could affect the awards that you receive. Accountant Shelly Goch, of New York's Garfield, Seltzer & Curcio CPA, points out, for example, that financial aid for-

Name of college or university: _____

Mail/Call Financial Aid Worksheet

Financial Aid Document (check if required)	Date Submitted	Date of Call Confirming Receipt	Name of Person w/ Whom I Spoke	Comments
☐ CSS/Financial Aid Profile				
☐ FAFSA				
☐ Family Federal Income Tax Return				
☐ CSS Business/Farm Supplement (this form only applies to parents who own an interest in a business or farm)				
☐ CSS Noncustodial Parent's Profile and Federal Income Tax Returns (this form only applies to divorced or unmarried parents)				
☐ Other (please specify):				
☐ Other (please specify):				

mulas make it more advantageous for assets to belong to parents than to a college-bound child. Transferring savings and other accounts out of your child's name and into yours before you complete your financial aid forms could make a difference in the amount of aid that colleges and universities give you. You can get a sense of what colleges and universities will expect you to contribute by using an Estimated Family Contribution (EFC) calculator on a Web site like www.act.org.

General Financial Planning Tips for College

Dwight Raiford, a financial planner for MetLife, emphasizes to families with college-bound children that they must predicate any financial plan for college on healthy, contributing parents. For that reason, a well-constructed educational payment plan also factors in disability, life, and long-term care insurance. Parents may also have to balance paying for their child's college education with providing for their own retirement, depending on their age.

Both Raiford and accountant Shelly Goch encourage all families with college tuition payments on the horizon to look into 529 savings accounts. Some families open these accounts early (Raiford has a client who started one when her son was first born), but you can accrue benefits even if you open one when your child hits high school. Goch likes the 529's flexibility. "It can cover tuition, room and board, books and supplies, and special needs," she points out. Better yet, "you can change beneficiaries." The 529 remains federally tax-free if you use it for a qualified educational expense at any postsecondary institution in the country. (Some of the 529's benefits require periodic reauthorization by Congress.) States offer their own 529 plans and investing in those can result in tax deductions at the state level as well.

Make sure that you distinguish between a 529 savings plan and a 529 prepaid tuition plan, as each one has different implications for financial aid. Financial aid formulas weigh family income more heavily than assets. Withdrawals from 529 savings plans, if used for eligible educational expenses, are not considered income and therefore have a minimal impact on a family's EFC. Withdrawals from 529 prepaid tuition plans, however, reduce financial aid eligibility dollar for dollar. Families at any income level can meet most if not all of their college savings needs through 529 plans. Those who have access to a financial planner should inquire about additional tools that can also help in certain circumstances.

DISCUSSING FINANCIAL AID WITH YOUR CHILD

The period during which your child is waiting for decision letters presents an ideal window during which you can discuss financial aid with him. Picture your child's financial aid package as a pie, with up to five slices:

1. Grants, which he does not have to repay;

2. Loans, which he does have to repay, generally at low interest;

3. Student contribution;

4. Family contribution; and

5. Student work-study.

The best-case scenario would make grants the largest slice of all, since he does not have to repay them. Many people feel apprehensive about packages that include a large amount of debt or that require students to work on campus and/or during school vacations. Colleges and universities will not put you in a position of having to sell your home to pay for your child's education. You may, however, have to make other sacrifices, such as taking out loans, having your child take out loans, eliminating family vacations, no longer sending your child to your home country during the summer because he has to work, etc.

Have some preliminary conversations about the scenarios that your child, you, and the rest of the family can accept while you are awaiting decision letters and financial aid packages, before their arrival adds time constraints and other pressures to the discussion. The process that you went through to fill out the CSS Profile and the FAFSA can prepare you for this kind of discussion with your child, as you have just gone through a thorough review of your family's financial situation and what colleges and universities will likely expect you to contribute. (Use an online EFC calculator at this point if you have not already done so.) Have a frank dialogue with your child about how much of his educational debt you will be able to help him repay, if loans look likely, and what kind of monthly loan payment he will be shouldering as he enters the workforce. Talk with him about how holding down a job for ten to fifteen hours a week on campus and working over his vacations will make him feel. Educate him about the typical components of a financial aid package so that he understands the implications of work-study and taking out loans.

I should clarify that I strongly agree with Spelman's Arlene Cash who sees a college education as the wisest investment a family can make. I, myself, paid off college loans over a twenty-year period (lengthened in part because lenders exempt you from payments and extend the term of your loan while you pursue graduate study). I also worked multiple shifts each week at a campus library job and full-time as a secretary during every winter, spring, and summer break during college. Looking back on my experience, I would not have done a single thing differently. I do wish, though, that I had taken on my educational loans with a full understanding of their long-term financial implications. Raising your child's consciousness about financial aid increases his financial literacy and lays the groundwork for mature decision making, both in the long term and when college letters arrive a few weeks later.

SEEKING SCHOLARSHIPS

Your child has the chance to reduce the amount of debt he may have to incur if he searches aggressively and submits applications for scholarships while he waits for college decision letters to arrive. Many scholarship deadlines fall in January and February, at which point they begin to drop off until the fall. Check with your employer and/ or union about monies for college that they may award, as well as with membership organizations to which you belong. These entities frequently sponsor scholarship competitions open only to the children of their employees or members. One young man I know won a $10,000 annual award from UPS, his father's employer, in addition to smaller scholarships that he found online.

Your child can also win scholarships based on personal and family characteristics, the type of college or university he plans to attend, his intended major, and more. Online search engines have made it possible for students to complete a personal profile and then wait no more than a few seconds to get hundreds of results. You can save your child a lot of time and frustration if you direct him to www. collegebroadband.com for free reviews of these search engines. The quality of their results varies considerably. Starting with an inferior one wastes your child's time and energy and could discourage him from

Financial Aid Road Map—Part I

GRADE NINE

- Open a 529 savings account if you have not done so already.

- Consider restructuring any investments you may have to use to pay for college to reduce risk. (Do not precipitously dump stocks that have temporarily lost value but that may come back.)

- Go to a Web site such as www.act.com and use an EFC calculator to get a preview of your expected contribution to the college bill.

- Contact your employer's Human Resources department or your union office to find out if they offer college scholarships to children of their employees/members.

- Students can earn scholarship dollars as early as age twelve! Have your child look for scholarships online, such as at www.collegebroadband.com.

- Conduct your own online scholarship search for your child. Consider joining social or professional organizations that award monies for college.

- Ask at celebrations and holidays for donations to your child's 529 account in lieu of gifts.

GRADE TEN

- Encourage your child to work during the summer, even just ten to fifteen hours per week, to get into the habit of balancing work with other responsibilities. (College financial aid packages frequently include work-study requirements.)

- Set up a schedule of regular contributions to your child's 529 savings account (if you have not already).

- Integrate creative ways to save money into your family routines, such as taking a five-day vacation rather than a full week.

GRADE ELEVEN

- Run an updated EFC calculation online. (Both parents should do this separately in the case of divorce.)

- Talk with a financial aid officer at one or two top colleges or universities on your child's list. Discuss your EFC and ask about the kind of aid that the institution would make available to you.

- Encourage your child to continue searching for scholarships online. He can make a chart of those to which he plans to apply, by award amount and deadline.

GRADE TWELVE

- Make sure your child has at least one college or university on his list that you can afford without any aid.

- Don't take institutions off the list just because you think they are too expensive. You may qualify for enough aid to make the net cost reasonable.

- If your child is applying early decision somewhere, check with the institution's financial aid office to see if, should he be admitted, the college or university will release him for financial reasons if necessary.

- File your CSS/Financial Aid Profile in early October, especially if your child is applying early.

- File your FAFSA on January 1 or as soon thereafter as possible. Use year-end figures to be as precise as possible, but estimate if necessary.

- Complete your tax forms as soon as you receive your W2s. You can hold off on submitting the returns to the Internal Revenue Service but still use them for financial aid purposes. (An award based on a complete tax return has more validity and less likelihood of being revised later than one based on estimates.)

- Make sure to include all pages, schedules, and W2s when you submit your tax forms to financial aid offices. Confirm that your name appears on everything.

looking further. Giving your child information on any family member who has served in the military (past or present, including branch of service and wars in which the person fought) and on any unions, social, or membership organizations to which you or your spouse belongs will enhance his search results. Many students lack these details when they sit down to enter their profiles and miss out on valuable scholarship opportunities.

Many scholarships ask applicants to submit an essay. Your child may find that he can use one of his college application essays, albeit perhaps with modifications. Even writing one from scratch does not seem that bad when you think of the possible return. As Spelman's Arlene Cash says, "Don't tell me you are not willing to write an essay—that essay could be worth $4,000!"

DECISION LETTERS

Every year, I correspond electronically with multiple parents while we all wait on pins and needles for decision letters to arrive (early-admission letters in the fall and regular-decision letters in the spring). I never check in with students at this time, as I want to give them their space, especially in those few days when some people have started receiving their letters while others are still waiting. To the extent that you can, try to show the same restraint with your child: give him room while he is waiting for his decision letters, reacting to them, and coming to his own conclusions. Let him know that you are there to help him in any way he needs as he sorts through his excitement and, if applicable, disappointment. Then close the door to your room and do a jig or scream into your pillow, if you need to; but let him get through his thoughts and decision process at his own pace. The eventual outcome will turn out much better for all concerned than it will if you hover over, pressure, or try to influence him in any way.[26]

Students who follow the steps in this book or the advice of a good guidance counselor generally end up with outstanding choices in front of them. They may have missed a reach school or even, occasionally, one of their targets. At the very least, though, they have four to five great options to consider.

My client, Seth, whom I mentioned earlier, reaped the benefits of having put together a fantastic college list. He got into all seven of

Name of college/university: _____   Date: _____

College Decision Checklist

Academics

Academic Area	# of Courses Offered That Interest Me
Possible college major #1 (please specify) :	
Possible college major #2 (please specify) :	
Other subject of interest (please specify) :	
Other subject of interest (please specify) :	

✓ Average student-to-teacher ratio: _____

Extracurricular Activities

Check the level of opportunity that this institution offers its students for each activity below:

Activity	Outstanding	Satisfactory	Poor	Does Not Matter to Me
Athletics				
Community Service				
Debate				
Journalism				
Student Government/Politics				
Theater				
Other (please specify) :				
Other (please specify) :				

Student Life

How comfortable do you feel with each aspect of the institution's campus life that appears in the table below?

Aspect of Student Life	Very Comfortable	Somewhat Comfortable	Not Comfortable	Does Not Matter to Me
Average # hours that freshmen study during the week				
Average # hours that freshmen study on the weekend				
Campus social life (too Greek, not Greek enough, etc.)				
Diversity of student population				
Dormitory conditions				
Geographic location (region, distance from home)				
Local setting (urban, suburban, rural)				
Religious life				
Other (please specify) :				
Other (please specify) :				

Additional Resources

Check the level of opportunity that this institution offers for each resource below:

Opportunity/Resource	Outstanding	Satisfactory	Poor	Does Not Matter to Me
Access to tenured professors				
Art studios				
Computer laboratories				
Dance studios				
Inter-college exchange programs				
Job externships and/or career counseling				
Libraries				
Media laboratories				
Music practice rooms				
Science laboratory research facilities				
Study-abroad programs				
Other (please specify) :				
Other (please specify) :				

the colleges and universities to which he applied and had a month to make a decision. Seth loved the places on his list so much that he initially had trouble eliminating any (even his safety). His mother e-mailed me in frustration to tell me that he wanted to visit all seven places, many of which he had already seen at least once in the fall! I suggested to her that she give Seth carte blanche to make as many college trips as he wanted to, after he had filled out the "College Decision Checklist" for each of the institutions he was actively considering.

Walking through the "College Decision Checklist" helps your child focus on whatever major areas matter to him—academics, extracurricular activities, student life, or something else. He can get down on paper the key facts and impressions about each college or university that he is considering, lay down all the pros and cons in front of him, and compare. Sometimes the simple act of writing things down helps a young person distill his thoughts. In Seth's case, he did not want to complete the checklist for seven institutions, which led him to clarify his thinking and eliminate some from his list right off the bat.

Having done thorough research when he compiled his list in the fall means that your child should not have much trouble narrowing the field to two serious contenders now (three at the outside). Seth decided to travel to two campuses in the end, both without his parents, and then surprised everybody by choosing a completely different place altogether. On his visits, he stayed in the dormitories and attended classes with his student hosts, two critical components of any campus stay at this stage of the process. He came back with solid, well-conceived reasons for his final decision and never wavered from that point forward. Seth's father e-mailed me after they dropped him off at school in the fall to let me know that he had settled in and "none of us has a doubt that he's in the perfect place."

Students who for financial or logistical reasons cannot travel to campuses should seek out other ways to get more of a feel than books and Web sites can give them for the places they are considering. Reaching out to recent graduates of their high school who attend a college or university can give young people personal and diverse perspectives on an institution. Your child can get back in touch with an alumni interviewer or contact the admissions office for a list of other graduates in the area. Members of major corporate or professional organizations that have mentoring programs would also, in many cases, gladly speak to your child about their experiences at a particular institution.

Not every student shares Seth's rock-star experience when decision letters arrive: rejection or wait-list notifications can leave a young person feeling crushed, even if the notifications only come from one or two institutions, let alone more than that. Although understandable, this reaction may compromise your child's ability to make a good decision for the following year. You and a guidance counselor can play critical roles in helping your child turn that corner and make sound decisions for his future if he finds himself in this situation. Consider it a priority to help your child redirect his energy in a positive way if you see him getting caught in the rejection trap. Go through the "College Decision Checklist" with him, for example, and point out positives at institutions that have extended offers of admission. Encourage him to visit at least a couple of those places. A positive experience on campus could change his whole outlook.

Annie, a client whom I mentioned in an earlier chapter, went through exactly this experience when she received her decision letters. She had come to me for help on her essay and for some general college counseling but did not work with me on putting together her list of colleges and ended up ignoring most of the advice that I gave her. The two rejection and two wait-list notifications that Annie received in the spring superseded in her mind her three acceptances. She felt completely downcast, until she visited one of the three colleges that had accepted her. Her mother told me later that the "great" campus experience had left Annie "very excited" upon her return home and had "clinched her thoughts" about that college.

Like Annie, a relatively small percentage of students in each admissions cycle receives wait-list letters in April, a scenario that can prove even more challenging than rejection. Wait-list letters do not extend an offer of admission but do not definitively reject a student either. Instead, they give an applicant the option of remaining on a list from which the admissions office draws names throughout the summer to fill slots that open up unexpectedly. Getting wait-listed presents young people with a unique set of challenges that can increase the stress of the college admissions process. "Think long and hard about whether or not it is a good idea to stay on a school's wait-list," Cornell's Doris Davis advises. "Sometimes it's not a good thing to do." The "Wait-List Survival Worksheet" can help you and your child decide if the wait-list sounds like a viable option for him.

Unlike the regular-admissions process that has a defined timetable with set notification dates, the wait-list process can drag on through-

Wait-List Survival Worksheet

In each of the boxes below, please check all options that apply.

Coping With the Uncertainty and Stress	Developing a Back-Up Plan
❑ My child can handle the extended uncertainty that comes with remaining on the wait-list (this means possibly not knowing anything until August).	❑ My child has accepted an offer of admission at another college or university, in case he does not get admitted off the wait-list.
❑ My child can handle the added stress that comes with remaining on the wait-list.	❑ My child will still be able to get excited about and develop a relationship with the college or university at which he has enrolled for the fall, even if he remains on the wait-list somewhere else.
❑ Remaining on the wait-list will not overshadow the end of my child's senior year or his summer.	❑ We are prepared to forfeit the deposit we put down at the college or university at which my child has enrolled for the fall if he gets accepted off the wait-list somewhere else.
Taking Proactive Steps	**Additional Considerations**
❑ My child has sought answers to logistical questions about the wait-list, e.g., how many wait-listed students the college or university accepted last year, whether or not the institution ranks its wait-list, when the admissions office expects to close its wait-list and not take any more students from it.	❑ We understand that the college or university that has wait-listed my child may not have any financial-aid dollars left to distribute, even if it accepts him.
❑ My child has inquired with the admissions office about what he can do to strengthen his folder and increase his chances of admission from the wait-list.	❑ We have researched the tuition and fees at the institution that has wait-listed our child and can cover those costs, even if they exceed the costs of the college or university that my child is planning to attend and even if we receive no financial aid.
❑ My child is following the instructions he received and has prepared and sent the appropriate materials to the admissions office.	❑ We are prepared as a family to change our plans at the last moment if necessary to conform to the academic calendar of the institution that has wait-listed my child, as well as to any corresponding change in travel plans if it lies in a significantly different geographic region from where my child is currently planning to attend.
❑ My child and I have met with his counselor to request that she also stay in touch with the admissions office and lobby for my child's admission off the wait-list.	

out the summer (see "Coping With the Uncertainty and Stress" section of worksheet). A student might get a call in May, in August, or not at all. Talk with your child to determine whether or not he is really prepared for this extended period of uncertainty and, possibly, stress. You want to make sure that staying on the wait-list does not overshadow the remainder of his senior year and/or his summer.

Anybody who stays on a wait-list must have a back-up plan (see "Developing a Back-Up Plan" section of worksheet). Your child needs to accept an offer of admission at another college or university and concentrate on picturing himself there in the fall. Spelman's Arlene Cash sees "developing a relationship with another college" as critical, since "more often than not the wait-list will not come through." Cash's staff, for example, may wait-list fifty students, and, when all is said and done, only accept five. Discuss with your child whether or not remaining on a wait-list will make it difficult for him to get excited about the college or university that he plans to attend if the wait-list does not come through. You and your spouse need to consider as well that accepting a spot off the wait-list somewhere else means forfeiting the deposit that you put down to hold your child's place in the freshman class at the college or university at which he has registered for the fall.

Students who really want to move off the wait-list and into a college or university's freshman class need to take proactive steps to increase their chances of doing so (see "Taking Proactive Steps" section of worksheet). Cornell's Doris Davis advises students and parents to stay in communication with an admissions office. "Find out if the number of students admitted from the wait-list has varied from year to year," she counsels. "Ask questions about the process, such as is your wait-list ranked? How many of your students got admitted from the wait-list last year? When do you expect to close your wait-list process?" Cornell, for example, "had lots of wait-list activity in 2004 but relatively little in 2003."

Communicating proactively with the admissions office also means finding out what your child can do to strengthen his profile. Spelman's Arlene Cash advises parents to step in and make a phone call to ask what a child can do to increase the chances of admission. Unlike rejected students, those on the wait-list have the opportunity to forward new information to the admissions office and still have it affect their outcome. Cash counsels students to take advantage of that opportunity and "send a little package with an update of what you have done since the application went in."

Students should "make clear that the school is your first choice! The better an admissions office knows your name, the more likely you are to get off that wait-list." I recommend going a step further and asking the guidance counselor to call on a student's behalf as well, if a college or university that has wait-listed him truly represents his first choice. A skilled guidance counselor has a platform from which to speak and relationships with admissions officers that parents do not. Set up a meeting with your child's counselor to see whether she will lobby proactively on your child's behalf. One family I know whose daughter got wait-listed found her counselor completely unhelpful. Understanding the reality of the situation, though, allowed them to take the counselor out of the equation and concentrate even more than they might have before on staying in touch with the admissions office themselves.

Families in need of financial aid must give special consideration to the realities of the wait-list (see "Additional Considerations" section of worksheet). The college or university that wait-listed your child may have already distributed its financial-aid dollars for the incoming class and not have any left to give him. That institution may also cost more than the one that your child had originally planned to attend; getting in off the wait-list, while uplifting news for your child, could significantly increase your financial burden. You should also not underestimate the potential logistical challenge of changing travel plans and estimated arrival dates if the institution that wait-listed and then accepted your child is located somewhere else or if its calendar differs from the calendar of the college or university that your child had planned to attend. All of these factors make it important for you and your child to discuss seriously whether staying on a wait-list represents a viable option for him and for your family.

FACTORING COST AND FINANCIAL AID INTO THE DECISION

You already had a preliminary discussion about financial aid with your child after applications went into the mail. Now the time has come to sit down and analyze the packages you have received and what they mean for your child's college decision. Colleges and universities anxious to get your child to enroll will sometimes offer scholarships

Financial Aid Road Map—Part II

- Evaluate financial aid offers when they arrive in the spring. Look at net cost (billed fees less grant aid) for each institution.

- Do not hesitate to contact an institution's financial aid office if you see differences in award packages and cannot figure out why. Ask them to look at the award again.

- Once your child has decided on a college, review what that institution needs you to do to finalize your award. Get it on the bill! Make it real! Remember that spring awards are normally tentative. Respond promptly and completely to anything the college or university needs you to do to finalize the award.

- Assume that you need to have everything in place no later than a month before the first bill arrives. Let them know about outside aid awards. Complete all loan paperwork before your child arrives on campus.

- Encourage your child to search the college's Web site over the summer for plum campus jobs, such as at the campus library where he can get some studying done.

- Review available college savings and withdraw as needed.

- Consider parent financing and parent loan options to fill any gaps.

- Get your child a credit card with a very low limit. Have him use it once and pay it off. Then take it away. Doing this will initiate a credit record for your child which may come in handy if he needs to take out a private student loan while in college.

- Help your child set up a tentative budget for the first semester and point out easy ways to save money, such as purchasing used books, sharing rides home, etc.

(outright grants that your child does not have to repay), even if a family has not demonstrated financial need. Those awards can be quite enticing for a family that does need the help. Chances are that your child has gained admission to at least one college or university that is offering more aid or that costs less than the others and you now must decide whether or not to ask him to attend that institution,

Emergency Educational Financing Plan*

Kevin just got into an Ivy League college, but with two other college-bound children right behind him, and a combined household income of $100,000 per year, his parents fear that they cannot afford the cost. Besides owning their small one-family house in a middle-income suburb, Kevin's parents have $15,000 in savings.

Initially, Kevin's first-choice school offered him $11,000 (net) in financial aid, with an EFC of $26,000. Kevin received $20,000 (net) in financial aid from a less selective institution and his first choice, in response, raised its aid level to $15,000. To send him there, Kevin's family still needs to come up with $7,000, in addition to the $15,000 they have in the bank.

MetLife financial planner Dwight Raiford thinks Kevin and his family have several options. First, he believes Kevin's parents should use their $15,000 savings for Kevin's first year, as the money will no longer remain in the picture when the financial aid office calculates next year's package. Raiford then recommends that Kevin himself take out a loan for the remaining $7,000. As a student, Kevin qualifies for a low interest rate. He also wants to go to law school and, as a result, will likely earn a comfortable living once he completes his education and be able to repay these loans over time without being completely handicapped by the payments.

If Kevin's parents do not feel comfortable using their entire savings, they can also take out several different kinds of loans themselves. Raiford would advise them first to consider a loan against a cash value life insurance policy, something that they would not have to repay because it comes out of the proceeds of a death benefit. They would lose access to that capital, though, as a source of emergency funding for something else or for retirement. As a second choice, Kevin's parents can take out a home equity loan. Raiford advises families to consider a loan against a 401(k) last of all because, once you borrow against the money, it reduces the return on your retirement investment.

---

* Dwight Raiford, of MetLife, put together this sample plan to illustrate that even families who have not done any advance planning whatsoever can pull together the resources to pay for a private college education if they so choose.

even if it ranks low on his list. Every family must make its own decision, but you have options that you may not realize and that you should explore before you formulate your final position.

Before you jump to conclusions, compare the actual net cost of attending each institution. (See "Financial Aid Road Map—Part II.") You calculate the net cost by taking the total amount for which a college or university will bill you and subtracting from it the grant aid portion of your package (dollars that the institution is giving your child outright that he will not have to repay). Let's assume that having completed this exercise, you see that your child's first choice comes in at a higher net cost than another institution. Call the financial aid office at the first-choice school and begin a conversation.

If you let an institution know that money is a barrier, Arlene Cash states emphatically, the people there "will bend over backwards to help you." I can think of multiple examples over the years in which a financial aid office raised the level of assistance it was offering, either in response to a more robust package from another institution or simply because a family made it clear that, without more support, a child could not attend. If you try to eliminate your child's indebtedness entirely, you will probably not succeed. If your child agrees to take out low-interest student loans, however, you leave yourself much more room for negotiation than if he refuses to do so.

You and your child may have access to more sources of loan money than you even realize. Before deciding that a college's price tag lies out of reach, review the borrowing strategies available to you. MetLife's Dwight Raiford can even come up with a college financing plan for a family with three college-bound children and $15,000 in the bank less than six months before the first payment is due. (See "Emergency Educational Financing Plan.") You may still opt for the higher net financial aid package of the two in the end. Make that decision in an informed way, though, after having fully reviewed all the options.

TAKING A YEAR OFF BEFORE COLLEGE

Many colleges and universities allow admitted students to defer for a year after high school if they do not want to move directly on to college. Even students who have gained admission to their first-choice institution sometimes want to do something different or adventurous for a year before embarking on their higher education. "Gap year" experiences could include working with a service organization like City Year, living abroad for a year through an organization like American Field Service (AFS) or English Speaking Union (ESU), or even taking a postgraduate high school year (especially helpful for students who want to bone up on skills or strengthen their academic transcripts).

Transferring After Freshman or Sophomore Year

With few exceptions, transfer students have a statistically lower admit rate to selective colleges and universities than those applying to enter as freshmen. At some institutions, such as Grinnell College, the faculty "has determined not to grow the college" while, at the same time, retention there has increased. These two circumstances have made it "definitely more difficult to get in as a transfer student than as a first-year applicant," according to Jim Sumner. Arnaldo Rodriguez at Pitzer College concurs: Pitzer limits transfer students to twenty per year, "out of more than 150 applicants. That's a 13 percent admit rate versus 40 percent for first-year students." At other colleges and universities, however, several deans of admission note that, admit rates aside, the quality of the transfer pool does not match that of the freshman pool. A strong transfer applicant would, therefore, have an easier time getting admitted than a strong freshman candidate, in spite of the statistics.

Deans of admission at a number of institutions find the transfer pool especially diverse and use it to recruit strong community college and/or urban students. Clark University actively recruits transfer students and offers merit-based scholarships to those coming from community college. Mount Holyoke College looks to transfer applicants "particularly to find students of color and first-generation college students," according to Jane Brown.

Anybody considering the submission of transfer applications should invest time in speaking to admissions officers about admit rates, the quality of the transfer pool, and what a student can do to strengthen his candidacy. The small size of the transfer pool and its off-cycle timetable means that a transfer applicant could have a substantive telephone conversation with an admissions officer. Encourage your child to make those inquiries and to obtain as much helpful information as possible so that he can rise to the top of the transfer pool and increase his chances for admission.

If your child would like to explore options for a year off, have him start by calling the admissions office at the college or university that he plans to attend to find out about their policies and procedures under these circumstances. Communicate with the financial aid office yourself (if you have received an award) to find out if a gap year has financial implications. In most cases, you will simply have to reapply for aid the following year, as you would for your child's sophomore year of college. I would also inquire with the sponsors of any scholarships your child has won, as they may require that he go directly on to college in order to receive the award.

Once you and your child have covered all the logistical bases, sit down and discuss whether a gap year sounds like it would work in his best interests. As a parent, you should focus on whether or not you feel comfortable with what your child would be pursuing during this year off, whether you feel it would benefit him educationally and personally, and whether or not your family can afford it. One student I know wanted very much to take a gap year. Doing so, however, would have thrown off the age order in his family and meant that three children would overlap in college at the same time, rather than two. His parents feared that even financial aid would not cover the full impact of that scenario and told him that a gap year would not work.

FREQUENTLY ASKED QUESTIONS

My daughter is a junior and is telling me that she does not need to apply to college next year because she wants to take a "gap year." Does this idea sound wise?

I always recommend that students go through the college admissions process while they are still enrolled at their high school, if at all possible. Your daughter, while attending school everyday, has contact with her teacher and counselor recommenders. She stands out much more freshly in their minds than she will after she has left the high school. People also naturally feel a greater sense of urgency to complete letters for students they see daily rather than for somebody with whom they no longer have regular contact. They will still write letters for her, but those letters may rank lower on their list of priorities than they otherwise would.

Your daughter may well decide to go through the admissions process again during her gap year if she thinks that her experiences that year will improve her college results. She has time to make that decision, though, and should leave it as one of several options for herself, rather than the only one that she has to consider. For your information and for your daughter's, the Newton North High School Web site offers useful information on the gap year: nnhscareercenter.home. comcast.net/gap-year.html.

My child got into the college that I think she should attend but she wants to go somewhere else. How can I talk some sense into her?

I would suggest having a dialogue with your child rather than trying to "talk some sense into her." Find out why the first choice she has identified appeals to her. Ask her to complete the "College Decision Checklist" and point out to you the specific institutional features that she finds attractive. You may find that, much to your surprise, you agree with your child's choice. If not, ask her if you can fill out the "College Decision Checklist" based on what you think your first choice could offer her. Point out to her the institutional strengths and ask if she would consider visiting both campuses (her first choice and yours) to compare the two. Approaching the topic in this manner will increase the odds that your child at least listens to what you have to say, rather than shutting down or focusing on her first choice even more determinedly than she otherwise might.

Our child got into her first-choice school but we cannot afford to send her there. How would you suggest we break the news to her that she will have to go elsewhere?

Given the options at your disposal that this chapter has laid out, I would suggest that you initiate a conversation with your daughter and see what she has to say. She may be willing to take on additional debt, work during all of her vacations, and aggressively seek scholarships. Her determination, if she demonstrates it, may sway you to explore some options that you had not yet considered. Make your daughter part of the decision process rather than somebody who just hears the news and has no input. Even if you arrive at the same conclusion in the end, getting there together will make a significant and positive difference for the entire family.

Our son has several wonderful college options in front of him but he refuses to share his thoughts with us or talk about his preferences. He says he will tell us when he makes his decision. We want to be part of the process but do not know how to do this without antagonizing him or encroaching on his independence.

Let your son know that you will not bring up the subject of college again until he feels ready to discuss it and that, when that time comes, you and your spouse would like to take him out to dinner at a restaurant of his choice (without any siblings, if he has any). At that dinner, you would like to make yourself available to listen to what he has to say and offer any feedback that he might find helpful. One of my favorite families tried this approach on my advice and it worked. The mother had to bite her tongue for several weeks, but in the end her son told both his parents that he was ready to sit down with them. At the restaurant, he unveiled his decision (a complete surprise to them!), explained his reasoning, and then asked them what they thought. They found themselves extremely impressed with the thought process through which he had gone and respected the choice he had made for himself. A little patience and self-restraint turned what could have amounted to several weeks of tension and conflict into a family experience that brought child and parents together.

STEP-BY-STEP CHECKLIST: WAITING FOR DECISION LETTERS AND FINALIZING WHERE TO ATTEND

❏ Use the "Financial Aid Calendar" at the start of your child's senior year. (You can update it as he adds colleges and universities to his list.)

❏ Complete the CSS Profile right away, if necessary, and file it as soon after October 1 of your child's senior year as you can.

❏ Go with your child to the FAFSA Web site in September or October to request your PINs, if you plan to submit the FAFSA electronically.

❏ Work on the FAFSA in the fall and submit it as soon after January 1 of your child's senior year as possible.

❑ Submit any other necessary financial aid documents as soon as possible after you have completed the CSS Profile and the FAFSA.

❑ Use the "Mail/Call Financial Aid Worksheet" in this chapter to confirm receipt of your financial aid paperwork at each institution and to document the conversations that you have with each financial aid office.

❑ Discuss your financial aid situation with an accountant and/or financial planner, if you have not already done so.

❑ Use an online EFC calculator, such as the one at www.act.org, to preview how much colleges and universities will expect you to contribute toward the bill.

❑ Discuss financial aid with your child, including debt level and work-study.

❑ Document for your child any family information that could assist him with scholarship searches.

❑ Give your child his space when decision letters arrive (no hovering or pressuring allowed!).

❑ Encourage your child to visit his top choices and to stay in the dormitories and attend classes while there.

❑ Help your child emerge from the rejection trap and/or figure out his wait-list options if necessary.

❑ Calculate the net cost of attending each institution that has accepted your child and explore and discuss with him all financing options before you reach a final decision about what you can and cannot afford.

Afterword

The college admissions process presents families with a series of simultaneous challenges that revolve around one young person but that bring parent-child relationships, family dynamics, household finances, and more under the microscope. Everybody involved faces some kind of stress, including the applicants themselves, their teachers, their counselors, and you—their parents. I opened my private practice and then wrote this book in the hope of minimizing stress for all involved by disseminating good information that simplifies and demystifies the college admissions process.

I, myself, have grown through these experiences, mostly through seeing and listening to my clients after they begin college. I used to focus on the percentage of my charges that matriculated at Top 20 schools as a sign of my success as a private counselor. Later, I substituted first-choice schools for Top 20. Most recently, I have simply marveled at the level of happiness and satisfaction my clients experience at any number of institutions, including schools that may not have sat at the top of their lists when the process started but that, upon further examination, grew into the schools of their dreams.

Therein lies the secret of this book: if you and your child follow the steps that it lays out, any college or university on your child's list could turn into the school of her dreams. Few things beat hearing the realization in a student's voice that she has arrived at just such a place when she settles into her new life on campus. I hope that this book makes it possible for you to hear that level of satisfaction and contentment in your own child's voice as her freshman year gets under way.

Best of luck as the process unfolds, and if you have any questions, remember to come visit www.collegebroadband.com, where you can hear more from me and some of the other experts quoted in this book. We look forward to seeing you there!

Notes

1. My thanks to Patrick Bassett of the NAIS for suggesting this idea.

2. Similar federally funded initiatives exist on college campuses around the country. The federal government also funds GEAR UP and Upward Bound Math-Science. To locate programs in your local area, go to the following U.S. Department of Education links and contact the appropriate program officer (based on geographic region). For GEAR UP, go to www.ed.gov/programs/gearup/contacts.html. For Upward Bound and Upward Bound Math-Science, go to www.ed.gov/about/offices/list/ope/trio/staffdirectory-cupt.html.

3. See www.heaf.org, www.nycmissionsociety.org/, and www.hcz.org/ for additional information on these three programs.

4. See www.summersearch.org.

5. See www.possefoundation.org.

6. My thanks to Mark Sklarow of the IECA for providing me with this yardstick.

7. The quotations from deans of admission that appear throughout this book come from formal telephone interviews in the summer of 2004 and subsequent follow-up conversations and exchanges of e-mail.

8. Statistics on dual enrollment programs come from the NCES April 2005 report entitled *Dual Enrollment of High School Students at Postsecondary Institutions: 2002–03*. Consult the NCES Web site at www.nces.ed.gov for additional information.

9. See, for example, Lillian Coltin's "Enriching Children's Out-of-School Time" (*Eric Digest*, May 1999), available online at www.ericfacility.net/ericdigests/ed429737.html.

10. Yale's Office of Undergraduate Admissions posts helpful advice on submitting supplementary materials that I have not seen on other admissions Web sites and that students considering a formal submission of supplementary materials to any college or university may want to read: www.yale.edu/admit/freshmen/application/supplementary_materials.html.

11. As of the writing of this book, ACT was aware of only ten institutions that accept the SAT and not the ACT: Art Institute of Boston at Lesley College, Boston; Central Maine Medical Center School of Nursing, Lewiston; Charles E. Gregory School of Nursing, Perth Amboy, NJ; CUNY–Bernard M. Baruch College, New York; CUNY–College of Staten Island; Harvey Mudd College, Claremont, CA; Johnson Technical Institute, Scranton, PA; Loyola College, Baltimore; Wake Forest University, Winston-Salem, NC; Webb Institute of Naval Architecture, Glen Cove, NY.

12. Go to www.collegeboard.com for details, including the current fee structure.

13. PSAT scores appear in two-digit format instead of three, so you need to add a zero to the end of each number on the score report to see what it would look like in SAT format. A 60 in mathematics on the PSAT, for example, would equal a 600 on the mathematics section of the SAT.

14. ACT has conducted a nationwide survey of colleges and universities and lists on its Web site which ones require the essay and which ones do not. Go to www.act.org to see the results. Individual colleges and universities usually specify in the admissions areas of their Web sites whether or not they require ACT takers to complete the essay portion of the test.

15. Both of these examples come from materials produced by the test makers themselves.

16. See www.collegeboard.com/press/article/0,3183,11147,00.html. (The College Board has since changed its American history Subject Test to U.S. history.)

17. The College Board publishes Subject Test percentile rankings on its Web site at www.collegeboard.com/highered/ra/sat/sat_data_satII.html.

18. See www.collegeboard.com for additional information on AP programs and www.ibo.org for details on IB programs.

19. Scores from tests that your child took before grade eleven provide a less useful basis for comparison, as she will not yet have covered major areas in the high school curriculum that appear on these examinations; the scores will not, therefore, provide an accurate reflection of what she will likely earn on tests that she takes a year or more later.

20. My thanks to Tim Levin, of New York City's Tim Levin Tutoring, Inc. (www.timlevintutoring.com), for contributing ideas to this chapter.

21. See Michael Luo's article "Taking Lessons from Another Culture," which appeared in the October 20, 2003, edition of *The New York Times*.

22. See Uri Treisman's article "Studying Students Studying Calculus: A Look at the Lives of Minority Mathematics Students in College," in *The College Mathematics Journal*, vol. 23, no. 5, November 1992, pp. 362–372, for additional information on his research.

23. Laura Clark's comments come from an interview (August 2004) and from ongoing conversations and e-mail correspondence thereafter.

24. These comments come from a telephone conversation with Ron Inniss, guidance counselor at the Jeremiah E. Burke High School, Boston, Massachusetts (September 1, 2005).

25. Over two hundred colleges and universities (including much of the Ivy League, the "Little Ivies," the "Seven Sister" schools, and HBCUs like Morehouse and Spelman) accept the Common Application™, available online at www. commonapp.org.

26. In this chapter, I refer to the regular-decision calendar for receiving and responding to offers of admission (letters generally arrive on or about April 1 and require a May 1 reply). Early-decision candidates who received a letter of deferral in the fall joined the regular applicant pool from that point forward and, if admitted in the spring, get the same deliberation time as regular applicants. Those who received an acceptance letter in the fall had already committed themselves to attending if admitted, so the spring decision period does not affect them. Early-action candidates made no commitment to attend a particular institution, even if it admitted them in the fall, so they also have until May 1 to accept or turn down an offer of admission.

Recommended Resources

As I conducted background research for this book, several resources stood out that could prove helpful if you want to gather additional information on specific topics. I have highlighted my favorites below, including books and Web sites.

Two books in particular helped me gain some valuable historical background on standardized testing, neither of which I could put down while I was reading it. Nicholas Lemann's *The Big Test: The Secret History of the American Meritocracy* traces the origins and development of the Educational Testing Service (ETS) and the use of standardized testing in college admissions. David Owen's *None of the Above: The Truth Behind the SATs* needs some updating (the last edition came out in the mid-1990s, well before the most recent version of the SAT) but still qualifies as a must-read for anybody interested in standardized testing and how it affects college admissions.

In the college guide department, two titles stand out as particularly helpful to parents and children. Parents in particular have appreciated Loren Pope's *Colleges That Change Lives,* a guide that focuses on lesser known institutions that provide a high-quality education. Pope's book has expanded into a resource-rich Web site (www.ctcl.com) and ongoing events around the country. *The Insider's Guide to the Colleges* (updated annually) has tremendous appeal for students because of its detailed descriptions of colleges and universities around the country, all from the perspective of college students who write for *The Yale Daily News.*

Anybody applying to selective colleges or universities should spend time at both www.act.org and www.collegeboard.org. In addition to

offering detailed information about ACT and College Board standardized tests, respectively, each Web site offers EFC financial aid calculators, test preparation resources, and more. The Singapore American
School, an international school with a particularly helpful college guidance area on its Web site (hseagle.sas.edu.sg/hscounseling/default.htm),
provides useful information on the PSAT, as well as a concordance
table that translates ACT scores into equivalent SAT scores and vice
versa. Newton North High School provides extensive resources on the
gap year, if your child is contemplating that option (nnhscareercenter.home.
comcast.net/gap-year.html). Students considering HBCUs can see a
complete list of colleges and universities (with live links) at www.smart
.net/~pope/hbcu/hbculist.htm. Last but not least, remember to visit
www.collegebroadband.com, where you can access multiple college
guidance resources and hear more from me and some of the other experts quoted in this book.

Index

DAVID ROTH—GREAT NECK, NY

EVA OSTRUM—an award-winning educator and filmmaker, respected author and consultant, and regularly cited media expert on education—is the founder and CEO of College Broadband, Inc. (www.collegebroadband.com), an educational media and consulting firm based in New York City. Eva also maintains a Manhattan-based private practice, through which she provides educational coaching and college counseling to parents and students. A sought-after guest expert and public speaker on education, Eva has been featured in media outlets around the country, including *BET Nightly News*, NPR, *Teen People*, and NBC's *Today* show.

FOR THE BEST IN PAPERBACKS, LOOK FOR THE

In every corner of the world, on every subject under the sun, Penguin represents quality and variety—the very best in publishing today.

For complete information about books available from Penguin—including Penguin Classics, Penguin Compass, and Puffins—and how to order them, write to us at the appropriate address below. Please note that for copyright reasons the selection of books varies from country to country.

In the United States: Please write to *Penguin Group (USA), P.O. Box 12289 Dept. B, Newark, New Jersey 07101-5289* or call 1-800-788-6262.

In the United Kingdom: Please write to *Dept. EP, Penguin Books Ltd, Bath Road, Harmondsworth, West Drayton, Middlesex UB7 0DA.*

In Canada: Please write to *Penguin Books Canada Ltd, 90 Eglinton Avenue East, Suite 700, Toronto, Ontario M4P 2Y3.*

In Australia: Please write to *Penguin Books Australia Ltd, P.O. Box 257, Ringwood, Victoria 3134.*

In New Zealand: Please write to *Penguin Books (NZ) Ltd, Private Bag 102902, North Shore Mail Centre, Auckland 10.*

In India: Please write to *Penguin Books India Pvt Ltd, 11 Panchsheel Shopping Centre, Panchsheel Park, New Delhi 110 017.*

In the Netherlands: Please write to *Penguin Books Netherlands bv, Postbus 3507, NL-1001 AH Amsterdam.*

In Germany: Please write to *Penguin Books Deutschland GmbH, Metzlerstrasse 26, 60594 Frankfurt am Main.*

In Spain: Please write to *Penguin Books S. A., Bravo Murillo 19, 1° B, 28015 Madrid.*

In Italy: Please write to *Penguin Italia s.r.l., Via Benedetto Croce 2, 20094 Corsico, Milano.*

In France: Please write to *Penguin France, Le Carré Wilson, 62 rue Benjamin Baillaud, 31500 Toulouse.*

In Japan: Please write to *Penguin Books Japan Ltd, Kaneko Building, 2-3-25 Koraku, Bunkyo-Ku, Tokyo 112.*

In South Africa: Please write to *Penguin Books South Africa (Pty) Ltd, Private Bag X14, Parkview, 2122 Johannesburg.*